CALLING OUT THE GOLD

CALLING OUT THE GOLD

*Equipping Millennials to be
the Next Church Leaders*

SARA BLAKENEY

credo
house publishers

Published in the United States of America by Credo House Publishers,
a division of Credo Communications LLC, Grand Rapids, Michigan
credohousepublishers.com

ISBN: 978-1-62586-230-3

Cover and interior design and layout by Frank Gutbrod
Editing by Stephen J. Grabill, PhD

Printed in the United States of America
First edition

This book is dedicated to the millennial generation.
May you know how valuable you are to the body of Christ.

CONTENTS

ACKNOWLEDGMENTS

I am incredibly grateful for my PhD supervisors at the University of Aberdeen, Rev. Dr. Kenneth Jeffrey and Dr. Marta Trzebiatowska, who believed in the merit of my research topic. Individually they are masterclass in their respective fields, and as a team they provided the wisdom and guidance I needed to succeed. They offered encouragement and pushed me further than I ever thought I could go academically. They became cherished friends along the way.

Thank you also to Dr. Kenda Creasy Dean and Dr. Léon Van Ommen, my PhD examiners, who encouraged me to turn my thesis into a published book. I highly respect their opinions, so I happily complied.

My deepest gratitude goes to Tim Beals, publisher at Credo House, whose expertise and godly character instilled confidence throughout the publishing process. Dr. Stephen Grabill was clearly the Lord's choice as editor for this project, and his passion and insight were greatly appreciated.

Thank you to my family for their love and support. They provided countless hours of proofreading, editing, moral support, and prayer and were my cheerleaders every step of the way. I share this accomplishment with them.

Finally, I would like to thank the millennials and ministry leaders at my fieldwork sites. It may have felt intrusive at times to see a woman walking around taking notes and photos, so I appreciate their patience during the research process. I am awed by the courage and faith of both communities. May the world see and emulate the amazing work they are doing for the kingdom of God.

FIGURE AND TABLES

CHAPTER 1

THE PRESSING NEED FOR DISCIPLESHIP

INTRODUCTION

"Discipleship [is] them calling out the gold in me." These are the words of a twenty-five-year-old millennial named Morgan.[1] Her words are telling: they indicate that she believes there are spiritual riches within her just waiting to be educed. Indeed, the process of discipleship is about following in the steps of Jesus so that one's value is recognized and one's giftedness is developed for the glory of God and the furtherance of his kingdom. Such edification of millennials is greatly needed, for they have too often been misunderstood. Popular media frequently has been guilty of painting them with a broad, derogatory brush.[2] Even academic assessments are varied and uneven, one moment casting millennials as altruistic and civic-minded and then as self-absorbed and fragile as "snowflakes" the next.[3] Such portrayals have implied, tacitly or perhaps unintentionally, that their contribution to society, much less the church, is somewhat dubious. The truth is that millennials have something crucial to impart, especially about the future of Christian discipleship. As Morgan said, there are things of value living within this generation. This book investigates how the church might bring those to light so that millennials can be equipped to be the next church leaders.

Throughout my twenty years in Christian young adult ministry, I have been fascinated by the uniqueness of the millennial generation. I found them eager to serve and zealous to make a difference in their world. However, I also sensed their growing discontent with the institutional church and the discipleship programs designed for them in which they were expected to be passive recipients of information more than active explorers of spiritual experiences. It is the paradox of millennials' discontent with the church, yet passion for doing good, that has led me to write this book. The apostle Paul said, "In him we live and move and have our being" (Acts 17:28). How can millennials "live and move" and discover their "being" for God in twenty-first-century America? What does discipleship for this generation look like in a changing ecclesiological landscape? These are some of the questions I have brought to my research and the reasons I have located that research within practical theology.

Gerkin calls the practical theologian an "interpretive guide," one who is able to "relate the normative source of the Christian tradition to the issues people actually face in their everyday lives."[4] It is important to know how to meet millennials in their everyday lives in order to make Jesus real and Christianity relevant. Part of being an interpretive guide is to engage in the "analysis and critique of the social systems shaping their interpretive patterns."[5] There is thus an iconoclastic role that practical theologians can play, one that "may well challenge and disturb certain accepted understandings and assumptions."[6] It is this role that I am particularly interested in playing with this study by challenging assumptions about both the millennial generation and normative practices in Christian tradition. John Swinton and Harriet Mowat write that "practical theology takes human experience seriously."[7] It is time to take seriously the human experience of millennials.

"EMERGING ADULTHOOD" AND THE MISSIONAL CHURCH

The millennial generation is unique in several ways. Born between 1980 and 2000, millennials are the first cohort to occupy an entirely new life stage.[8] Psychologist Jeffrey Jensen Arnett identified this stage as "emerging adulthood," a discrete phase between adolescence and full adulthood characterized by identity exploration, instability, self-focus, transition, and hope.[9] Whereas previous generations usually moved straight from adolescence to adulthood, emerging adults are often delaying the five adult milestones: graduating, leaving home, achieving financial independence, getting married, and having children.[10] The years between 18 and 30 have always been a formational time of faith, when individuals assess their worldview and determine for themselves what their spiritual and religious beliefs will be. Emerging adulthood, however, has its own set of challenges and opportunities because there is more time to consider alternative viewpoints. The uncertainty, while allowing freedom on the one hand, causes anxiety or feelings of being morally adrift on the other. Some are concerned that this freedom to focus on the self has devolved into full-blown narcissism.[11]

Another unique characteristic of the millennial generation is that it is the first fully postmodern generation. Millennials reflect a larger epistemological turn from Enlightenment to post-Enlightenment thinking in the West.[12] Some speculate that there has been a failure to fully understand the magnitude of the epistemological turn, which is the reason for so much misunderstanding about millennials. For example, David John Seel writes that this is

> why so much of the research done on millennials is distorted. Most millennials resist being called millennials because the national narrative on them is so pejorative, patronizing, and just wrong . . . Moreover, the litany of stereotypes used to describe millennials make it nearly impossible to appreciate their positive insights.[13]

The church, by not understanding the turn, has accidentally pushed this generation away. A bastion of Enlightenment thinking, the evangelical church has remained too entrenched in rational, analytical, left-brained processes, while eschewing right-brained imaginative, intuitive, relativistic thinking.[14] This has made it difficult to reach postmodern millennials. Reengaging them will thus require more than a retooling of techniques; a larger paradigm shift will be necessary.[15] The answer for the church lies in finding "on-ramps" for millennials to engage their faith "in lived experiences outside the institutional church."[16] What is needed are new discipleship models, those that are based—at least in the initial stages—more on right-brained presence, empathy, and relationship than on left-brained mastery of knowledge.[17]

These unique demographic features of the millennial generation have implications for the best methods of discipleship. The church is at a crossroads, wrestling with whether to ask millennials to change their spots so they can be assimilated into the existing form of church or to modify long-established customs, rituals, and practices in order to accommodate their new life stage and postmodern orientation. The task before the church is to know how to innovate without compromising the Christian faith and tradition. It is a fine line to walk.

Many millennials have not rejected their Christian faith wholesale but simply have become disenchanted with traditional congregations.[18] Alternatively, some are finding a sense of belonging and spiritual community in the burgeoning missional movement, defined by Darrell Guder as a "profoundly theocentric reconceptualization of Christian mission" where "mission is not merely an activity of the church" but "the result of God's initiative, rooted in God's purposes to restore and heal creation."[19] Derived from the Greek *missio*, meaning "sent," the movement is, as Alan Hirsch writes, essentially about "taking the church to people rather than bringing people to church."[20]

The missional movement is predicated on the notion that the West has lost the centrality of the gospel and has itself become a mission field.[21] Most major denominations are in decline, and the Western church is faced with the challenge of reaching people for Christ in culturally relevant ways.[22] This challenge has been met by the establishing of Christian faith communities that are noninstitutional in form and contextualized to the culture, known as missional communities.[23] Situated outside the four walls of traditional church buildings and established in third-place settings, missional communities are an attractive option for Christian millennials because of their organic, noninstitutional atmosphere.[24] Consequently, many of these missional ministries are designing discipleship programs for the purpose of developing the faith of their millennial members.

THE LOST ART OF DISCIPLE-MAKING

Hirsch boldly asserts in his book *The Forgotten Ways* that the American church in general has "lost the art of disciple-making."[25] Theological titans such as Dallas Willard and John Stott voiced similar concerns in recent years, lamenting that many churches focus on making new converts without the necessary follow-up of training disciples.[26] Rather than being the costly enterprise that "bids [us] come and die," as Dietrich Bonhoeffer so eloquently wrote, discipleship in the United States lacks depth, resulting in churches full of superficial believers.[27] Author Rachel Held Evans articulated the same viewpoint from a millennial's perspective:

> You can't hand us a latte and then go about business as usual and expect us to stick around. We're not leaving the church because we don't find the cool factor there; we're leaving the church because we don't find Jesus there. Like every generation before ours and every generation after, deep down, we long for Jesus.[28]

Evans expressed in millennial language what scholars and ministry practitioners have been contending for some time: that emerging adults are longing for mentors who will invest in discipleship to facilitate their personal relationship with Jesus.

Some have grown concerned that today's churches are filled with those who are either un- or under-discipled.[29] Further, there is concern that even the churches that are investing in discipleship are placing an undue emphasis on programs or techniques rather than on a relationship with Christ.[30] Theologians such as David E. Bjork theorize that one of the primary impediments to effective discipleship in American churches today is the institutionalization of faith communities—the tendency to relegate discipleship responsibilities to the paid clergy and/or church staff rather than equipping lay leadership to go and make disciples.[31] This renders discipleship, at least from an institutional perspective, entirely optional, stifling the replication function.

Millennials, meanwhile, are the most unchurched generation in the United States today, with a full 65 percent rarely or never attending a Christian place of worship.[32] The American church, in fact, is experiencing a "dropout phenomenon" among an entire generation of people in their twenties and thirties.[33] The reasons for this mass exodus are varied, but principal among them is that this age group tends to have an aversion to institutions of any type, and this includes the church.[34] Recent sociological research reveals that the emerging adult generation is disconnected from and unsympathetic toward Christianity and the church.[35] Instead, the majority subscribes to what Christian Smith in his landmark book *Soul Searching: The Religious and Spiritual Lives of American Teenagers* has termed "Moralistic Therapeutic Deism" (MTD), which views God as a distant creator who wants humans to be "nice" to one another and intervenes only to help them attain happiness and fulfillment.[36]

Based on 3,300 interviews with American teenagers, Smith codified MTD with five tenets: (1) "A God exists who created and orders the world and watches over human life on earth"; (2) "God wants people to be good, nice, and fair to each other, as taught in the Bible and by most world religions"; (3) "The central goal of life is to be happy and to feel good about oneself"; (4) "God does not need to be particularly involved in one's life except when he is needed to resolve a problem"; and (5) "Good people go to heaven when they die."[37] Smith claims that MTD, however, is not just a young adult phenomenon; millennials are adopting the belief system being modeled for them by older adults.[38] They are, as Smith writes, "reflecting the contours, priorities, expectations, and structures" of American society to which they have been inculcated.[39]

The lack of discipleship within the American church remains one of its most concerning issues; however, the missional movement is beginning to take the problem seriously and make discipleship a central focus of its strategy.[40] Discipleship, as a result, is currently in the process of being reframed along missional dimensions so that leaders can adapt traditional Christian practices to the specific cultural milieu of their constituents.[41] Missional theologians such as Dwight J. Zscheile have been instrumental in developing a missional theology of faith formation in order to address the problem of deepening "the church's Christian identity in a post-Christendom world."[42] Part of the problem is that millennials are no longer coming to church, so they are unable to hear for themselves the difference between MTD and authentic Christianity. For discipleship to happen, the church must go to them.

AN ACUTE SPIRITUAL CRISIS

The need to reach the millennial generation for Christ has reached "an acute level of spiritual crisis," and it is possible that the continued failure of the church to disciple young adults could have serious consequences.[43] The millennial generation is growing up and is quickly arising as the "most pressing mission field."[44] In response, many ministry leaders and practitioners are developing new ways of discipling millennials that are proving effective. Innovations are taking place, especially in the missional church movement, that are worth acknowledging, studying, and responding to. All of this led me to ask: What does it mean for millennials to follow Christ today in missional communities? The primary purpose of my research was to study the ways in which millennials experience faith formation through discipleship in missional communities. My research aims were:

- To explore the spiritual experiences of millennials participating in discipleship relationships and programs in missional communities.
- To chart the pedagogical, relational, pneumatological, and replicating aspects of discipling programs of millennials in missional communities.
- To identify what millennials and their leaders perceive as the most beneficial practices of discipleship in their respective missional communities.
- To investigate the effects of deinstitutionalization and contextualization of missional communities on the discipling of millennials.

I chose this particular context because research suggests that missional churches are gaining so much momentum that they will eventually supplant institutional forms in the West.[45] It appears that the missional model is proving effective; the few denominations that do report church growth attribute their success to the increase in missional church plants.[46] It is important to understand how millennials are responding to the discipleship approaches designed for them, the ways in which they perceive their faith to be growing, and the larger implications of how the missional movement is influencing the spiritual development of this demographic.

ETHNOGRAPHIC FIELDWORK AND METHOD

My research aims were achieved through a year of ethnographic fieldwork at two sites in Fort Worth, Texas. Both ministries contained 85 to 90 percent millennial constituency and were missional in nature, situated outside the four walls of traditional church buildings and established in third-place settings contextualized to the surrounding culture. Both sites offered the discipleship of millennials through their programs, practices, and/or services with the goal of faith formation. The research sites differed from one another, however, in that one was in a middle-class / upper-middle-class nondenominational church, while the other was a ministry focused on a marginalized, disenfranchised population in an urban setting. The purpose in selecting two disparate sites was to create a "comparative puzzle," a qualitative research schema that explores differences and similarities among social phenomena.[47]

Site 1: Urban Life Church

Urban Life Church was founded in 2011 in downtown Fort Worth by a pastor, his wife, and roughly twenty-five other adults. By 2018 the congregation had grown to approximately two hundred members, 80–85 percent of whom were millennials. Seventy percent of these millennials lived within a three-mile radius of the church, so it was very much a young, urban setting. Ten to 12 percent of members were baby boomers, with Generation X and Generation Z cohorts making up the remainder with 4–5 percent each.[48] Their missional approach was based on making an impact in the marketplace and downtown community, a theme discussed in greater detail in a later chapter. Urban Life held four core values that helped them fulfill their mission:

1. Legacy: We value, equip, and fuel the potential of the next generation.
2. Influence: We measure our success by marketplace and community impact.
3. Intention: We value bold, creative strategies that focus our efforts on possibilities yet unseen.
4. Presence: We highly value the presence of God, while striving to walk in unity and harmony with one another.

I attended Sunday worship services and visited other ministry events and programs in order to gain a thorough understanding of their congregational life and discipleship efforts.

Site 2: Strip Club Church

The second site for my research was Strip Club Church, a ministry dedicated to reaching out to those in the sex industry. Their mission statement reads, "We exist to show the unconditional love of Christ to women and men who work in the sex industry and to renew and reaffirm hope and a future to them." Each week a ministry team, called a Go Team, visited strip clubs in the Fort Worth area. They had begun a discipleship program and provided resources to those wishing to leave the sex industry. I joined one of the Go Teams and ministered alongside them in the strip clubs every Friday night for a year.

Strip Club Church was part of a larger organization founded in 2002 in Las Vegas and had expanded to be an international network of like-minded ministries dedicated to reaching (primarily) women in the sex industry. At the time of this writing, they had partners in over one hundred cities in the United States, Canada, the United Kingdom, and Australia. Local ministries could apply to become part of the network and have access to resources and training. Thus, the Fort Worth chapter was a network affiliate, and part of my training, participant observation, and interviewing was conducted within this larger network.

At both fieldwork sites, "access" included online content. I was permitted to join the closed Facebook page of the Strip Club Church Network, which allowed me to read posts and correspond with affiliates in other locations. This proved very helpful to me when amassing my interviewees, as I will explain below. I was also given online access to a closed Facebook page at Urban Life Church, where I was able to read prayer requests from congregants, as well as receive scheduling updates on meetings being held by the church.

Fieldwork conducted at these sites provided data to answer my primary research question and satisfy my research aims through following a model of practical theological interpretation put forth by Richard Osmer. Using a rubric of "four tasks of practical theology interpretation," the model is designed to aid ministers in connecting method and practice in order to solve problems and improve ministry.[49] This model has four tasks, each with a corresponding question to be explored:

1) The Descriptive-Empirical Task: "What Is Going On?" The descriptive-empirical task involves the gathering of information from the research setting and examining that information for patterns and/or dynamics present.[50] Regardless of the scope and duration of the setting, the objects of study are the "social and natural systems in which a situation unfolds."[51] These systems are comprised of the lives and behaviors of individuals and their contexts.

2) The Interpretive Task: "Why Is This Going On?" The second task in practical theological inquiry is the interpretive task, which requires understanding and explaining why particular patterns and dynamics are present. It utilizes theories from other disciplines, such as the arts and sciences, to discover the reasons certain behavior patterns and dynamics exist.[52] This is the interdisciplinarity aspect of practical theology, where practitioners may draw from a host of other disciplines to aid them in interpretation.

3) The Normative Task: "What Ought to Be Going On?" Osmer states that, as beneficial as theories from other fields are, practical theology interpretation must go a step further to guide the Christian community into faithful practice. Thus, a normative task is crucial; it involves interpreting situations using a theological rubric and then formulating norms to determine the best course of action. Osmer's normative task involves three steps. First is theological reflection, the process of "using theological concepts to interpret particular episodes, situations, or contexts, constructing ethical norms to guide our responses, and learning from 'good practice.'"[53] The second is to identify principles and guidelines that can be applied to the situation to guide behavior. Third, the normative task involves examining Christian practices, both past and present, that can act as an authoritative standard in shaping future patterns.[54]

4) The Pragmatic Task: "How Might We Respond?" The final task in Osmer's model of practical theology is the pragmatic task, which asks how we as the Christian body might respond to the discoveries made.[55] This task involves determining specific actions that may be taken in order to positively influence future Christian practice. Research is viewed through the lens of theology, with an eye toward shaping the field in which the study is being undertaken.[56]

Some practical theologians, such as Pete Ward, see limitations with Osmer's approach, noting that its orientation toward problems and conflicts within the pastoral setting separates it from the normal, everyday life of the congregation being studied, thus stifling the ability to connect theology and practice in the ordinary.[57] However, it was precisely this focus on the problematic that made it well suited for my study.

As previously noted, the contemporary American church is facing several challenges: a dropout phenomenon among its younger members, a changing ecclesiological landscape, and a persistent discipleship problem. The pastoral cycle provided the framework within which to investigate these problems with depth of insight. Osmer's process of practical theological hermeneutics was particularly relevant; namely, the notion of "being brought up short" as "preunderstandings" are challenged, a dynamic that was at play in my research as the emerging data confronted previously unquestioned methods of discipleship of young people.[58]

Further, Osmer's emphasis on interdisciplinary dialogue was appropriate for my integration of theology and sociology.[59] The importance placed on the interplay between the "worldly wisdom of the arts and sciences" and the wisdom of God was a helpful guide as I engaged in both cultural and theological exegesis in my fieldwork.[60] This dialogical interplay led to a "fusion of horizons" whereby preunderstanding merged with new discoveries, resulting in fresh ideas for transformed praxis.[61]

Thus, my study followed the four tasks of the pastoral cycle sequentially. In order to address Osmer's first and second questions,

I employed the methodologies of "big ethnography": participant observation, interviews, and document analysis. The primacy of contextualization in missional theology made ethnography a particularly suitable approach. I was able to study millennials in their ecclesiological and relational ecosystems, considering how the third-place settings formed and informed discipleship practice. Ethnography "always implies a theory of culture."[62] Culture is a concept of meaningful symbols; therefore, ethnography helped me determine what millennials deemed meaningful in their own cultural contexts.[63]

In answer to Osmer's third question, I selected Bonhoeffer's "religionless Christianity" as a theological framework for my study. Religionless Christianity was Bonhoeffer's new theology for a world that no longer found religion credible. In answering the question "What is Christianity, or who is Christ for us today?" Bonhoeffer was reframing core tenets for a new era.[64] These concepts made Bonhoeffer a suitable dialectical partner for several reasons. First, Bonhoeffer's religionless Christianity dealt with the recovery of the meaning of the gospel for a new philosophical context, just as the church is doing today with the turn to postmodernism. He saw a need to translate theological forms and constructs for a contemporary world that no longer found religion relevant, famously asking, "What does a church, a congregation, a sermon, a liturgy, a Christian life, mean in a religionless world?"[65] Similarly, the church today is asking, "What does a church look like in a postmodern world?" in an attempt to translate discipleship for a new epistemological era. Bonhoeffer's ideas offer valuable answers to this question

Second, Bonhoeffer's religionless Christianity is very much in line with missional theology. It created a world-centered ethic for the church that pivoted away from inner preservation and toward a concern for "the other."[66] It is ethical at the core. When the church is open to the world, especially to the oppressed and suffering, then there is a shift in the way of being "church." Thus, religionless Christianity becomes a theology that has fundamental reorientation to the world, undergoing what Bonhoeffer called a *metanoia*.[67] Similarly, missional-incarnational ecclesiology espouses taking the church to others, establishing local bodies within the cultural contexts of its constituents, often in third-place settings. Thus, the missional movement is creating a *metanoia* of the church (conceivably, one could even categorize it as a reformation; time will tell), just as Bonhoeffer wrote about. I hope this book will in part answer his question "What does a church . . . mean in a religionless world?" with missional ecclesiology, a new theology resulting in a fundamentally different way of being the church.

Third, I believe it to be a suitable rubric because Bonhoeffer espoused his new theology with future generations in mind. He viewed his theology as one of taking responsibility to mold history for the next generation. By recovering the meaning of the gospel for a new historical context, he hoped to set the stage for younger generations to embrace Christ.[68] In today's context, as in Bonhoeffer's, the task is to ensure that the faith being handed down to the next generations is true, authentic Christianity, not a set of heterodoxies that have insidiously made their way into the minds and hearts of believers. This was the task of undoing religion in Bonhoeffer's day, and it is the same task with millennials and MTD today. In this way, his framework provides a significant overlap with the topic of the discipleship of millennials. For these reasons, Bonhoeffer's ideas made for thought-provoking and lively discussion as I reflected theologically on my research findings.

Finally, Osmer's fourth question was addressed by linking key themes in research findings with recommended corresponding practices. The goal was to offer concrete suggestions on how the church might respond faithfully and effectively as it considers renovating its approach to the discipleship of emerging adults. The desired outcome was a model of "good practice" implemented in the context of "servant leadership."[69] The Christian practices of testimony, hospitality, and discernment were identified as three of the most effective ways to disciple millennials. My intention is that the unique contribution of this research will inspire innovative thinking and robust discourse among church leaders as they develop emerging adult discipleship into the future.

THE AUDIENCE

My hope is that this work will be helpful to fellow evangelical audiences.

Ministry Practitioners. In my own ministry to the millennial generation, I have often felt stuck between two conflicting motives: my desire to share the love of Jesus, on the one hand, and their reluctance to be associated with a church they deem judgmental and hypocritical, on the other. This internal conflict has too often resulted in my refraining from engaging in a spiritual conversation or initiating a discipleship relationship. My hope is that, by pinpointing practices that are effective with young adults in their own cultural contexts, using a missional framework, I may equip leaders in the United States—whether academics, church leaders, or millennials in peer leadership positions—with a guide that will aid them in discipling young adults.

The Millennial Generation. There is a need for new voices in the area of ministering to millennials, voices that can revision discipleship for this unique generation living in this unique time in history. As postmoderns living in a time when the church is still largely entrenched in Enlightenment thinking and practice, millennials are often expected to conform. A conceptual niche needs to be carved for them, one that accommodates their epistemology while retaining the essential tenets and practices of the Christian tradition.

The American Evangelical Church. Like their baby boomer predecessors, millennials are so large a cohort that they have a "pig in the python effect" on the culture, reshaping society as they move through it; thus, it is inevitable that they will influence the church of the future by virtue of their sheer size.[70] The practices instilled in them by the church today will have a profound effect on the trajectory of American Christianity in the years to come. Further, young adults throughout history have tended to be what Andy Crouch calls "culture makers," birthing many great social causes, revivals, and spiritual renewal movements, so millennials hold great promise and potential for the church of the twenty-first century.[71]

Academics and Scholars of Practical Theology. Much has been written on those of the millennial generation and their relationship with the Christian faith: specifically, their disillusionment with organized religion, their their perception of the irrelevance of the institution of the church, and the resulting dropout phenomenon of young adults from traditional forms of congregational life. However, the topic of the discipleship of millennials remains underexplored, particularly the practical aspects of effective ministry to young adults in postmodern, post-Christendom cultural contexts. Important advancements have been made in the scholarly conversation; overall, however, the relationship between young adult faith formation and the missional movement has been underdeveloped.

Prior research has produced several important insights regarding discipleship among millennials and discipleship in missional contexts; however, scant attention has been devoted to the relationship between the two topics—a relationship that is conceptually intriguing because it has implications for future praxis.[72] Thus, my work provides a unique theoretical contribution by advancing our understanding of the connection between millennial discipleship and the missional church movement. Research has focused up to this point either on the relationship of millennials to discipleship or the relationship of millennials to the missional movement, but a paucity of research exists that focuses on the confluence of all three subjects. This provides an opportunity to contribute new data and insights to the current body of work by identifying transformational aspects of discipleship. Thus, my work concentrates on exploring the discipleship of the millennial generation in missional communities.

CHAPTER PREVIEW AND ORIENTING ROAD MAP

Chapters 2, 3, and 4 provide reports of my findings, arranged by theme. The three principal themes that emerged were: (1) discipleship among millennials in missional communities was facilitated by opportunities to become engaged in ministry and mission in the world; (2) discipleship among millennials in missional communities was facilitated by authentic, caring, and loving relationships; and (3) discipleship of millennials in missional communities included a belief in the activity of the Holy Spirit. Chapter 5 reflects theologically on the findings, critically correlating the themes with biblical principles and theological writings. Chapter 6 addresses the implications for practice derived from the study and makes recommendations for future praxis based on specific ministry strategies.

CONCLUSION

No longer are churches able to assume that millennials will eventually return to church, as previous generations have done. They are not coming back.[73] Some churches are recognizing this shift and are adopting a more missional approach to millennials. My research demonstrates that the missional movement holds great promise for the discipleship of millennials. The church need not consternate about how to restore its young adults, nor lament their absence. Instead, it can be encouraged as it is reminded of the essence of the Great Commission: Go. Jesus specified the location of disciple-making as "all the world," and the church can establish a missional ecclesia that is inviting to millennials who have strayed from their church home. I call this act "repatriation," the calling back of exiled millennial Christians into the body of Christ. This repatriation is taking place in the most exciting and unexpected of places.

However, although the church is in the process of shifting to a more missional approach to attract and retain millennials, the church is not adequately addressing the *other* shift, the turn to postmodernism. Still stuck in Enlightenment-based thinking, churches are hoping to retrofit millennials into the Age of Reason. The mission field, therefore, entails not only going to the next generations physically, but also philosophically. What is needed are voices who know how to create Jesus followers within this generation, using language they can understand. Thus, the original contribution of my research is reimagining discipleship methods and practices in postmodern terms within missional contexts so that the traditions of the Christian faith can be "translated" into epistemological forms and symbols to which millennials can relate. In doing so, I will view the uniqueness of this generation as an asset to be mined and developed: "calling out the gold" of the abilities and gifts within them.

CHAPTER 2

MISSIONAL DISCIPLESHIP

INTRODUCTION TO THEMES

The millennial generation is a mission field. David John Seel, in his book *The New Copernicans*, has gone so far as to say that they are the "most pressing mission field" today.[1] The reason for the urgency is that millennials have reached the age of being the church leaders, transmitters of the gospel for the future, yet they remain the most unchurched, dechurched generation among us.[2] The West as a whole has been drifting away from Christianity for some time; in fact, decades ago the renowned missiologist Lesslie Newbigin recognized that the West was itself becoming a mission field and advocated for believers to take a missionary stance within their own culture.[3] But the "dropout phenomenon" of the millennial generation has created a tipping point of that drift, decisively shifting us into a post-Christian era.[4] The Western church, as a result, is in a critical moment, and the need to innovate is urgent.

If the millennial generation is a mission field, then they need to be approached as an indigenous people group with their own language, customs, and cultural symbols. In short, Christianity needs to be contextualized for these inhabitants of the post-Christian world. No longer can we expect to inculcate them into our current form of church, because the dropout phenomenon proves this is not working. The following chapters set out to show how this contextualization can take place, and indeed, already is taking place in two important ways. First, millennials are responding to ecclesiological contextualization. As the church embraces the missional-incarnational impulse through the burgeoning missional movement, they can take church to millennials rather than expecting them to come to church. Second, millennials are responding to philosophical contextualization. As Christian practices are translated into postmodern forms, the church is learning to speak millennials' epistemological language.

So, how are millennials being discipled in missional communities? What is proving effective and why? These are the questions I brought to my research as I spent a year with Urban Life Church and Strip Club Church. This is what Osmer calls the descriptive-empirical task, which seeks to discover what is going on in a particular setting. The descriptive-empirical task involves "priestly listening," which goes beyond gathering data.[5] Instead, listening becomes a spiritual act, even an intercessory act, whereby the researcher listens to others "in their particularity and otherness in the presence of God" with great attentiveness, openness, and unconditional acceptance in a way that creates a sense of communion.[6]

Osmer points out that it can be challenging to truly listen to another because it is natural to be preoccupied with other thoughts or even to rush to judgment without ever pausing to listen in order to understand.[7] In my estimation, millennials too often have been talked about, but rarely have they been listened to with such spiritual attentiveness and lack of prejudice. It was important for me to listen to millennials in order to understand what it meant from their perspective to be a disciple of Jesus in missional communities. The ethnographic methods of participant observation, interviews, and document analysis enabled me, as far as possible, to see the world through their eyes and from within their cultural context, allowing for the generation of thick description. Only then could I proceed to the second step in the pastoral cycle: the interpretive task, which asks the question "Why is this going on?"

As a result, three key themes emerged from my analysis of the data collected: Theme One: Discipleship among millennials in missional communities is facilitated by opportunities to become engaged in ministry and mission in the world; Theme Two: Discipleship among millennials is facilitated by authentic, caring, and loving relationships; and Theme Three: Discipleship among millennials in missional communities includes a belief in the activity of the Holy Spirit. Over three chapters I will present these themes, each with several subthemes, that emerged from the data. The voices of millennials and their leaders will address the descriptive-empirical task, followed by analysis and correlation with secondary literature to address the interpretive task. The purpose of collecting data and generating themes ultimately is to answer my central question, "What does it mean for millennials to follow Christ today in missional communities?"

THEME ONE: ENGAGED IN MINISTRY AND MISSION IN THE WORLD

The first finding of my research was that discipleship among millennials in missional communities was facilitated by opportunities to become engaged in ministry and mission in the world. Millennials engaged enthusiastically in activities that were missional in scope, including going into the surrounding culture, proclaiming the gospel, and serving others.

Both fieldwork sites self-identified as missional communities. It might help for me to explain what this meant. Urban Life Church based their missiology squarely on the Great Commission and the Great Commandment. Thus, the mandate to "go and make disciples" was an expression of love of God and others. Missional methodology was built on this foundation. Their mission statement was:

> Developing followers of Jesus who impact and shape culture. With intention, we fuel a long-term strategy of legacy by actively making Jesus known through influence in our neighborhood and around the world. We

believe the presence of God in us will result in a greater measure of the Holy Spirit activity in the culture. We are passionately evangelistic. We are boldly gospel centered. This embodies our call to fulfill the Great Commission and the Great Commandment.

Thus, "mission" to Urban Life Church meant being sent into the surrounding culture to establish relationships, share the gospel, and make disciples through the power of the Holy Spirit, so that lives are changed, culture is transformed, and the city is "healed" of the destructive effects of sin.

Strip Club Church, meanwhile, framed their missiology in terms of the ministry of reconciliation, based on 2 Corinthians 5. God is reconciling himself to the world through Christ, and believers are called to participate in his work through acting as his ambassadors. Strip Club Church described the ministry of reconciliation as one of their "biggest purposes," saying, "We are called to the ministry of Christ, which is love and reconciliation." Their missional methodology was to enter the world of the sex industry and demonstrate the love of Christ in word and deed, and then to let the Holy Spirit convict of sin, knowing that he was working in the hearts of the recipients to receive the gospel.

Thus, the missiology of both sites was centered on the *missio Dei*, viewing the church as empowered and sent by the Father, Son, and Holy Spirit into the world as missionaries of God's redemptive work through Jesus Christ. The goal, then, was to equip their millennial constituents to be missional themselves as an act of replication in the discipleship process. Missional equipping was implemented in three ways: providing opportunities for incarnational engagement of culture, proclaiming the gospel through testimony, and being mobilized immediately for ministry.

OPPORTUNITIES FOR THE INCARNATIONAL ENGAGEMENT OF CULTURE

The Descriptive-Empirical Task: What Is Going On?

Both fieldwork sites encouraged millennials to go into the surrounding culture to participate in the work of Christ, incarnating his life, teachings, and love through word and deed so that others may know, believe in, and follow him as Lord and Savior. Each site had their own unique expression based on their cultural milieu: Urban Life focused more on going into the marketplace because of their fixed downtown location, while Strip Club Church based their outreach on a population rather than a location, with millennial volunteers dispersing into clubs, expos, and events in order to enter the sex-industry subculture. Fieldwork at both sites generated data supporting the idea that millennials were enthusiastic about the incarnational engagement of culture.[8]

Urban Life Church was explicit in their incarnational orientation, stating that "influencing the culture" by "making Jesus known" was one of their primary missions. One of the pastors, named Mark, provided the church's definition of culture: "the observable byproduct of beliefs; including speech, traditions, customs, collective behaviors and expressions of life that make up an area/neighborhood." The implication of this definition is that every neighborhood or geographical area has a distinct expression, based on its underlying worldview. To engage the culture incarnationally, therefore, is to enter a particular locale and bring a Christian worldview, using contextualized expressions of the customs, language, and behaviors of that area.

Pastor Jim explained that the church's philosophy "is that ministry happens outside the walls of the church building." Being a downtown church made it uniquely positioned in the culture, he explained, because sociological research has shown that whoever is present and active in the cultural center of a city (what he called "upstream") will have inordinate influence on the rest of the city ("downstream").[9] Further, the unique downtown location of Urban

Life enabled it to develop relationships with the culture-makers. Pastor Jim elaborated: "It's about getting involved in people's lives where you are leading them—other people—to Jesus, because when you begin to impact the culture-makers, the people who create culture here in this neighborhood, then that's when the cultural shift happens."

As individuals are transformed through knowing Jesus, their influence flows "downstream." Thus, the believer becomes a co-laborer with God in healing the city. The disciple-making process he referred to here has a distinctly incarnational flair: the process of impacting culture, then, was first going into the culture; second, forming relationships; and third, discipling others so that they encounter Jesus.

Urban Life had a well-organized discipleship framework for incarnational ministry. First, congregants were encouraged to find their unique position in the culture to which they were called, the place where they were distinctively suited to be an incarnational expression of the knowledge of Jesus. This was accomplished through completing a questionnaire that helped identify areas of passion and ability. They

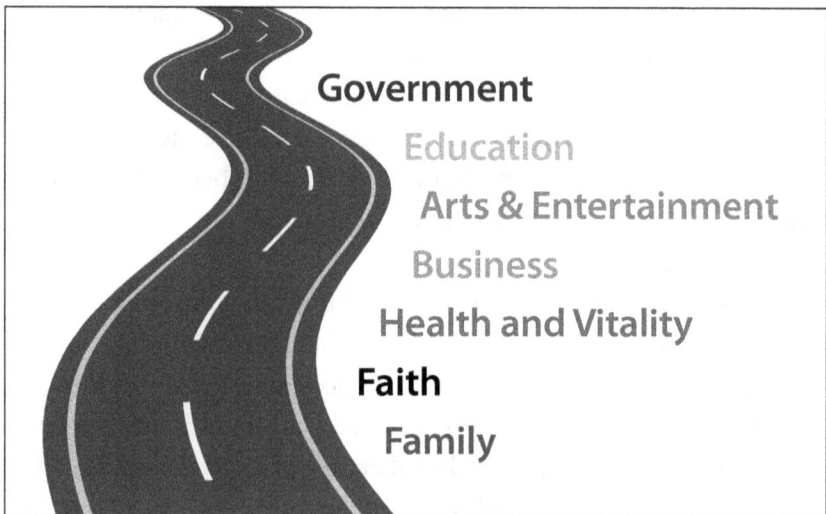

Government
Education
Arts & Entertainment
Business
Health and Vitality
Faith
Family

Figure 2.1 Seven Cultural Streets

were then introduced to a conceptual framework called "The Seven Cultural Streets" to help them implement their mission. Cultural streets were spheres of society where individuals were placed to do the ministry of Jesus. The seven spheres were: Government, Education, Arts and Entertainment, Business, Health and Vitality, Faith, and Family. The goal was to "make Jesus known" on their "street."

Second, congregants were deployed to their respective "streets" to incarnate the life of Christ through using their abilities and forming relationships. The purpose was to share "God's heart" for people, bringing "Christ's culture" to them. Pastor Mark explained that "there are hurting and broken people on every street in this world." Without Jesus, the individual is naturally self-focused, which can lead to unhealthy, "toxic" behaviors. Urban Life listed five of these behaviors of the human condition: "critical negativity," based on the belief that "I need to focus on myself"; "draining grouchiness," resulting from the belief that "someone owes me something"; "projected phoniness," based on the belief that "people's perception of me is everything"; "repulsive lethargy," which means engaging with others only when it fits one's agenda, based on the belief that "everything depends on me"; and "dreary consumerism," stemming from the belief that "my life is all about me." These are the issues in the culture that are making people miserable without Jesus.

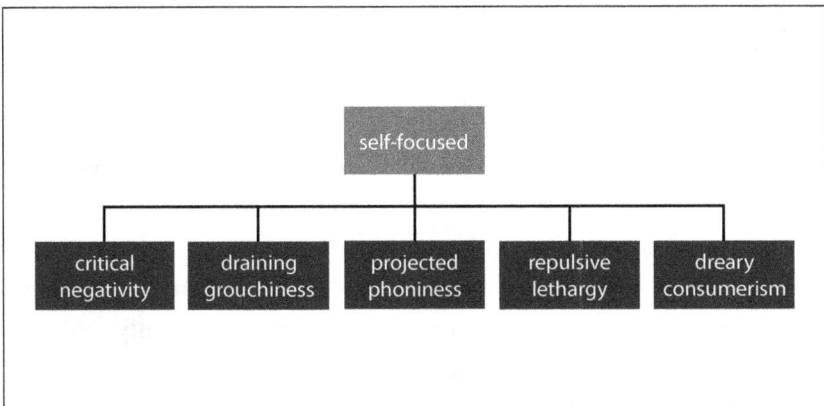

Figure 2.2 Toxic Behavior Based on the Human Condition

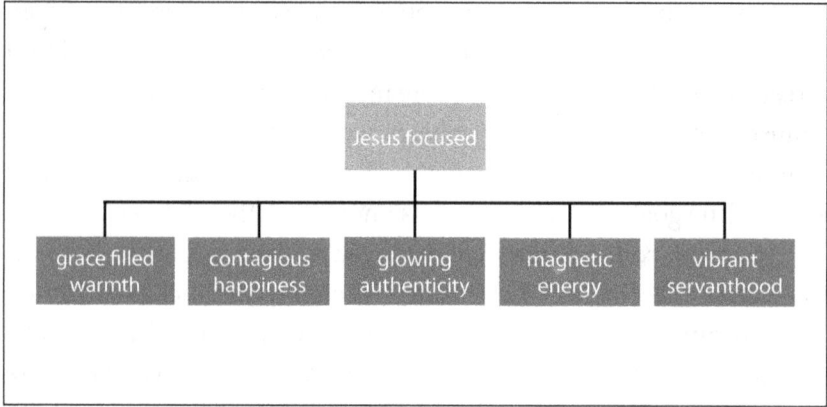

Figure 2.3 How Urban Life Behaves Based on the Unique Edge

Urban Life believed that, as millennials disperse into the surrounding culture, they can be agents of healing and transformation through incarnating the foil of the self-focused individual, which is the "Jesus-focused" disciple. They were to "fight toxic culture by doing the opposite." The Jesus follower will exhibit five characteristics that contain culture-transforming efficacy, called the "Unique Edge." First is "grace-filled warmth," based on the belief that "every person is valuable to me because every person is valuable to God." The individual will "pick people up rather than picking them apart." Second is "contagious happiness," which believes that "nobody owes me anything because Jesus gave me everything." The corresponding behavior is "wherever we go, smiles and laughter follow." Third is "glowing authenticity," based on the belief that "his [God's] strength is valuable to me because every person is valuable to God." The resulting behavior is that "we don't puff up, we don't slouch down, we stand on sacred ground." Fourth is "magnetic energy," based on the belief that "greater is he that is in me than he that is in the world," and behavior signaling that "we leave people better than we found them." Fifth and finally, "vibrant servanthood" is based on the belief that "today is less about me than I think it is" and the resulting behavior that "we are the first to spring into action on an opportunity to serve." As millennials were dispatched into the surrounding culture equipped with the beliefs and behaviors borne out of a life focused on Jesus, they began to transform lives they encountered, and healing of the city took place.

A millennial named Michael reported that Urban Life helped him find his place on the Arts and Entertainment Street and turn his artistic ability into a ministry. "I love making things," he said. "I actually went to welding school." He went on to explain that the streets concept "gave me a bit more direction in life." He created a ministry plan he called "Creative Outreach," which he described as "a group of creators dedicated to building the church and community through craft and trade." He was in the process of building a website where costumers, video makers, speakers, writers, and other artists could offer their creativity. "Think Amazon but for services," he explained. He viewed his profession as a ministry, thanks to the cultural-influence teaching of Urban Life Church. Michael had caught the vision of impacting the culture and felt that he had been given the direction he needed.

The Seven Cultural Streets concept also resonated with a millennial named Savannah. "There's these different areas and spheres of cultural influence," she explained. "Through my real estate work . . . [I] just knew that I was called to the business sphere of influence. So, when I went to Urban Life seven years ago, [I felt] that there was support for that." Savannah viewed her real estate job as a platform for ministry and felt encouraged to develop that idea. Her mission, she said, was "bringing the kingdom and shaping the culture in our city" through her work.

Like Urban Life Church, Strip Club Church also had seen millennials responding positively to the calling of incarnational ministry. The incarnational orientation to the ministry's training and equipping they offered was outlined on their website:

> What if Jesus was serious when he identified you as the "light on the hill," the one who is meant to "go and be a light unto the world?"

What if he had a plan to deeply impact the lives of hundreds
    or thousands of women through you? Would you want to
    be part of that plan?
We believe that's exactly what he desires.
We believe God wants to equip you to meet the needs of the
    women in your city by his love and connecting in ways
    that allow you to speak life and bring encouragement.

Strip Club Church believed that they provided skills to equip others
to "go," so that Jesus could be incarnated and "deeply impact" others.
Danielle, one of the volunteers with Strip Club Church, described it
this way: "We're walking in the ministry of Jesus . . . his hands and
feet going physically into a place and loving on them." Her hope was
that her actions would be received by the dancers as the actions of
Christ himself, impacting them with his love.

A millennial named Emily, one of the founders of Strip Club
Church in Fort Worth and a former dancer, made weekly visits into
the very strip club where she used to work, bearing gifts for the
dancers and speaking of the love of Jesus. Specifically, she wanted to
be an agent of healing for those who had experienced sexual abuse.
She herself had been sexually abused and considered stripping a
"fruit" that had come from "the root" of the abuse. In her estimation
the vast majority—99 percent—of the women there had been
sexually abused, and they, like her, became "hypersexual" to "fill
that void or take that pain away." Her mission was to go into the
clubs as an incarnational presence "to bring healing to that place."
"I just wanted to be Jesus," she said.

The Interpretive Task: Why Is This Going On?
The incarnational approach employed at both fieldwork sites is one of
the central tenets of missional theology.[10] Theologian Darrell Guder
defines incarnational mission as "the understanding and practice of
Christian witness that is rooted in and shaped by the life, ministry,
suffering, death, and resurrection of Jesus."[11] Jesus sorrowed along
with the world at the reality of injustice, violence, and tragedy and was

passionate about seeing lives redeemed. The word "incarnational" is based on John 1:1–18, which describes the action of Jesus, who came to earth and "made his dwelling among us" (*eskeonsen*, verse 14), what Hirsch describes as Jesus "moving into the neighborhood" and identifying with humanity.[12] This stands in contrast to a church that is separatist, extractional, or withdrawn from the surrounding culture. The incarnation of Christ is thus the "what" of the gospel, the defining event of God's salvific actions.[13]

Incarnational mission calls Christians to go beyond orthodoxy—right believing—and to give full expression to orthopraxy by joining God in his restorative work.[14] Jesus's incarnation is the example for the church of how to engage the world. More than words, the gospel must be a "demonstrated message,"[15] and the purpose of the church is to be an instrument of the kingdom inaugurated by Jesus.[16] This is what N. T. Wright calls "putting the world to rights" through acts of justice, peace, and compassion.[17] The purpose of salvation is not just about spending eternity in heaven but about bringing heaven to earth by going into the world to "reclaim, reform, and restore it for Christ."[18] By extension, spreading the kingdom is more than evangelistic efforts to save souls, as crucial as that is. It is also "working for the healing of persons, families, relationships, and nations."[19] Christian practices become "key elements of the calling to work for his kingdom within the world."[20]

Bonhoeffer did not use the term "incarnational," but his writings placed great emphasis on the concrete ethics of living out one's faith as a reflection of Jesus. In *The Cost of Discipleship*, he wrote,

> The bearers of Jesus' word receive a final word of promise for their work. They are now Christ's fellow-workers and will be like him in all things. Thus, they are to meet those to whom they are sent as if they were Christ himself. When they are welcomed into a house, Christ enters with them. They are bearers of his presence. They bring with them the most precious gift in the world, the gift of Jesus Christ.[21]

These words echo those of Guder and Hirsch by emphasizing that the presence of the believer is the presence of Christ himself. Bonhoeffer goes so far as to say that "the church is the church only when it exists for others"; that is, it is in the act of sharing the gift of Jesus that its function is made manifest. He continues that the church "must not underestimate the importance of human example (which has its origin in the humanity of Jesus); it is not abstract argument, but example, that gives its word emphasis and power."[22]

To Bonhoeffer, as well as to Guder and Hirsch, incarnational ministry means going beyond doctrinal abstractions and going into the surrounding culture to embody Jesus to others in concrete actions. In my fieldwork, millennial members of both groups embraced this outward trajectory of ministry and were eager to influence the culture by incarnating Christ in their respective spheres, or "streets." This notion is reminiscent of Bonhoeffer's words that the church "must tell men of every calling what it means to live in Christ, to exist for others."[23] It was the express purpose, especially of Urban Life Church, to equip millennials to use their vocation as a means of ministry in every sphere of society.

OPPORTUNITIES TO PROCLAIM THE GOSPEL THROUGH TESTIMONY
The Descriptive-Empirical Task: What Is Going On?
A second subtheme that emerged from the data was the effective use of millennials' personal narratives in discipleship. Their stories were firsthand accounts of their encounters with Jesus and choosing to become his disciples. Millennials at both fieldwork sites were enthusiastic to tell their stories as part of the discipleship process.

Urban Life Church emphasized the importance of telling faith stories. This was done through teaching and preaching, videos, and seminars. Pastor Jim emphasized that the Bible is a book of stories, true stories of "normal people" who "walked in their purpose" and "were on mission" and who demonstrated that we "can live on mission with purpose" as well. Thus, the missional impulse was explicitly tied to the telling of personal narratives.

One of the activities designed for this purpose was a feature on the church's online app called "Share Your Story." Members could log in and submit their story about how their life and faith had been impacted at Urban Life Church. A screenshot of this feature is in Figure 2.4 below.

Congregation members completed the form and submitted their stories, which became videos that were shown in Sunday morning worship services and posted on social media. The stated purpose was "to inspire others to make an impact in the

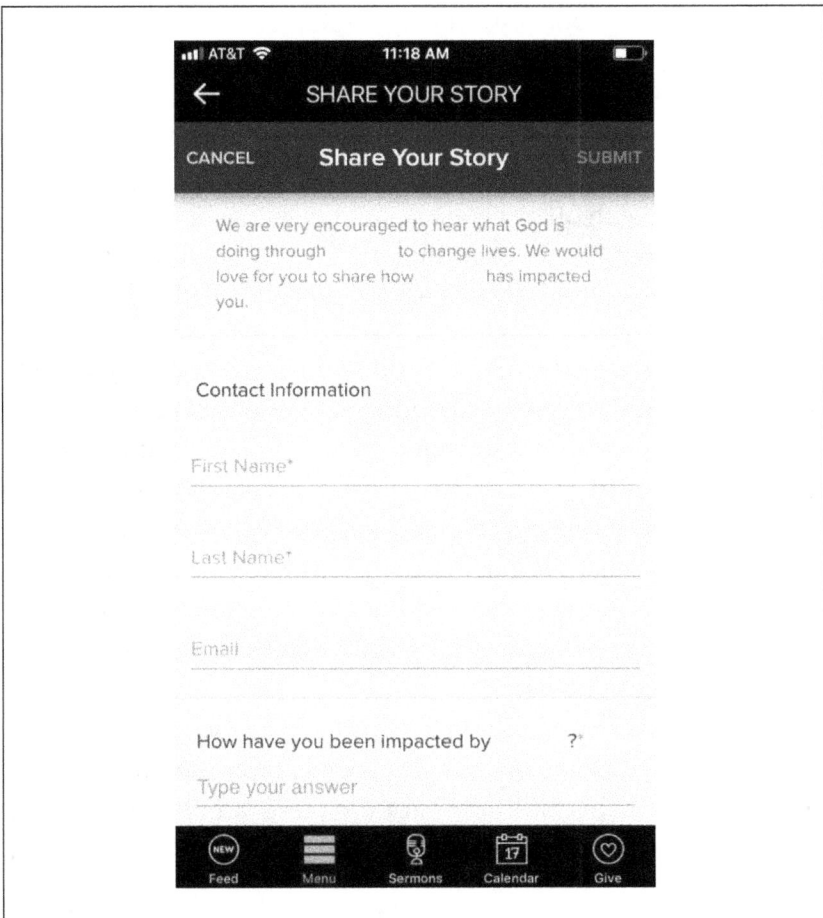

Figure 2.4 Screenshot of "Share Your Story" on the Church App

community." One of these video stories was about a millennial named T. J., who shared that he was a former homeless veteran and drug addict. When he eventually hit rock bottom, he said, "[I] let go of everything and surrendered my life to God." He went on to explain, "I knew that the void I had in my heart was for Jesus" and that he needed to "get plugged into a church." He started attending Urban Life Church because it was near the rehab center in which he was staying. As a result of rebuilding his faith, he and his wife reconciled and started attending church together. He is now attending seminary in Fort Worth.

T. J.'s video made a strong impression on a millennial named Morgan, who shared that

> hearing about how God just completely transformed his life, it strengthened my faith . . . I felt more comfortable speaking with other people about my faith, and I wanted to reach out and be like, you know, how I can know who I can have coffee with this week that I don't know.

Several important themes are present in this passage. First, Morgan's own faith was strengthened as a result of hearing T. J.'s story about the transforming power of God. Second, she felt greater freedom to speak about her faith because of the modeling by T. J. Third, she was inspired to "reach out" to others and initiate conversation so that she could make a positive impact on others. In fact, as a result, Morgan reached out to a millennial named Amy. They became friends and began weekly one-on-one discipleship meetings with each other.

The subtheme of personal narratives emerged in my work with Strip Club Church as well. Former dancers used their stories as a source of hope to others; an example is a millennial named Melissa, who recounted that

> God commissioned me to share my testimony, and so that is a part of my ministry. And so, God uses like,

my testimony [with] people who have struggled with addiction, or prostitution, or loss, or brokenness, or dysfunctional [sic] or anything . . . because ultimately . . . it gives them the hope that I have in Christ.

Melissa's use of testimony was to incarnate the ability of Jesus to heal, thus providing hope to those who were still in the throes of life in the sex industry and feeling hopeless. When I asked how she counseled dancers when they were open with her about their problems, such as with money and relationships, she reported, "I just address it by sharing my testimony."

Emily, the former stripper mentioned earlier, explained that she had the words "I am her" tattooed on her arm to show that she has a story similar to those of the other strippers. She elaborated:

I just wanted them to know . . . I don't think anything less of you . . . I've been in this club; I've done the things you're doing; I've sold my body; I've done things I'll never be proud of. But it led me to this point to come back to be able to say to you, "I'm not any better than you." That's why I have this "I am her" tattoo, like, I am her. I've been right exactly where you're at. And I've gotten that a lot: "Well, you don't know." You think I don't know—you don't know that I've been on that stage, this exact same stage. That's why there's certain clubs I like to go to because I can say "Yeah, I've been on the stage right where you're at."

I offered a summary of her comments: "So, that's a real point of connection with them, when they realize, oh my gosh, she's been there?" She answered, "For sure." My follow-up question was, "When I say the word 'discipleship' or 'discipling,' what does that mean to you?" Her reply was, "Tell somebody about Jesus, give my testimony, to share with you my walk." Simple but powerful: Emily's definition of discipleship was to tell her story.

The Interpretive Task: Why Is This Going On?

Theologian Kenda Creasy Dean observes that, although the practice of testimony has been a part of "missionary history," it has become "mostly rusty from disuse" in Christian spiritual formation.[24] She notes that the results of Christian Smith's NSYR study (see chapter 1) suggest that young adults, in particular, have "enormous difficulty" articulating their faith.[25] As a result, Dean advocates for a recapturing of the practice of testimony for young people because it can help them "confess their identity as Christians in the presence of those who are 'other,'" thus giving it missional purpose.[26]

Dean wonders, however, whether the NSYR measured the faith of young adults or, in reality, just their ability to talk about faith in a way that met the approval of older generations.[27] I would argue based on my research findings that the latter is true. I found millennials eager to tell their stories using the vernacular of their own cultures; an example is Emily, who used her "I am her" tattoo as a conversation starter to share her testimony. By contrast, I observed several times in my fieldwork that, when young adults used the lexicon of the traditional church, they themselves would label it "Christian-ese"—such was the case with Noah at Urban Life Church—or apologize for "sounding churchy" when they spoke, such as with John, who was speaking from the platform at a Sunday service at Urban Life.

To Dean's point, it might make some members of the traditional Christian subculture uncomfortable to hear language that is contextualized or indigenized to the culture; a notable example is a devotional written by Strip Club Church for dancers:

> You see, the Bible says we've all blown it. Whether we are stripping, working at a coffee shop or running a church, we are all sinners who have "stuff" we need to clean up . . . The good news is that Jesus knows this and loves us anyway. It doesn't matter if you got high yesterday or masturbated five minutes ago. He still loves you.

These words might be off-putting to some, but in order to reach the unchurched or dechurched, some cultural translation like the above may be required, even if it makes the traditional church or older people squirm.

Hirsch and Hirsch put it this way:

> Our message is heard properly only when we have gone through the process of identifying with people, hearing them . . . and knowing how they experience and express their search for meaning . . . If we don't do this, we will simply impose a cultural Christianity on them.[28]

Identifying with people includes understanding the meaning they ascribe to symbols such as language. By contrast, imposing cultural Christianity runs the risk of turning the missional movement into another form of ecclesiastical colonialism. Missiologist Anthony Siegrist makes this point directly: "To avoid colonializing missions, missionaries must learn a new culture and a new language."[29] In recapturing the art of testimony, it is important to avoid a new form of colonialism by assuming or demanding an adherence to a traditional "Christian-ese" lexicon within missional settings.

Dean says that testimony is one of the practices that can help young people develop missional imagination so they can resist Moralistic Therapeutic Deism.[30] I agree, but based on my research I would go a step further and argue that missional imagination must include incarnational language rather than adopting the vocabulary of the traditional Christian subculture. Dean asks an important question: "Where is the line between faith formation and religious indoctrination when it comes to forming a missional imagination?"[31] I contend that there is a fault line and that, while cultural forms of language are on the missional-incarnational side of the line, "Christian-ese" is on the indoctrination side.

It appears from the data that millennials were using narrative and testimony as methodologies for discipleship. The individual faith stories became contextualized sermons to the hearers. Cultural forms and symbols such as tattoos, vernacular expressions, and subjective spiritual experiences became vehicles of the gospel proclamation. Millennials forewent the use of doctrinal statements or proof texts in favor of being living epistles to those around them (see 2 Corinthians 3:2 NKJV).

This finding is in line with previous research on two important points. First, that millennials are inclined to communicate narratively and are "culturally attuned to communicating through the means of shared experience."[32] Second, this inclination extends to the spiritual dimension of life. My findings were in line with those of others who posit that stories are preferable to stand-alone truth claims and doctrine detached from personal experience.[33] Overall, my research found that there is a shift taking place from attractional to missional-incarnational discipleship approaches, and narratives are part of that shift.

OPPORTUNITIES TO BE MOBILIZED IMMEDIATELY FOR MINISTRY

The Descriptive-Empirical Task: What Is Going On?
Millennials at both sites reported that leaders made it easy for them to begin serving. Neither time nor lack of experience was a barrier, and individuals were mobilized for service with no delays. Several attendees of Urban Life Church expressed how quickly they were positioned for service. An example is Olivia:

> The first day that I joined the church they [said], like, "Hey, do you want to serve?" and "Here's where you can serve," and I was like, *Oh, they're not going to call me,* and they called me like two days later and they were like, "Okay, we have you signed up for this!"

Olivia had the expectation that they would not follow up with her after her orientation at the Welcome to Church Lunch and was amazed when they contacted her within a short time period.

Her reaction was not that they were being pushy or presumptive by asking her to get involved; rather, she viewed it as a pleasant surprise. She added, "I love volunteering so much!" indicating that she neither considered service to be compulsory nor felt pressured to enlist but deemed it as something that brought her joy.

Similarly, when I asked a millennial named Zach, "It seems like you got involved pretty quickly?" he replied that he did, and that from his perspective this was unusual for churches:

> We started serving within like the first week or two . . . which is great because you know, there's not too many churches that will do that . . . My wife's done missions work. I really have a heart for it as well, and we want to go somewhere that we can be used that can be important, you know, make a difference when you have weight to it.

He equated being able to serve quickly with being appreciated and valued. Like Olivia, he did not consider immediate recruitment as off-putting but considered it "great" and something that most churches do not do.

Several respondents at Urban Life Church similarly reported that they were not required to have a lot of previous knowledge or skill in order to begin serving. For example, Kara said:

> That's one thing that Urban Life does differently. I really felt like I didn't need to be qualified to serve. Like, I felt like at other churches I had to have some background or, I don't know, I kind of thought that I had to be like a really churchy person to, like, volunteer at church. But they kind of make you feel like "We don't really care about that, we just care about your heart for serving," which is really cool.

Kara stated that she did not need to be "qualified" by having a background in a particular area of skill or ability. She also alluded to another factor, spiritual maturity, which she called being "a churchy person." She appreciated the fact that she was recruited for her "heart" (desire) to serve and not her level of religiosity. Pastor Jim verified—as an intentional strategy of Urban Life Church—one did not have to achieve a certain level of spiritual maturity in order to "qualify" to serve. Jim explained, "So, they can come and be a part and hang out here, and even serve in some lower-level areas here in the church without even having to have made that profession of faith at that point." Being mobilized for service even before making a profession of faith is what Pastor Jim called "the pre-conversion part" of discipleship. Service, then, became a means to, as opposed to merely a result of, spiritual maturity.

Participants at Strip Club Church had similar responses regarding the elimination of barriers to serving. One volunteer, a millennial named Jennifer, spoke about the obstacles she had encountered trying to join other strip club ministries. She had found the application process to be cumbersome and prohibitive to the point that she felt unwanted: "They were like 'Well, this is kind of how we do things. If you could just fill out the application first, and then we'll be happy to meet up and talk.' So, I was kinda like, 'All right, I'll think about it.'"

"I'll think about it" was Jennifer's polite way of saying "I'm not interested." She was unwilling to take the time to move through a preliminary application process she considered to be laborious. By contrast, Strip Club Church provided a low barrier to entry because one of the leaders "reached out" to her "right away," and "she kinda told me, 'Come meet us—come see what we're about. You can't really go out for your first time but just come meet us and then we'll take it from there.'" Thus, the ministry made it very easy for her to begin to engage. She was able to observe firsthand the hearts of volunteers as they met up and prepared to minister, and her response was, "Like, man, these people really love these girls! . . . I couldn't think of a better way to spend a Friday night."

The ministry did have a few qualifications for Jennifer:

> So then after that she asked me if I was still interested
> and I said yes and then we did meet one-on-one, and she
> heard more, like, about my testimony and just gauged
> where I was at spiritually and [what my] interests were
> for wanting to become involved in the ministry. And
> then they did have a little manual they had created just of
> events and expectations and implications of the outreach
> and what happens at the clubs, but then also as somebody
> going into the clubs what they would like to see.

This application process was effective because it allowed Jennifer
to immediately enter the world of the ministry, experience the
ethos, and catch the passion and the vision of the volunteers; yet the
ministry itself was protected until they could complete their vetting
process.

The rest of Jennifer's account introduced another eliminated
barrier to serving: ministry experience. Jennifer was willing to
comply, and the process continued:

> Because before that I had never in my life been inside a
> strip club, it was a little nerve-wracking for me at first.
> But the next time we met up for the prayer night and we
> went in one of the vehicles on the outreach, but I still
> didn't go inside the club yet . . . I went with them in the
> car, and I stayed in the car so I could get more familiar
> with how things go and just get more comfortable, and
> then [it was] not until the third time that I went inside
> one of the clubs.

Thus, the process of being in full-blown ministry entailed progressive
steps of preparation, yet Jennifer did not feel put off but wanted,
needed, and engaged. "It definitely helped me to feel more equipped
. . . to actually be prepared to go for ministry," she said. Strip Club

Church allowed her to be involved from the very beginning, but she received "on the job" training by being allowed to pray with the team, ride in the car, and later enter the clubs. Equipping was a process, not an event. The barrier to entry was removed, yet she received the necessary training for ministry.

A similar instance of a low barrier to entry involved an account I read on the Strip Club Church's Facebook page. One chapter of the organization had an "expertise advisory board" populated by women who were current and ex-members of the sex industry and who could give input on best practices for ministry in strip clubs. Some of these women were still working in the strip clubs and had made no profession of faith. I found this to be an ingenious strategy for learning how to be missional in the strip club culture. The women did not have the requirement of being "churchy," as Kara put it—spiritually mature—or even of being professing Christians to serve on the advisory board.[34] The barrier of spiritual maturity had been removed.

The Interpretive Task: Why Is This Going On?
The above approaches employed by both Strip Club Church and Urban Life Church of removing barriers to serving is reminiscent of the missional theologian Alan Hirsch and his Forge Mission Training Network's approach, called "action-learning discipleship."[35] Action-learning discipleship is based on the idea that spiritual events, principles, and truths can be processed along the way, in real time.[36] The rationale is that individuals are much more open to learning when they are placed in situations beyond their current expertise or level of skill.[37] This approach stands in contrast to the information-based, classroom-style discipleship approach that has dominated the church and the academy in Western Christendom, where learning is removed from everyday, ordinary life. In formal pedagogical settings, "discipleship" becomes an abstraction, separated from an active environment. It comes to be about a successful transmission of concepts and ideas disconnected from ethical expression. Hirsch argues, "We cannot continue to try and think our way into a new

way of acting, but rather we need to act our way into a new way of thinking."[38] Activity and discipleship go together.

The action-learning discipleship model is based on Jesus's relationship with his disciples. He had his followers out in the world ministering with him immediately after having called them; as Hirsch writes, "Straightaway they were involved in proclaiming the kingdom of God, serving the poor, healing, and casting out demons."[39] The barriers of time, experience, and spiritual maturity were removed, just as in my fieldwork sites. Jesus engaged his followers in "active and direct disciple-making in the context of mission."[40] Likewise today, when discipleship is "organized around mission," even the newest convert can participate.[41] This is in line with my research findings in which Urban Life Church and Strip Club Church removed spiritual maturity as an impediment to serving.

In fact, my fieldwork sites took this concept even a step further, allowing millennials to serve even before having a conversion experience. Both Strip Club Church and Urban Life Church provided the possibility of serving without having made a profession of faith. This approach is what Dallas Willard termed "discipleship evangelism."[42] It intends, as Willard writes, "to make disciples and let converts 'happen,' rather than intending to make converts and letting disciples 'happen.'"[43]

Historically there has been a bifurcated view of evangelism and discipleship.[44] As missional leaders Maddix and Akkerman write, "evangelism in many circles has stressed belief before belonging: one must accept the gospel before becoming assimilated into the church. Missional engagement reverses the trend, stressing belonging first . . . trusting that belief will follow."[45] Reframing this concept in discipleship terms, it is what Pastor Jim called the "pre-conversion part of discipleship," where individuals can serve "in low level areas" before making a profession of faith. The discipleship that happens "along the way" is action-learning discipleship, also described as "missional discipleship."[46] This approach broadens the view of discipleship, making it more holistic and inclusive.[47]

Based on the reactions from respondents at both sites, discipleship that is based on action, regardless of conversion status, and mobilizes individuals for service immediately was a highly effective method of engaging millennials and equipping them to follow Jesus. Removing barriers to entry resulted in the recruitment and retention of millennials in missional communities, leading to greater opportunities for discipleship.

CONCLUSION

Discipleship among millennials in missional communities was facilitated by opportunities to become engaged in ministry and mission in the world. Ministry and mission were expressed in three ways. First, through the incarnational engagement of the culture. Urban Life Church used the framework of the Seven Cultural Streets as an aid to help millennials find their niche. Strip Club Church dispatched volunteers among sex-industry workers to engage them directly in their cultural milieu. Millennial members of both groups embraced the outward trajectory of ministry and were eager to influence the culture by "putting the world to rights" through incarnational ministry.

Second, millennials were enthusiastic about telling others about their faith. Sharing testimonies was a prominent activity at both sites, with training provided on how to tell one's faith story. Third, providing opportunities to be mobilized immediately for ministry resulted in an effective way to disciple. Barriers to serving, such as time, experience, and spiritual maturity, were removed, so that service could start immediately. Millennials were enthusiastic to learn along the way.

This chapter has provided an account of the first of three key findings from my ethnographic fieldwork. The generation of these findings was implemented through the ethnographic inquiry, including the methods of participant observation, interviews, and document analysis. The purpose was to carry out the descriptive-empirical task of the pastoral cycle so that I could address my central question, "What does it mean for millennials to follow Christ today in missional communities?" along with corollary research aims. The effective discipleship of millennials in missional communities, therefore, includes providing opportunities for ministry and mission in the surrounding culture. The bottom line? We need to disciple millennials to be missionaries.

CHAPTER 3

LOVING DISCIPLESHIP

THEME TWO: AUTHENTIC, CARING, AND LOVING RELATIONSHIPS

In my interviews and participant observation, it was striking how many millennials at both Urban Life Church and Strip Club Church identified love as an important component of their discipleship relationships. No matter the type of discipleship relationship— whether between ministry leaders and millennials, within a group, one-on-one, in the context of "pre-conversion" discipleship, or with the spiritually mature—the vital aspect of this finding was that millennials responded to messages they decoded as loving words, actions, and attitudes of others in the context of discipleship. The entry for "love" in the *International Standard Bible Encyclopedia* states, "Love, whether used of God or man, is an earnest and anxious desire for and an active and beneficent interest in the well-being of the one loved."[1] This section will discuss the nature of this concept. The theme "discipleship among millennials was facilitated by authentic, caring, and loving relationships" contains the following subthemes: millennials contrasted experiences of love and judgment by Christians and/or the church; millennials developed friendship love (philia) through commonalities and authenticity; and millennials responded positively to overtures of the agape love of Jesus.

LOVE INSTEAD OF JUDGMENT
The Descriptive-Empirical Task: What Is Going On?

Both fieldwork sites stressed the importance of showing love to those to whom participants were called to minister in order to reverse previous feelings of judgment conveyed by Christians and/or churches. Millennials responded positively to these overtures of love.

Olivia at Urban Life Church said that, for a while, she had stopped going to church because her previous church had become "legalistic." She explained that there were "unspoken rules, like, how you should dress, how you should look, or 'Oh, that person had a kid when she was sixteen.'" "I didn't care for that," she said. She wanted "to make it better," but her mom, who served as an elder at the church, "never really listened to me." "I was having to develop my relationship with Christ myself," she said, through "listening to sermons online and podcasts" because "I wasn't trusting of the church." She began attending Urban Life Church, and, when her father passed away, some of the members came to her house to pray for her. "I felt that they really, truly, genuinely cared," she shared. As a result, she joined the prayer team, where she could "[be] there for other people in their time of need," as they had been for her.

Zach felt judged simply for being a millennial. He recounted that in "past churches I've been at there's definitely an age gap" and that as a result "it's really easy to not be involved or to be in a place where you don't feel relevant." "What is the point of me going if I'm just going to sit in the chair for an hour or two," he lamented. "It seems like a lot of other people" at Urban Life "have had the same experience, the same feeling, so they make an effort not to treat you that way" and "not to be judgmental." Instead, he considers it a "big thing" that Urban Life Church "has hope for the future generations and for my age group." "What's really unique about this place is that everybody here wants . . . to know more about you, and you know they want to see what your life is like, and they care," Zach concluded.

A particularly powerful example of this theme was a Sunday sermon given by Pastor Jim at Urban Life Church in which he

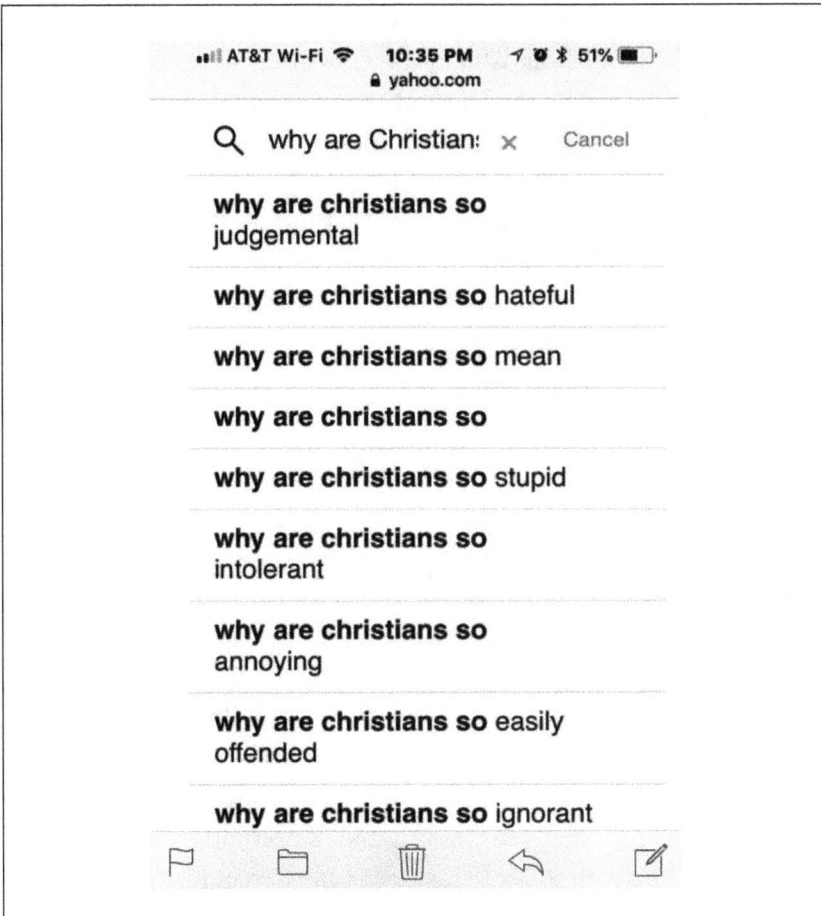

Figure 3.1 Screenshot of Pastor Jim's Phone²

addressed "what our culture is asking about Christians." He began his sermon by saying, "Christianity gets a pretty bad rap . . . in our culture." As evidence for his assertion, he did a real-time Yahoo search on his phone, typing "Why are Christians so . . . " and projecting the result on the screen at the front of the church auditorium. The search engine automatically completed the sentence based on the most popular previous searches, and the very first result generated was "Why are Christians so judgmental?" The full results can be seen in Figure 3.1 above, which included other phrases, such as "Why are

Christians so hateful?"; "Why are Christians so mean?"; "Why are Christians so stupid?"; and "Why are Christians so intolerant?"

Pastor Jim agreed that he had "known quite a few" Christians who fit the above description. He asked, "How do Christians get so jacked-up like that?" and continued, "We are not good at letting people know about the causes that Christianity is really all about" because many Christians "come to faith and then isolate themselves or insulate themselves from the culture." As a result of pulling away from the world and cloistering away in a Christian subculture, the believer "will become stagnant and really can't be the essence of Christ," which is "life, love, and the power of God flowing out of us." Pastor Jim seemed to be asserting that a lack of mission will result in an inert, stale faith that stifles the ability to demonstrate the love of Christ to the world. The antidote, he said, is that believers "need to be on mission" to "allow God to work through you," to "let his love flow through you." He concluded, "All you can do is try to make an effort, and God's going to do the rest." By being "on mission" and letting God flow through us, each of us can be a conduit of his love and power to others. This is the way to overcome the "bad rap" Christians have within the culture.

Emily from Strip Club Church shared opinions and sentiments that were in line with the conclusions of the Urban Life pastor as she explained the common expectation that the strippers will be judged by the church and/or Christians: "People expect you to go in and . . . throw a Bible at them and [say], 'Hey, this is what you're doing wrong' and it's like, 'I love you no matter what . . . I'm not here to judge you, I don't think anything less of you.'" A former dancer herself, Emily knew firsthand about the expectation of feeling judged for her profession. She considered demonstrations of love to be imperative for counteracting the presumption of judgment:

> You know for sure that they're not really here to judge somebody, like "Hey, I gave up my Friday night to come out of my comfort zone into this club with you," versus like

in a church you're not sure what you're walking into, you
know what I mean—like the judgment . . . because I chose
to come bring this love to you. I didn't have to . . . versus
me trying to walk into a building where I'm, like, not sure
what they're thinking, or do they know I'm a stripper?

Emily was connecting missional action with love in this explanation.
The fact that volunteers were going cross-culturally into the strip
clubs of their own volition was proof to her that they loved the girls
and were not there to judge them. This is reminiscent of Pastor
Jim's point that Christians often get a "bad rap" because they
remain insulated in their own subculture, but that when they are
"on mission" they allow the love of God to flow through them, thus
overcoming the negative stereotypes.

One of the more dramatic examples of showing love instead
of judgment was the story of Liz, who visited a drag show once a
month to share the love of Jesus. She had such a good relationship
with the club manager that he invited her to speak during the show.
She was surprised the first time the manager called her up on stage:
"I never expected to get up on stage . . . The manager said, 'Well, I'll
bring you up on stage in a little bit,' and I said, 'Wait, what?' I said,
'What do you want me to do up there?' and he said, 'Just talk about
your ministry and let us know why you're here.'" Liz used this as an
opportunity to talk about love versus judgment:

I get up there and I just let God lead me . . . I always
make it a point to try to say, "Jesus loves you, we're not
here to judge you . . . I know that others in the Christian
community have told you that . . . the way you live your
life is a sin and that Jesus doesn't want anything to do with
you. I'm not here to judge whether what you do is right
or wrong, I'm just here to let you know that, no matter
what, Jesus loves you and wants to have a relationship
with you."

Liz's message of the love of Jesus was so well received that she was invited to speak at each visit. Furthermore, when the promoters of the drag show learned that that she was using her own funds to run the ministry because she received very few donations from churches, they gifted her with a monthly stipend for gasoline and contributed several one-hundred-dollar donations to her ministry so that she could keep coming and sharing the love of Christ from the stage.

Similarly, one of the cofounders of Strip Club Church in Las Vegas, named Greg, explained that other well-known ministries had in the past criticized Strip Club Church for ministering in "sinful" places like strip clubs, porn conventions, and sex-industry expos. He attributed their judgment to their lagging behind in understanding Jesus's missional mandate upon the church. He testified to seeing young adults ages 25 to 35 "leaving the church but not leaving faith," so he considers Strip Club Church "ahead of where the church is at" in terms of reaching these dechurched millennials through the ministry's missional approach. As a result, he said, "he doesn't think about the ramifications of judgment" by the mainstream Christian church or worry about "marketing" to the Christian culture in order to be accepted by them. He said, "Back in '02 churches wouldn't touch the ministry," but now, because the dropout rate of millennials is so high, a "shift is happening" whereby churches are more open to groups like Strip Club Church.

The Interpretive Task: Why Is This Going On?

My findings were consistent with recent research indicating that millennials consider the church and Christians to be judgmental. In 2019, the Christian research firm Barna Group, in cooperation with World Vision ministries, conducted an online survey of 15,369 respondents ages 18 to 35 in twenty-five countries about their "goals, fears, relationships, routines, and beliefs."[3] The sample distribution included two thousand respondents from the United States.[4] Of these two thousand Americans surveyed, 64 percent were considered "church dropouts," which Barna defined as "respondents who either grew up Christian and no longer affiliate with the Church or still identify as Christian but attend a place of worship infrequently (less than every few months)."[5] There were several notable results germane to the topic of judgment versus love.

According to Barna, 77 percent of church dropouts considered present-day Christianity to be "judgmental," and 67 percent agreed with the statement "people at church are judgmental."[6] Of those who claim to have "no faith," responses to these statements were 88 percent and 78 percent, respectively. Of those respondents who claim to be of "other faith," responses were 74 percent and 61 percent, respectively. And of those respondents who self-identify as Christian, responses were 61 percent and 47 percent, respectively.[7] Barna Group concludes: "Young adults with some proximity to religion in general or Christianity specifically hold respect for the church, while those furthest from religion—and particularly those who have detached from it—show great opposition."[8]

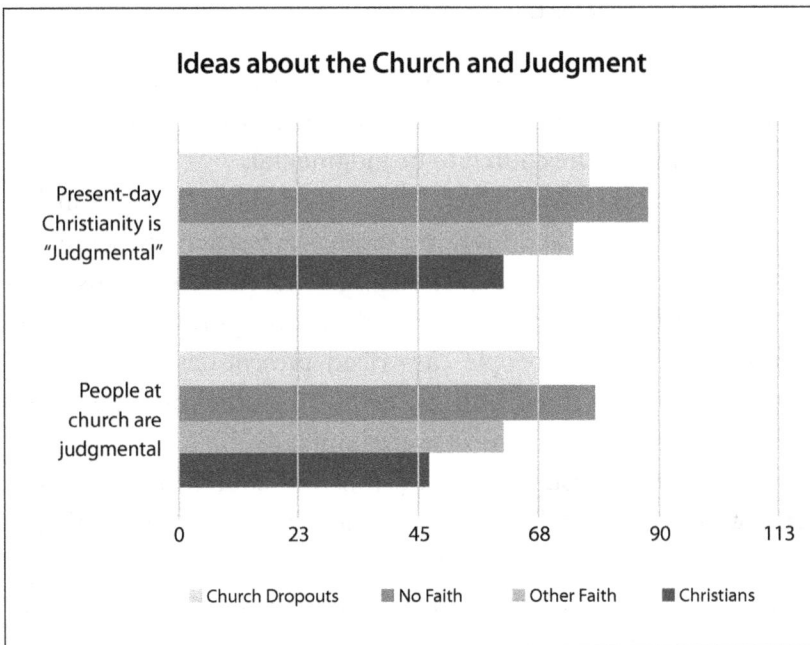

Figure 3.2 Ideas about the Church and Judgment

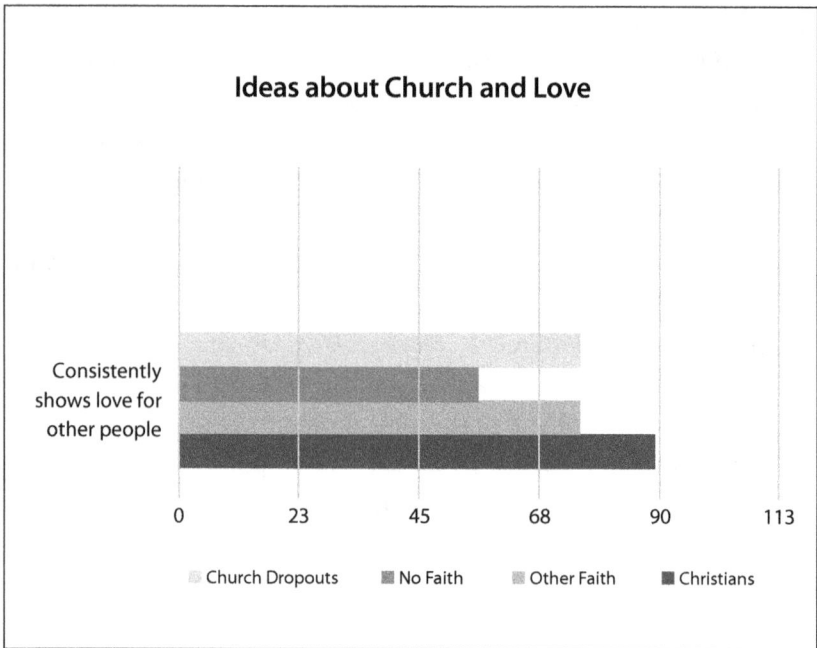

Figure 3.3 Ideas about the Church and Love

Those respondents who were part of the dropout phenomenon were second only to those with no faith when it came to considering Christians and/or the church to be judgmental.

Curiously, however, when Barna asked about the relationship between the church and love, the responses were overwhelmingly positive. Seventy-five percent of millennial church dropouts answered "a lot" or "some" when asked to what degree the phrase "consistently shows love for other people" described present-day Christianity.[9] Fifty-six percent of those with "no faith," 75 percent of "other faith," and 89 percent of Christians answered similarly.[10]

The Barna Group concludes that the church has a "mixed reputation" among millennials, who view present-day Christianity as simultaneously judgmental and loving.[11] The ambivalence demonstrated in the Barna study is consistent with my findings. Millennials in my study often assumed that they would be judged by Strip Club Church and Urban Life Church but were pleasantly surprised when they received love instead. The love opened the door for discipleship to those who had dropped out of the church but considered themselves Christians. Discipleship was facilitated by exhibiting love instead of judgment.

LOVE AS PHILIA

The Descriptive-Empirical Task: What Is Going On?
Philia love emerged as a prominent subtheme in my fieldwork. Philia, or friendship love (Strong's Concordance, 5368 *philéō*), is defined as "to show warm affection in intimate friendship, characterized by tender, heartfelt consideration and kinship."[12] Philia was developed among millennials at both sites through discovering commonalities and fostering authenticity. In fact, most interviewees—twenty out of thirty—talked about the importance of authenticity among the friendships in their Christian communities. The activities that most often cultivated friendship love were small groups, missional outreach, and one-on-one interactions.

Several of the respondents from Urban Life Church emphasized the common ground they found with others in their small groups, which they called Connect Groups. These were affinity groups, meaning that they were established around common interests and goals. For example, Jesse started a connect group for people who, like himself, desired to take more risks in life. He had dreams of expanding his real estate profession and wanted support from Christian friends. As he talked with others at Urban Life Church, he discovered that they too had dreams of risk-taking, whether personal, vocational, or spiritual, and were not finding the support they needed from friends or family. As a result, Jesse created a connect group so they could meet regularly to support and encourage one another in their common goal.

Kara described how a professional crisis acted as a catalyst for her to open up and be authentic with her friends at Urban Life Church: "It took a rough patch of my job to really be vulnerable and real with people. and when I was, then people responded well, and I felt that community," She went on, "I was just so drained and overwhelmed, so I brought it up during [small group]." As a result, she "became closer to the community at church" and learned to "rely on my faith and get to know God more." The risk Kara took by being authentic paid dividends in both her relationships with others and her relationship with God.

Similarly, Morgan reported that she had "real relationships" at Urban Life Church, in contrast to previous church experiences:

> What sets this church apart from other churches [is that] it's very authentic . . . You don't have to hide behind a fake smile or happiness. You know, if you're having a rough week, you can be like, "Hey, my week has been crap," and people aren't afraid of you having difficulties.

Morgan's implications were indicting. She was in essence saying that at her former church others had been afraid to be authentic and talk about feelings, forcing Morgan to pretend to be happy when she really was not. Even worse, Morgan seemed to be generalizing, claiming that most churches shun emotional intimacy. In contrast, she felt welcomed to share her true feelings at Urban Life Church. "It is a very warm and welcoming environment where you can be yourself and you can be real," she concluded.

Noah also spoke of the importance of authenticity in missional outreach, about building friendships with those whom he wanted to reach for Christ:

> Just build a relationship first . . . I think it all has to do with relationships. So, if you have somebody that's hurt by the church . . . if they know you as a person who loves them rather than a Christian who is always trying to save them, it's going to be way easier, because then they don't think you have an agenda other than to just be friends with them and to get to know them.

Noah appeared to imply that there are those who have been hurt by Christians who have operated with a hidden agenda. He said, it is imperative "to start with you deciding to treat them like a person rather than a project, which I've seen happen a bunch in church." He viewed authenticity as the gateway to Christian community and discipleship:

> I know [it's important] relationally for us to be friends before I can even start to try and ask them, like, "Hey, would you like to come check out my church?" . . . because I don't think I have any social equity with them until I felt that friendship . . . Really, in a sense it feels oversimplified, but like, "Are you ready to change your life?" which is really what it is, but, I mean, they have to know that you want that for them and that you aren't getting anything out of it.

Noah did not want to lead off with invitations to come to church. He felt that he had not earned the "social equity" to make such a request until he had firmly established a friendship and proved to them that they were more to him than spiritual conquests. The phrase "social equity" is loaded with meaning because it has to do with fairness and equality; Noah implied that pressuring his companions with the gospel before establishing friendships would have been unfair to them, would have been treating them as less than equals. This speaks of the respect and dignity he desires to show others.

Noah also shared his sentiments about authenticity in his connect group:

> That's how I got some of my best friends . . . Nobody's perfect; we all go through the same struggles, but we're also still trying to do better. I feel like that's just the easiest way to see how human people are and that we're not just trying to put on a show for people . . . I think we all go through the same things, but you don't have to do it alone.

Noah touches on a significant aspect of discipleship in his words "you don't have to do it alone." Overcoming isolation and creating community underscore the importance of fostering a sense of philia as part of the discipleship process.

Philia was also developed at Strip Club Church through expressions of commonality and authenticity. Annette connected the concepts of love and finding commonality: "The language of love will lead you to be relatable to people . . . If you go into a strip club and have nothing to say to them except to preach Jesus to them, you are basically saying that you have nothing in common. So, you must establish a common ground." She explained why she believed this foundation to be important:

> In order to offer Jesus, you first must find something you can relate to. Preaching at them doesn't change lives; discipleship changes lives. So, the time spent outside the clubs with the women, that's where you're establishing a relationship; that's where you're going to make a difference in their lives.

Annette highlighted the relational value of finding common ground. She gave the simple but effective example of discovering that she and a dancer friend were both vegan, so she took the girl out to eat and then invited her to church. A ministry approach of "preaching at" someone, which carries the connotation of lacking intimacy, equity, and reciprocity, she considered to be ineffective, while she pointed out that discipleship that "makes a difference" will happen by taking the time and effort to get to know the person and their personal preferences. Common ground is the place of belonging and intimacy, Annette explained: "When women trust you, that's when you can be open and honest . . . This is where ministry will happen."

In my fieldwork with Strip Club Church, I observed what I would call a pseudo-friendship among the dancers, who often formed a community marked by commonality but based more on survival than philia. For instance, a former strip-club worker named Roxy described the dancers as having "loyalty among thieves" when it came to protecting one another, especially in keeping the secret that they were working as prostitutes. She referred to their affiliative communication as the "code of the street" and gave the example of the moniker "bottom bitch," a woman in charge of being a liaison between the dancers and the pimps. The girls must report "everything" to this woman, and Roxy concluded that the whole enterprise is "dangerous" for them. Hence, while there were protective measures among the dancers—while it seemed at first glance that they had shared affinity based on common goals—the community was fraught with hostility.

Jennifer similarly reported an account of going into a dressing room at a strip club and encountering an "alpha" dancer—one who is a "bully" who "pulls rank" and will not let the other dancers interact with her. She said:

> It broke my heart . . . because I just feel like they're already battling so much, the last thing they need to do is battle each other. Like they should be there to support one another because they're the only people really in the world who understands what each other's going through.

It is powerful to say that these girls are the "only people in the world" who understand each other. What could be an opportunity for deep connection, support, and empathy among the girls is squandered, which Jennifer attributed to competition for attention and money.

Unfortunately, love was not generated from these associations, which resulted instead in feelings of isolation. This dynamic created opportunities for Strip Club Church to step in and offer an affiliative alternative that drew the girls out of isolation and into the warm philia of Christian fellowship. This was addressed explicitly by Samantha, who stated of her relationship with Barbie and Holly at Strip Club Church that "[they were] loving" by "making me feel comfortable and like I'm not going to be isolated" or "by myself." Over time, Samantha developed philia toward the Strip Club Church Go Team. She said, "I always feel, like, the love, you know, and like they love seeing me." Their visits to her strip club on Friday nights formed a place of affiliation for her within the larger, often hostile work environment. It appeared that the discipleship efforts were bearing fruit by introducing her to the ways of philia.

The Interpretive Task: Why Is This Going On?
The above discussion can be interpreted using the theology of C. S. Lewis in dialogue with the psychosocial framework of psychologist Erik Erikson. C. S. Lewis famously wrote about love in his work *The Four Loves*. These four loves, as outlined by Lewis, are *storge, philia, eros*, and *agape*.[13] Philia is based on companionship and common interests that are unique to the relationship. According to Lewis, this companionship might be based on "common religion, common studies, a common profession, even a common recreation."[14] This kind of bond is forged when two people discover a commonality that previously "each believed to be his own unique treasure (or burden). The typical expression of opening Friendship would be something like, 'What? You too? I thought I was the only one.'"[15] Lewis's little phrase "What? You too?" beautifully encapsulates the sentiment of many in my interviews.

As commonalities were established and intimacy developed among millennials at my fieldwork sites, former feelings of loneliness, fear, or disenfranchisement diminished, and philia emerged. This process of overcoming feelings of isolation and discovering intimacy with others during young adulthood is a dynamic famously outlined by the psychologist Erik Erikson. Erikson wrote about the primacy of love in young adulthood in his famous work on ego development, *The Life Cycle Completed*.[16] Erikson believed that love, which he defined as "mutuality of mature devotion," was the basic psychosocial strength that arises from this life stage.[17] This definition is akin to philia in that both concepts stress relational equity and emotional connection.

With Erikson, the strength to love arises from the individual's struggle between intimacy and isolation. As young adults emerge from adolescence, Erikson observed, they search for a sense of identity and "can be eager and willing to fuse their identities in mutual intimacy, who, in work, sexuality, and friendship promise to prove complementary."[18] Intimacy is formed by identity groups, or "concrete affiliations," that encourage sharing and community.[19] Using this framework, it is possible to see how in my fieldwork the shared activities of community groups, missional outreach, and one-on-one relationships could provide the context for intimacy, ultimately leading to expressions of philia. Erikson warns that, when intimacy is not successfully attained, isolation can set in, which is "the psychosocial antithesis to intimacy."[20] Young adults experience fear of remaining "separate and unrecognized," rendering them unable to develop the strength to love.[21]

From a missional perspective, churches place a high priority on community, believing that living incarnationally as participants in the *missio Dei* is not meant to be a solitary endeavor but develops within the context of fellowship. Missional leaders such as Michael Frost and Alan Hirsch often use the term *communitas* to describe the ethos to which missional communities aspire. *Communitas* refers to a strong sense of belonging and cohesion by members of a group that is situated "outside" society, a position known as liminality.[22] The bonds of *communitas* are often formed around shared religious rituals experienced in a liminal state.

My fieldwork sites both contained aspects of liminality, as they were located on the frontiers of the Western mission field outside the four walls of institutional churches and, in Strip Club Church's case, situated among a marginalized and disenfranchised population. When Christian community can live as *communitas*, according to Frost, it can propel society forward as it lays hold of a "grand sense of purpose" for the sake of the kingdom of God.[23]

This was the aim and purpose of both fieldwork sites. Based on this data and this discussion with the secondary literature, it is apparent that "what was going on" and "why" were that the discipleship of millennials in missional communities was being fostered by authentic relationships built around common goals and interests, which overcome feelings of isolation and marginalization.

LOVE AS AGAPE

The Descriptive-Empirical Task: What Is Going On?

To the millennials in my fieldwork, agape (unconditional) love meant loving people just as they were, no matter their behavior, just as Jesus did. Agape is defined by Strong's Concordance as "affection or benevolence; charity; love." Its lexical relative, *agapao*, means "to love in a social or moral sense."[24] It is a love that is unconditional and self-sacrificing, expressed in both feeling and action.[25] It loves everyone equally, regardless of position or status. This agape love, what Lewis calls "charity," is unselfish, desiring "what is simply best for the beloved."[26] Lewis wrote that agape is "Gift-love," originating with God's very essence, for God is love and, as Lewis states, "In God there is no hunger that needs to be filled, only plenteousness that desires to give."[27] It is a love that is willing to give without receiving anything in return. In short, agape is the unconditional love of Christ.

Barbie, the director of the local Forth Worth chapter of the Strip Club Church network, stated explicitly that the ministry "exists to show the unconditional love of Christ to women in the sex industry." It is the foundation upon which the entire ministry is laid. All their other noble and notable activities, whether helping with social services, providing gifts to the dancers, or prayer, radiate from the center that is the love of Jesus.

Agape was a powerful theme with Strip Club Church in particular, because unconditional love stood in stark contrast from the dancers' lived experience, which was full of abuse and trauma. For example, Barbie explained that, in her estimation, 70 to 80 percent of the women had a pimp, "which is generally this boyfriend type person, this 'Romeo' guy . . . that just starts pampering them with all the things that seem like love." The man is "in it for the money" because "he has ten girls that he splits time with" who all must "give [him their] money." The girls are "being abused" but think it is love. Melissa, a former dancer, verified this by sharing her story:

> Women in the industry . . . struggle with feeling not whole and empty as a woman, and not complete because they don't have a man. And so, the Lord walked me through that and said, Melissa, I will be your husband, I will be your provider . . . I will be your father . . . I will be all the things you think you are lacking. And if we allow God to love us in that way, if we allow God to take the place of what we're [idolizing], . . . then [men] do not complete me. Jesus Christ completes me.

"Love" had been a misunderstood and confusing concept to Melissa because of the way the men in her life had misrepresented it. The love Melissa was looking for was found in the agape love of Christ.

A bold and enterprising example of how volunteers communicated the love of Jesus was through a line of products used by Strip Club Church bearing the slogan "Jesus Loves Strippers." One of these products was the *Jesus Loves Strippers Bible*, which contained commentary, as well as the testimonies of former dancers woven throughout. The commentary touched on themes related to love, such as: Jesus loves everyone equally, Jesus loves you no matter what you have done, and Jesus was radical and countercultural in his love. The back cover contained the following copy:

> Jesus loves you. "Jesus Loves Strippers." We say it a lot here at Strip Club Church. It's kind of our thing. But what does it even mean? Sure, it gets a lot of attention, and it generates a lot of disbelieving chuckles, some of them shocked at the audacity of such a statement, some of them wondering whether it might be true. It is.

To be "shocked" by the love of Jesus is significant. Too often Jesus is portrayed as an effete, mild religious leader or an inanimate, two-dimensional, stained-glass image. The Jesus that is "shocking" and "audacious" is one who is fully alive with love, daring to consort with tax collectors, sinners, and yes, strippers.

In addition to the Bible, Strip Club Church produced other items, such as T-shirts and drinking cups printed with the "Jesus Loves Strippers" message, that were disseminated all over the country through their network affiliates. The response to the "Jesus Loves Strippers" products among millennial volunteers and sex workers was overwhelmingly positive, opening the door for further ministry and discipleship.

For instance, Melissa described an occasion when she took a stack of cups into the clubs and asked a young employee and her boyfriend if they would help pass them out to the dancers. They agreed, the young woman exclaiming, "That's so cool!" Melissa said the positive response created rapport with the girl, which opened a dialogue about the love of Jesus that would not have happened otherwise.

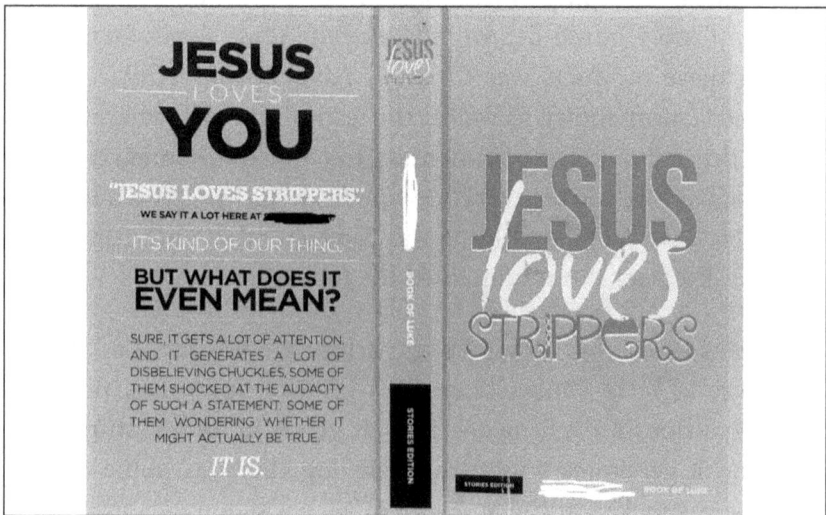

Figure 3.4 Jesus Loves Strippers Bible, cover

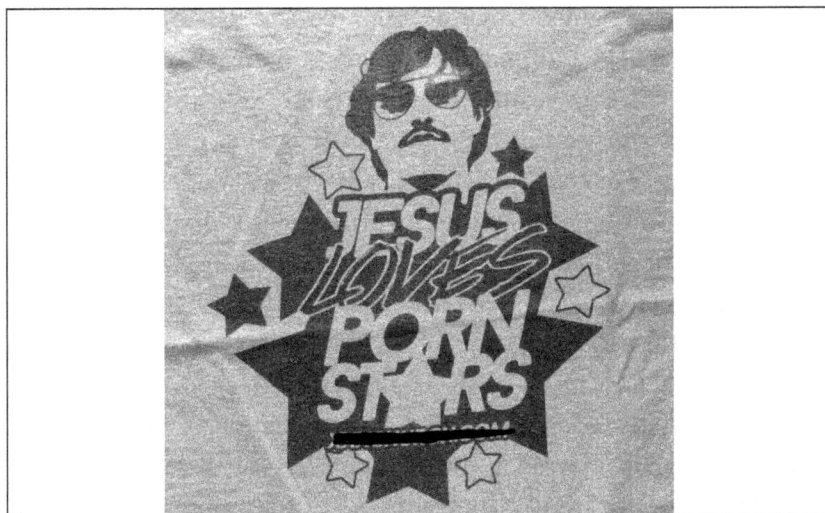

Figure 3.5 Jesus Loves Porn Stars T-Shirt

Another chapter of Strip Club Church distributed sixty copies of the *Jesus Loves Strippers Bible* in one of the strip clubs. One of the dancers was visibly touched as she read the cover, saying, "Thank you for not calling me a whore." Other dancers requested additional copies to distribute to their friends and family. Even the clubs themselves on occasion requested copies to distribute to their employees.[28]

I was able to witness the popularity of these Bibles firsthand at a sex-industry convention in Chicago sponsored by Strip Club Church. The ministry rented a booth in the middle of the exhibition hall and set up a display of the Bibles for anyone to take. They also had a T-shirt printer and a volunteer who printed custom-made T-shirts that said "Jesus Loves Strippers" and, since this was a sex-industry convention that included workers in the pornography business, T-shirts that said "Jesus Loves Porn Stars." Over the course of the approximately three hours I was at the convention, a line formed for the Bibles and shirts that wrapped around the entire booth—at least a hundred people. Other ministry volunteers mingled with those in line, answering questions about spiritual matters or simply establishing relationships. It was at this venue that a millennial named Annette, who was a porn star, met a pastor named Rachel. The two made a personal connection that became a lasting discipleship relationship, ultimately resulting in Annette leaving the industry and starting a ministry of her own.

Showing unconditional love was especially effective with the drag-show ministry. Liz adapted the "Jesus Loves Strippers" message for her ministry to drag queens. She purchased a device that enabled her to print her own customized products, which she passed out at the drag-show club, such as lighters with the message "Jesus Loves LGBTQ," as well as cups and mugs that said "Jesus Loves Drag Queens." She reported, "They just go crazy over them. The manager has on display at the bar everything we've ever given."

The responses were enthusiastic and invited engagement with those with whom she desired to have a discipleship relationship. She reported that "they always ask a lot of questions" about who she is, what her ministry is about, and what the message "Jesus Loves LGBTQ/Drag Queens" means. This opened the way for dialogue about the person of Jesus and his love for them. She reported that the bartender, dancers, and drag queens all felt comfortable asking her about spiritual matters because she emphasized the love of Jesus. She often asked for their phone numbers and would continue the spiritual conversations between visits to the club, providing counsel and sharing Scripture as the Lord led.

Because of her loving approach, Liz was able to form a discipleship relationship with a millennial drag queen named Rosie Mystique:

> He grew up in a Christian home and he wanted to know what our agenda was, and I told him we didn't have an agenda, it was just to let him know that Jesus loves him. And he said, "Well, the reason I ask is because my father doesn't love me. When he found out I was gay and that I wanted to do drag he didn't want anything to do with me anymore." And so, we just had a conversation about how

. . . we were not there to do anything but [to] tell him Jesus
loves him no matter what . . . and we're there for [him].[29]

The phrase "no matter what" meant "unconditionally," even if Rosie
was gay or a drag queen. His life choices did not negate God's love
for him. By contrast, those choices *did* negatively affect his father's
love for him. It was important for Liz to communicate that, although
Rosie had been rejected by his father, he was still accepted by Jesus.
Liz sought to reflect this agape love of Jesus in her relationship with
him and to undo the conditions placed on him for love. Rosie had
grown up in a Christian home, so he knew the gospel, but Liz was
careful, out of respect, not to pressure him on spiritual matters. "All
they want," Liz said of the drag queens, is for me to be "open to
learn" about them "and not judge them." She told Rosie, "You want
to talk, we'll talk. If you don't want to talk, we will walk away. You
know, it is totally up to you; you are in charge of the relationship
with us. And that was very appreciated."

As a result of the unconditional love Liz showed Rosie, they
formed an ongoing friendship. They communicated regularly, often
about Rosie's career but also about spiritual matters, renewing Rosie's
faith in the idea that God loved and accepted him unconditionally.
Another positive result of their friendship was that, since Rosie was
a very popular performer, even gaining a national following online,
he had a lot of influence in the drag club. Once he had accepted Liz
into the community others did too, which gave Liz more influence
among that population.

The Interpretive Task: Why Is This Going On?
My findings were consistent with prior Christian research, which
found that most millennials have a positive view of the person of
Jesus Christ. A 2011 study of 1,500 millennials conducted by church
leaders Rainer and Rainer found that 57 percent agreed or strongly
agreed with the statement, "You have made a personal commitment
to Jesus Christ that is still important in your life today."[30] Similarly,

Kimball, who interviewed 18- to 35-year-olds for his book *They Like Jesus but Not the Church*, found that emerging generations "like and respect" Jesus, while criticizing the church as largely "judgmental," "homophobic," and "negative."[31]

Kimball, a pastor who has spent many years studying the millennial generation, believes that before we can engage today's emerging adults in a conversation about personal sin and repentance, we must first build trust through relationship, restoring the reputation of the church and Christians.[32] Kimball uses the familiar Bridge Illustration to explain the difference. The Bridge Illustration was a popular twentieth-century visual aid to explain the process of salvation. Under this paradigm, humankind is separated from God by a vast chasm of sin. Faith in Jesus "bridges the chasm."[33]

However, Kimball revised the Bridge Illustration because those ministering to young adults in post-Christian America encounter a second chasm: the negative perception of Christianity and the Christian subculture. What is needed, Kimball asserts, is to build trust in order to change this perception. Building trust is accomplished through friendship and community. Only then can we address the problem of sin and the need for the salvific work of Jesus.[34]

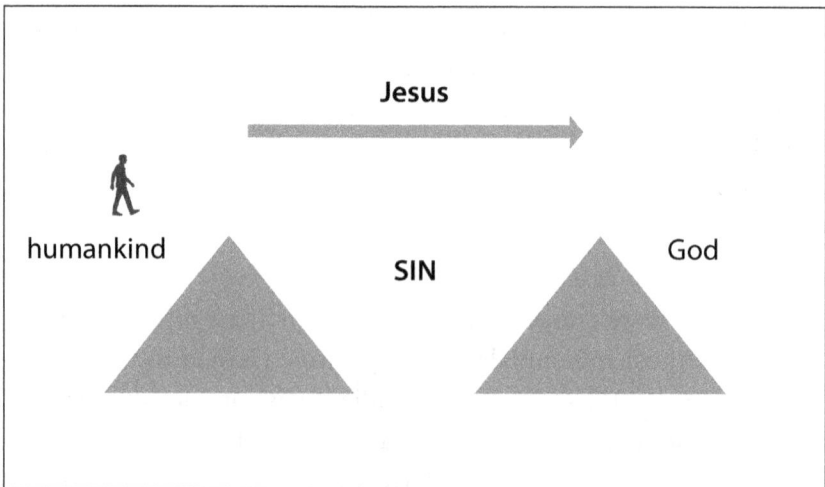

Figure 3.6 Traditional Bridge Illustration

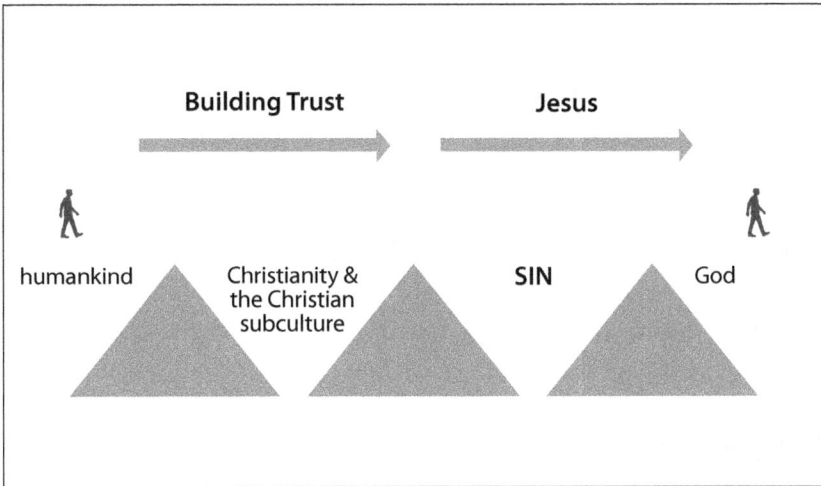

Figure 3.7 Kimball's Revised Bridge Illustration

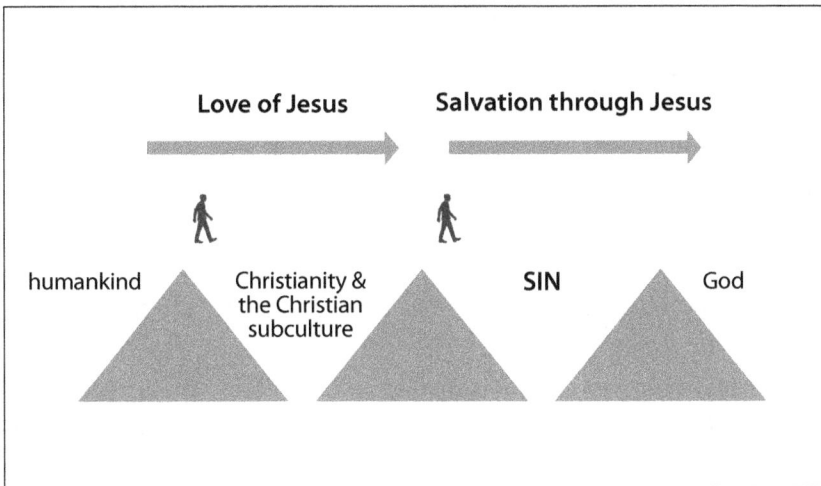

Figure 3.8 Proposed Revision Based on Findings

Based on my findings on the positive response to the love of Jesus, I would modify Kimball's figure. The first "bridge" is built through the demonstration or incarnation of the agape love of Jesus so that trust can be established and discipleship can take place. In fact, "bridge" was the exact word used by one of the Strip Club

Church interviewees, named Elaine, as she talked about reaching out to the dancers and "loving them right where they're at." She recounted a time when one of the dancers had asked her to help untie a knot in her G-string:

> She was like, "Will you help me get this knot out?" and I remember as I'm standing there, I'm like, "Lord, is this really what you would be doing?" And I just felt that peace, like "Yes, you are building a bridge with this woman," and it opened a conversation.

Elaine felt a modicum of reluctance because she was so far out of her comfort zone, afraid that she might be somehow condoning wrong or sinful behavior. But entering the dancer's world, however foreign or even offensive it might have been to her, allowed her to start a conversation about Jesus. Her actions were a demonstration of agape because she was willing to feel uncomfortable, choosing to incarnate the love of Christ "on the cultural and social terms of those" to whom she was sent, and not on her own terms based on what would have made her feel comfortable.[35]

In conclusion, one of the findings of my research was that expressing the agape love of Jesus, explicitly using his name, was highly effective in forming discipleship relationships with millennials. Leaders felt compelled to enter missional settings with Christlike boldness and compassion, and the millennials were responsive. In this way, the discipleship of millennials in missional communities was empowered by expressions of agape.

CONCLUSION

Discipleship of millennials in missional communities was facilitated by authentic, caring, and loving relationships. Love was expressed in three principal ways: love instead of judgment, love as philia, and love as agape. Love in place of judgment was communicated through the missional activity of entering the culture of millennials and reversing previously held negative stereotypes about Christians and the church. Philia was shown to millennials through commonalities and authenticity, often through the formation of affinity groups. Agape was demonstrated to millennials in the name of Jesus, incarnating his love through unconditional acceptance, frequently with the use of products bearing the message of his love. The result was an openness by the millennials to explore and develop their faith. If we are to distill the findings down to one main point, it would be this: disciple millennials with love.

CHAPTER 4

SPIRIT-LED DISCIPLESHIP

THEME THREE: BELIEF IN THE ACTIVITY OF THE HOLY SPIRIT

In my efforts to answer the question "What does it mean for millennials to follow Christ today in missional communities?" the agency of the Holy Spirit emerged as a key theme.[1] This was a surprise; although I had included an interview question about the Holy Spirit, I did not expect such robust responses. Osmer calls it being "brought up short" when the research data makes us question our preunderstandings of something usually taken for granted.[2] Being brought up short affects the interpretive process and elicits two possible responses: we either deny the threat to our understanding in order to maintain the status quo or accept the challenge to create a new understanding. This new understanding is what Gadamer called a "fusion of horizons," the emergence of a previously unknown interpretation of the world that can be applied to everyday life.[3] My previously held prejudices—that millennials were either unaware of the Holy Spirit or suspicious of him and the ministries that stressed his activity—were challenged by the findings, causing me to revise my understanding and think expansively about the role of pneumatology in discipleship.

The third finding, then, was that discipleship among millennials in missional communities includes a belief in the activity of the Holy Spirit. Findings fell into three subthemes. First, millennials believed that the Holy Spirit prepared them for discipleship relationships through prevenient action. Second, they believed in the Spirit's gift of discernment as a guide in discipleship efforts—specifically, with whom to engage in conversation, how to go about it, and what to say. Third, the presence of the Holy Spirit was a recurrent topic among millennials, with fifteen out of thirty interview respondents referring to his presence, often as a means to inner healing. Both Urban Life Church and Strip Club Church affirmed that they successfully discipled millennials in their missional communities through the agency of the Holy Spirit. As with the other themes, the question "What is going on?" is answered by the firsthand accounts of millennials and their leaders, while the question "Why is this going on?" is addressed through secondary literature that helps to interpret the findings.

BELIEF IN THE PREVENIENT ACTION OF THE HOLY SPIRIT IN MISSIONAL ADVANCE

My research found that participants believed that the Holy Spirit prepared dechurched millennials for discipleship relationships through prevenient action.[4] In concert with my own findings, I discuss the work of missiologist Lesslie Newbigin, who wrote on the prevenient action of the Holy Spirit in the advancement of mission.

The Descriptive-Empirical Task: What Is Going On?

Katherine was a millennial who had "a bad Catholic" experience and became a casualty of the dropout phenomenon before attending Urban Life Church. "I felt like every little sin was being counted," she said, "and that's when I got really upset." When I asked whether that had kept her from wanting to attend any church for a while, she answered, "Definitely . . . I read the Bible on my own and watched YouTube videos." Eventually, however, she decided "to find a local church to get involved in" and visited Urban Life Church. She explained how the situation unfolded:

So, I was unchurched and praying for a church and God had me Yelp search "best church Fort Worth" and theirs was number one and I read reviews and decided to go the next week. And when I got there, I met all my closest friends the first day. The Holy Spirit was all over that!

In saying that the Spirit "was all over that," she meant that God's coordination of the events was undeniable and obvious to her. She felt that finding Urban Life online, and subsequently meeting new friends, had been orchestrated by God's preparation. Her belief that the Holy Spirit was working behind the scenes was bolstered further by the fact that she immediately connected with others in the faith community upon arriving: "When I got there, the Holy Spirit had told the woman in front of me that a new person was coming, and she needed to ask her to sit with her, so she asked me to sit with her! That day I met three of my closest friends, including Charlotte."

Katherine believed that others were being prepared by the Holy Spirit for her arrival. The woman's prompting to ask Katherine to sit with her made a huge impact on her, so much so that she reiterated to me that she wanted me to include this vignette in my account.

Similarly, Gabby believed that it was the Holy Spirit who had led her to become involved at Urban Life Church after a period of churchlessness two-and-a-half years prior. She reported that she "didn't have connections with people" at her previous church. She attended for a while but became discouraged when she "tried to join a connect group at this other church and they were like, 'you can't' because they were too full." She chose her words carefully, saying that she did not want to "speak ill of other churches," but it was clear by her demeanor and tone of voice that she had found the experience disheartening. As a result of feeling disconnected, she had left the church. When she visited Urban Life Church one Sunday morning, Gabby said that the Holy Spirit "pointed out" a woman in the crowd, and she felt that the Spirit "was like, just go over there and talk to her."

One of the things Gabby had been praying for was a mentor:

> My mom passed away when I was like nineteen, almost twenty, so I haven't had like that female . . . that is, like, a maternal figure [who could] slap you on the head when you're doing something wrong but then also be like that encourager and give you that maternal type love.

Hoping that the Lord was perhaps answering this prayer, Gabby approached the woman whom she felt the Holy Spirit had highlighted. "She prayed for me immediately," Gabby reported, "and I was like, 'Yeah, this is the right person.'" From that point on, Gabby committed to being part of the Urban Life community. This woman became Gabby's mentor for the next two years, meeting with her regularly to "encourage" and "challenge" her in her faith. As a result of this relationship, Gabby began mentoring two women younger than herself. "It's like a stair step, like, she pours into me so I can forward to them."

Gabby credited the leading of the Holy Spirit in helping her go from being disconnected from a church to being involved to the point that one of her deepest desires had been granted. He had gone before her, answering her prayer for the mother figure for which she had prayed for years. This, in turn, led to Gabby replicating the discipleship relationship with younger congregants.

Strip Club Church also reported instances of the prevenient work of the Holy Spirit in the dechurched. A dramatic example of this theme is the story of Annette, the former porn star who became a volunteer with Strip Club Church. She recounted,

> I was in the industry for seven years, but I took a break at year three. During my break, I went to church with my grandpa and his wife and received Jesus as my Lord and Savior . . . However, I got connected with the wrong group of people and did not go back to church for a while . . . I got involved with a pimp and got right back into the industry.

Annette returned to the porn industry, leaving the church behind. She reflected, however, that "this time something was different . . . I had the Holy Spirit in my heart." Four years later, she was headed to Las Vegas to film a pornography movie and felt an "urge" to take her Bible with her. She said she later realized that the "urge" was the direction of the Holy Spirit. Sitting on the airplane, she turned in her Bible to Revelation 2:20–23, which speaks about an adulterous woman. She recalled that, as she read, she "felt the Holy Spirit come over" her "with great conviction" about her life in the sex industry. She shared, "The Scripture I read on the plane that day changed my life. It is a hard Scripture; however, the Holy Spirit spoke to me through it. He said, 'Annette, I have a far greater life in store for you. If you would just give up everything and follow me, you won't regret it.'"

That was the last pornography movie she ever filmed. This encounter with the Holy Spirit coincided with meeting at the sex-industry expo a Strip Club Church volunteer named Rachel, who would become her discipleship mentor and help her transition out of the sex industry. Annette said she "felt so loved" by Rachel, who encouraged her to "take a step of faith" and leave the porn industry once and for all. Strip Club Church continued to disciple her, along with her local church, so that six months later she felt ready to begin sharing her testimony and attending porn conventions on the "other side," as a minister of the gospel. Annette now has her own ministry to girls in the sex industry. Annette's story demonstrates that, once again, the Holy Spirit worked providentially in the life of the dechurched in preparation for an encounter with her future discipler in the missional community.

Emily described a similar experience with the Holy Spirit while working in the clubs. What Annette described as an "urge," Emily called a "tugging" and "stirring," explaining, "I remember feeling that tugging, like 'Hey,' God is stirring in me, like 'Hey, this is not where you belong.'" Emily had a Christian background, having grown up in a household where her "mother was a believer but ha[d] never taken me to church." She noted, ironically, that it was the mother of a friend who had sexually abused her who first took her to church. The situation "was kind of awkward," she said, but, ultimately, she was "grateful" because "where my faith came from was just being little and being in the church." Thus, when she started working in the clubs years later, she already "had a faith."

She found it difficult to attend church regularly because of her sixty-hour work week, so she joined the ranks of the dechurched. But she recounted that, after a period of time, "I could feel God trying to pull me out of that club." She befriended Barbie, who began a discipleship relationship with her, helping her address her addiction and underlying trauma from the sexual abuse she had endured. In addition, Barbie encouraged Emily's relationship with the Holy Spirit. Emily reflected on her belief that the Holy Spirit had been speaking to her all along, saying she now realizes that "you don't have to be perfect to have the Holy Spirit living in you or around you or near you . . . You can be from the club, in the club, and he can be right in this club with you right now."

Thanks to Barbie's encouragement, Emily realized that the Holy Spirit had "always" been a part of her faith. The two went on together to found Strip Club Church in Fort Worth, and Emily reentered a faith community. This is another example of belief in the Holy Spirit preveniently working in the heart of the dechurched in order to prepare them to meet an individual in the missional community who can facilitate their reengagement with the body of believers.

The Interpretive Task: Why Is This Going On?

Preeminent missiologist Lesslie Newbigin expounded on the Spirit's prevenient action in mission in his work *The Relevance of Trinitarian Doctrine for Today's Mission*. He shared a personal experience from the foreign mission field that led to his "clear convictions" on how to understand the role of the Holy Spirit in "missionary advance."[5] Groups from neighboring villages would often come to the place where Newbigin was ministering and ask for instruction on Christianity. "Invariably," Newbigin wrote, "it was found that, behind such a request, there was some experience which had prompted a desire to know more of Christ," such as a dream, a "chance" reading of Scripture, or an answer to prayer.[6] As Newbigin reported, "Questioning would bring out the fact that the Holy Spirit had, in this way, touched the life of a man or a group of men, to a new desire of God."[7]

He called this touch the work of "the prevenient and sovereign Spirit" and advised that it must be acknowledged by the evangelist and accepted as the guide in her efforts.[8] His advice was to "find out what the Holy Spirit has done among them and build on that."[9] This became one of his core missional convictions. Taking Newbigin's concepts and overlaying them on my findings, it is evident that the prevenient action of the Holy Spirit in missions was being reframed from evangelism to discipleship at my fieldwork sites and that Newbigin's advice for the evangelist in the foreign mission field applied as well to the discipler in the missional community: find out where the Holy Spirit is already at work and build on it.

This idea is a central doctrine of the missional movement, the *missio Dei*.[10] Latin for "the mission of God," *missio Dei* underscores the idea that God himself is a missionary at work in the world. Guder describes it thus:

> We have come to see that mission is not merely an activity of the church. Rather mission is the result of God's initiative, rooted in God's purposes to restore and heal creation. Mission means "sending," and it is the central biblical theme describing the purpose of God's action in human history.[11]

This theme of God's mission, Guder writes, can be observed throughout Scripture, culminating in the sentness of Jesus Christ to earth to redeem humankind.[12] God is a missionary God, and his people, the church, are to be a sent people. As Christ said, "As the Father has sent me, I am sending you" (John 20:21).[13] God is always at work in the world, and the church is given the choice to join him in his work.[14] The Spirit of God is the agent of transformation, and the discipler simply comes alongside in cooperation with his work already in progress.[15] Thus, the work of God is accomplished through the church but also beyond it.[16] This sentness is what Hirsch calls the "missional impulse," and it stands in contrast to the prevailing attractional model of church, a "come-and-get-it" approach so prevalent in Christendom.[17]

BELIEF IN DISCERNMENT THROUGH THE HOLY SPIRIT

A second prominent pneumatological theme that emerged from the data was a reliance on the Holy Spirit for discernment. The belief in this pneumatic function of providing insight and sound judgment was prevalent throughout my fieldwork. In particular, respondents emphasized their confidence in the guidance of the Holy Spirit on how to engage missionally with those to whom they were ministering and discipling, including whom to talk to and what to say (and, at times, what not to say). Prayer was viewed as a means of connecting with the Spirit in order to receive the guidance needed, as was the corporate act of discernment.

The Descriptive-Empirical Task: What Is Going On?

One of the main themes throughout the interviews with volunteers from both sites was their reliance on the Holy Spirit for guidance both in preparation for ministry and during ministry. Several respondents spoke of seeking the Spirit's guidance in advance of encountering individuals in ministry. For example, Charlotte and her husband, Tom, both millennials, were directors of the prayer team at Urban Life Church, and part of their weekly preparation for Sunday morning was to share with the rest of the leadership what they were "hearing from the Holy Spirit for that day, and then pray together over the services." Charlotte explained how she relied on the Holy Spirit to help her be an effective leader:

It's kind of like that readiness as a Christian that you must be prepared to minister to somebody or just be like a light, and like keeping your ear tuned to the Holy Spirit. Being a leader . . . helped us to hone that because you feel the weight of the responsibility and it's like, "Okay, yeah, like this is serious, this is people's spiritual lives" . . . We've been given a platform and a position to have a level of influence in that area, and so it's like, "Okay, Holy Spirit, like what are you saying right now and what are you saying for this situation?"

Charlotte prayed before the Sunday service so that, if she were asked to pray for someone during the service, she would be ready to be a "light" to them. Her level of commitment was admirable, wanting as she did so to faithfully bear the "weight" of her responsibility as a leader. It stands to reason that operating under the guidance of the Holy Spirit—to hear what he is saying in each situation—is evidence of good stewardship, while failing to do so would have been failing to take her position seriously.

She shared that, indeed, one Sunday she prayed for a millennial named Katherine who was experiencing sleeplessness and feelings of depression, and the Holy Spirit brought her "a new level of freedom" through her prayers. This is the same Katherine we read about earlier, who felt that the Holy Spirit was leading her to a particular woman. Charlotte was that woman! Their encounter began a mentoring relationship in which Charlotte helped Katherine "grow and find joy in Jesus." Thus, Charlotte's prayers for discernment eventually led to an opportunity for discipleship.

The above example is about how the ministries sought discernment from the Holy Spirit in preparation for ministry; however, they also spoke of how they continued to seek guidance from the Holy Spirit even during ministry. Charlotte let the Holy Spirit lead her to whomever it was she needed to minister to at Urban Life Church:

[I was] listening . . . and saying, "Okay, I really feel like I would feel uncomfortable if we don't say, go visit [with] this person. I would feel like something is off, but I feel at peace when I think about going and seeing them." And so, a lot of times it's as simple as following that peace.

Charlotte was "listening" to the Holy Spirit during the Sunday worship service, asking for direction in terms of whom to pray for. As she did so, she felt increasingly "uncomfortable" about the prospect of choosing not to speak with a particular individual; she deemed this discomfort a spiritual leading. When she made the decision in her heart to speak with that individual, on the other hand, she felt peace. She concluded, "I don't mean emotion, but it's a feeling, like within you to follow that peace," presumably drawing a distinction between an emotional response and peace as a fruit of the Spirit (Gal 5:22). She credited the Holy Spirit as the agent of this peace.

A millennial named Jennifer was a volunteer with Strip Club Church who spoke about using discernment when going into the strip clubs. She said,

Once we're in [the clubs, we have] an individual discernment when we're talking to the girls, as far as what to say, what to ask, how far to push in things because we don't want to push them away, but we also want to get to know them. We want to be intentional to talk about meaningful things when the opportunity arises or having the boldness . . . according to how the Spirit is leading to ask to pray with them.

Spirit-imparted discernment aided Jennifer in approaching others with intentionality and boldness. It is interesting that she used the phrase "how far to push," implying that she was willing to step out of her comfort zone in order to be obedient to the Spirit's promptings that might lead her to take a conversation deeper or even ask if she could pray with a dancer.

The above examples are about individual discernment, but Jennifer and others also talked about the importance of corporate discernment through praying together as a team, either in meetings or even in the car on the way to the ministry venues. Jennifer elaborated on the corporate role of the Holy Spirit in her ministry: "We all must agree if one person . . . is [like] 'I just don't feel right about it tonight; I just don't feel comfortable,' we would be like, 'Okay, then let's just pray over the club. We'll go to the next club.'"

Jennifer's group relied on the guidance of the Holy Spirit for direction. This corporate act of discernment entailed God either guiding the entire group of people or guiding an individual within the group experience. The ministry teams sought such discernment in order to make decisions together about how to best engage when there was not necessarily a clear-cut course of action.

Several members of Strip Club Church reflected on the negative consequences of failing to seek the guidance of the Spirit. Liz said that she specifically asks the Holy Spirit to "speak through me" during the conversations with the dancers and drag queens because "my own words . . . will not be good." Rozelle similarly said, "We have to have the Holy Spirit to lead us to do everything . . . because I'll mess up." Lynette explained that the Holy Spirit

> would be the one to illuminate for us, you know, what needs to be said, when and where and who we know we need to be having a conversation with, because if he's not driving it, you'll do like I did when I first started going . . . I'm just standing at the back . . . before realizing that I needed him to be leading me—I was just a wallflower . . . I just went in there in my own power.

All three of these volunteers, Liz, Rozelle and Lynette, said that, had it not been for the aid of the Holy Spirit, their words would not have been what the hearer needed. Discerning the presence of the Holy Spirit helped them feel more effective in ministry and better able to connect with others.

Mary from Strip Club Church agreed that being led by the Holy Spirit is paramount but expressed frustration when others were intent on relying on human effort and agendas:

> We want to be Holy Spirit driven all the way . . . but I think putting that into practice is harder for some people than for others. I think some people want this very clear step-by-step [ministry plan], when I see—I think—the Holy Spirit gives us like those plans, but I also think that sometimes he's like, "You know, can you just trust me for the next step? Can you just trust me for the next time?" because I think that gives him greater glory, as well, when we do that. Instead of "Look what we planned," we say, "Look at the steps that he took us through," and I think there have been team members who struggle with that, and I think that that has caused rifts and not as intentional participation in ministry.

Mary preferred abandoning human agendas for the spontaneous discernment of the Holy Spirit. To be sure, this was a risky endeavor that made others feel uncomfortable. Nevertheless, she showed boldness in her willingness to forgo the predictability of a human plan or technique in favor of the wild adventure of following the Spirit. In summary, the practice of discerning the Holy Spirit in both Urban Life Church and Strip Club Church, whether by millennials being ministered to, millennial volunteers, or their non-millennial leaders, was believed to be a means of making purposeful connections where relationships could be established for ongoing discipleship.

The Interpretive Task: Why Is This Going On?
Theologian John V. Taylor writes that the Holy Spirit is the "current of communication" that connects the believer with Christ and with others in the context of mission.[18] Like an electrical current, the

Holy Spirit acts as an "invisible go-between" to help us discern God's will for a certain situation.[19] The prerequisite of receiving such discernment, writes Taylor, is attention.[20] When one attends to the reality of the Spirit's presence, she becomes attuned to the direction in which the Spirit is moving. Attention requires awareness and intentionality, both of which were exhibited by the respondents in my research. Volunteers prepared themselves by giving attention to the Spirit's guidance ahead of time in prayer; they also maintained their focus on the Spirit while ministering. This allowed them to remain in the flow of the "current" of God's intended purpose for a particular person or interaction. Taylor's point is that the Holy Spirit is the "chief actor" in mission, the "director of the whole enterprise."[21]

Taylor writes that, unfortunately, Christians too often "have turned the divine initiative into a human enterprise," substituting human ingenuity and strength for movements of the Holy Spirit.[22] Jesus never intended it to be this way. Taylor points out that Jesus's missional mandate was given simultaneously with the empowering of the Holy Spirit, thereby inextricably linking the two.[23] Jesus forbade moving ahead of the Spirit, instructing his disciples to "wait" for empowerment from on high. Not to do so results in a flesh-driven ministry.

Similarly, in *Life Together* Bonhoeffer contrasts the fellowship of the Spirit with mere "human community"—that which is a "psychic reality," as opposed to a spiritual one.[24] The existence of Christian community is based on the ability to discern between pneumatic and flesh-driven ideals. The health of the church is dependent on this discernment; indeed, Bonhoeffer states in strong terms that "the life or death of a Christian community is determined by whether it achieves sober wisdom on this point as soon as possible."[25]

For Bonhoeffer, the goal of proper discernment is for the development of authentic *koinonia* of the church community, so that it can bear witness of Christ to the world by its spiritual health.[26] Taylor, by contrast, writes about the importance of discernment in missions. The missional impulse today, says Taylor, must be carried out effectively by waiting upon the Holy Spirit to lead rather than forging ahead in one's own thinking, efforts, or agendas.[27]

Thus, there is a tension in discernment that must be navigated: on the one hand, Scripture affirms that "God is not a God of disorder but of peace" (1 Cor 14:33); on the other hand, as Hirsch and Hirsch note, missional discipleship often requires "untamed, Jesus-like disciples" who are willing to follow the wind of the Spirit as it blows.[28] This tension seemed to be resolved when the ministries exercised corporate discernment. When this discernment was effectively exercised as a group, *koinonia* and unity followed. Even standing at the front entrance of a club, for example, they were willing to turn their attention to the Holy Spirit and wait on his direction. I interpreted such restraint as an act of obedience and surrender to the Lord's leading.

BELIEF IN THE PRESENCE OF THE HOLY SPIRIT

My research found that belief in the presence of the Holy Spirit in the context of discipleship was a prominent theme at both fieldwork sites.[29] The presence of God was described in language that emphasized his immanence and his ability to supply inner healing, thereby preparing the hearts of millennials to engage in further discipleship. This section will elaborate on these findings, using the writings of theologian David Watson as a dialectical partner.

The Descriptive-Empirical Task: What Is Going On?
Jesse at Urban Life Church told me that he had never known his biological father. He had abandoned Jesse and his mother when Jesse was very young, which had always been a source of great pain. But at the church service on Father's Day, Jesse had what he described as an "emotional" encounter with the Holy Spirit:

> On Father's Day was the first time I truly felt it . . . I got very emotional, I got filled with tears of gratitude . . . [realizing] that had my father not done that to my mom

she probably never would have gotten out of her comfort zone [and] gone to the U.S. . . . so, I felt like that was one of the first times that the Holy Spirit really touched me.

He said he felt God's "hand on my heart" in a way that healed emotional wounds inflicted in childhood from not knowing his biological father. He described feeling "joy" in that moment, realizing that the Lord was behind his move from Mexico to the U.S., adding that the "Holy Spirit really touched me and made me realize, like, be grateful." Jesse explicitly credited the presence of the Holy Spirit as the agent of his transformation.

Savannah similarly shared that, when she felt the presence of the Spirit, she felt "transformed" as "someone who has purpose and meaning, and that you matter, that you are valuable. In a world where there is so much noise and anonymity, . . . it's easy to feel lost." Savannah credited the presence of the Holy Spirit in the healing of her assaulted self-esteem that had convinced her that she was not valuable. The clamor of the world had robbed her of feeling special in God's eyes, and the Holy Spirit restored her spiritual vision. Whereas she had felt lost, she now felt found. Noah from Urban Life Church similarly described a recalibration of vision, reflecting that "the presence of God . . . reshapes your focus on what you see for your life and how God sees things for your life." The role of the Holy Spirit as a helper (paraclete) is to lead the believer to the truth, and Noah and Savannah's accounts point to this role. In their estimation, he was removing the self-deception and helping them see themselves as God sees them: as valuable and having purpose.

Morgan at Urban Life Church also touched on the world's ability to emotionally wound and the Spirit's ability to heal. She shared that Sunday services at Urban Life had "impacted her the most." "Throughout the week you just notice, like, how much negativity gets spoken through media and through people, and it kind of wears on you . . . and then you're able to come on Sunday and get refreshed through the Holy Spirit."

Morgan's reference to the negativity in the world contains echoes of the teaching on the "Unique Edge" discussed in Theme 1—specifically, that the world is full of "hurting and broken people" who exhibit "critical negativity" and "draining grouchiness." If this is accurate, it stands to reason that Morgan would have been drained by such encounters as she was out on her "cultural street," endeavoring to impact culture in her job. The "refreshing" of the Holy Spirit, then, was welcomed by Morgan as a source of rejuvenation, like a drink of cool water in the desert of a hostile world.

Noah, Ryan, and Savannah all mentioned that they "felt" the Holy Spirit. I asked Noah from Urban Life Church, "Will you describe for me how you know when you're feeling the presence of God?" He answered, "I usually just count it as, like, do you feel joy in the setting that you're in, or do you feel like some type of peace . . . Are you finding that you're coming in a bad mood and leaving in a good mood, feeling lighter . . . even more optimistic?" Noah described an emotional healing by the Spirit, manifested in a change of disposition and attitude. The result was greater peace and joy. Similarly, Ryan from Urban Life Church shared that he felt "an overwhelming calm" when he experienced God's presence and that this was "a big reason" he "kept coming" to Urban Life Church. Savannah provided a similar description. I asked her what the presence of God "felt like," and she replied, "So, usually the presence of God and Jesus is just—there's this warmth, there's just a genuine like, peace . . . the fruits of the Spirit of just peace or joy or love." She explicitly named the feelings as "the fruit of the Spirit," implying that she had a biblical framework for the sensations. It was also notable that she used the word "usually," thereby indicating that awareness of God's immanence was for her a standard or common occurrence.

The presence of the Holy Spirit was discussed among respondents from Strip Club Church, as well. Melissa described an interaction with a group of strippers in which she was invited to a housewarming party for an employee of one of the clubs she served. She was asked to pray a blessing on the house, and "it was one of those Spirit-led moments where I just started praying . . . I saw like all the girls who were next to me just in prayer over the house, they're all weeping, and they were like, 'Melissa, that was so beautiful,' and I'm like, 'I wasn't trying to pray a beautiful prayer or whatever, but just praying God's Word and just praying and inviting the Holy Spirit in that moment, and [the Spirit] touched these girls to tears.'"

The emotional response of the girls, according to Melissa, happened because "they're thirsty" for the Holy Spirit. As the girls joined Melissa in prayer, they were "touched" by the Spirit. Their hearts were softened, and their protective masks came off. Melissa paraphrased their thoughts: "'I feel emotional when I'm trying to be emotionless,' like 'we tried, you know, to kind of be hard, you know, on the outside.' [But] when the Holy Spirit is in contact with you, he's going to touch you. He's going to bring out those things that are true."

This particular experience with the Holy Spirit opened the door for further discipleship between Melissa and the girls. She explained that, as a result of this encounter, she could go deeper with the girls, talking about areas that needed "healing," such as financial problems or sexual addiction, because the Holy Spirit had tenderized their hearts and made them receptive. She told me that she planned on starting a group using a curriculum for freedom from what she called the "big issues" in their lives, which were "money, men, and self-worth." Melissa credited the presence of the Holy Spirit for penetrating the emotional armor of the women and preparing them for discipleship.

Annette from Strip Club Church also spoke about the feelings she experienced as a result of the Spirit's healing touch. She reported that he had helped her "have a smooth transition" out of the sex industry and into recovery. She subsequently started her own ministry to sex workers and preached about the importance of "God's presence" for transformation: "Please, I beg you, get into God's presence every single day! You need him . . . God's presence gets us through the worst of times with an overwhelming sense of peace and comfort . . . I don't know how I ever survived without his presence."

It was the Spirit, Annette said, that made her aware of the presence of God, and she credited him with giving her a peace that helped her survive the onslaught of a hostile world. As a former porn star who struggled with drug and alcohol addiction, she viewed the presence of God as the source of inner healing:

> I walked into [church] drunk and high on prescription pills. In that moment, everything began to change for me. I felt God's presence. You know those warm tingles that consume you from head to toe? No, it wasn't the drugs— it was God, and I was in awe. I have not backslid or fallen back into addiction because God's presence (and grace) gives me the strength to stay set free.

Annette recognized the presence of God's Spirit as keeping her from experiencing the typical "yo-yo" pattern of sex workers in and out of the industry.[30]

The Interpretive Task: Why Is This Going On?

One of the essential functions of the Holy Spirit for the modern disciple, according to Watson, is to foster spiritual growth, while one of the most important aspects of the Holy Spirit's agency in spiritual growth is healing.[31] Watson writes that the Spirit's role of healing is often misunderstood or neglected.[32] Biblically, however, whenever Jesus commanded his disciples to preach the gospel, this was almost always accompanied by the command to heal the sick.[33] Thus, to be a disciple of Jesus means to take seriously the idea that God heals.

Watson gives particular emphasis to emotional healing, or "inner healing."[34] The havoc of sin causes all humans to be "emotionally fractured, wounded, and scarred," writes Watson, "and so in need of inner-healing."[35] He goes on to explain that "we need to open our lives to God and to one another for his Spirit to heal our inner hurts and to renew us in God's love."[37] Watson suggests three means of accomplishing this. First, remove the "protective masks" that act as defense mechanisms and impede emotional transparency, perhaps even with ourselves. Second, engage God in prayer with our true selves, asking for forgiveness and healing by the Spirit. Third, openly share our lives with others in loving Christian fellowship.[38] When the Holy Spirit brings his healing touch, protective measures fall away, and the true self can be seen and thus healed.

Watson explains that, when one is touched and healed by the Holy Spirit, the fruit of the Spirit is made manifest, such as in the presence of love, joy, and peace.[39] As the Spirit heals and his fruits are made manifest, the believer is conformed to the image of Christ.[40] Watson summarizes the experience of the healing presence of God by saying, "Unless God is manifestly in our midst, the world has no time for the church."[41] The world has tired of dry doctrine and meaningless gatherings; "people are looking not for religion but for reality."[42] They are looking, Watson says, for an experience of the living God.

Savannah from Urban Life Church made an assessment that was uncanny in its similarity to Watson's:

> If people don't encounter the presence of God when they come to Urban Life, then everything we do is in vain, and we can look polished and produced . . . but if they're not experiencing the presence of Jesus, then it doesn't matter what we do. So, everything we do is to break down barriers so that people can encounter the presence.

For both Savannah and Watson, the immanent, manifest presence of the Holy Spirit was superior to rote liturgy and glossy production. The task of the church, then, is to break down barriers that keep individuals from experiencing the fullness of a transforming God, so that they can be healed and conformed to the likeness of Christ.

For millennials in my work, healing was clearly viewed as an area of the Holy Spirit's action experienced as part of the discipleship process. As the Holy Spirit was given room to move among the missional faith community, they believed that he brought his healing presence to refresh and gently deal with past hurts, resulting in greater freedom to follow Christ. The effective discipleship of millennials in missional communities, thus, means allowing them to explore the person and work of the Holy Spirit, both in mission and in ministry. This has important implications for ministering to postmodern millennials: his active presence replaces static, formulaic programs; a relationship with him replaces stale religion; and his healing transformation replaces mere transmission of information.

CONCLUSION

The research revealed that discipleship among millennials in missional communities was believed to be facilitated by the work of the Holy Spirit by acting preveniently in mission, providing discernment, and offering inner healing. The Spirit was credited with working preveniently by drawing unchurched millennials back to communities of faith, often through answering prayers and bringing conviction in a way that was perceived as obvious action in millennials' lives. Meanwhile, missional community volunteers and their congregants sought discernment from the Holy Spirit, leading to relational connections with God and others and resulting in fruitful discipleship encounters. As millennials were brought into the community of faith, they continued to seek the Holy Spirit's ministry. They reported experiencing the Holy Spirit's presence, bringing inner healing or manifestations of the fruit of the Spirit, such as peace and joy.

What is clear from the data is that following the leading of the Holy Spirit as the discipleship "program" or "curriculum" was exponentially more effective than human effort alone, because there was an assumption that he had already been working on the hearts and minds of those who were ready to engage. We can draw the conclusion from the research that we need to disciple millennials through the presence and power of the Spirit.

CHAPTER 5

RELIGIONLESS DISCIPLESHIP

INTRODUCTION

Millennials are a mission field. If this is true, then it is important for the church to learn how to translate Christianity into their cultural vernacular. But in doing so, how do we ensure that the essential tenets of the faith are not lost in translation? How can we contextualize the gospel without veering into heterodoxy? This is again where Osmer's pastoral cycle is a helpful guide. Doing practical theology well, according to Osmer, involves four critical tasks. The descriptive-empirical task asks "What is going on?" while the interpretive task asks "Why is it going on?" As important as these questions are, practical theologians must go a step further to guide the Christian community into faithful practice. Thus, a normative task is crucial; it asks the question "What ought to be going on?"[1]

I have attempted to answer the first two questions in the previous chapters. This chapter seeks to explore the answer to this third question through theological reflection. Theological reflection is the process of "using theological concepts to interpret particular episodes, situations, or contexts."[2] It is a hermeneutical activity that understands particular situations by critically examining them "in light of scripture and tradition" in order to enable faithful practice.[3] As we consider what it means for millennials to follow Christ today in missional communities, it is not enough to know what activities and practices are taking place and why. There must be an interpretive step, one that delves into the theological interplay between divine and human action. This chapter aims to explore and explain such a relationship so that foundations for transforming practices can be laid.

Given these considerations, the significance of Osmer's third question for my research is "What ought to be going on with the discipleship of millennials in missional communities? How has God revealed himself through Jesus Christ to this cohort in this setting that should become normative for future praxis?" To answer these questions, I have chosen Dietrich Bonhoeffer's concept of "religionless Christianity," along with biblical passages and secondary sources, to interpret the findings of my fieldwork.[4]

The choice to employ religionless Christianity was based on two considerations. First, the concept is grounded in Bonhoeffer's concern that the church had become disconnected from the surrounding culture.[5] This echoes the contemporary issues of the perceived irrelevance of the institutional church with millennials and the need for a missional, world-centered ethic. Second, religionless Christianity was the antidote to a prevailing imposter religion of the day, which Bonhoeffer called "the God hypothesis."[6] It bears a striking resemblance to Moralistic Therapeutic Deism, the dominant belief of millennials today.

BONHOEFFER AND RELIGIONLESS CHRISTIANITY

The theology of Dietrich Bonhoeffer is best understood in the context of his life and the era in which he lived.[7] Bonhoeffer was a theologian and pastor in Germany in the 1930s during the time of the Third Reich. He considered the German church to have closed itself off from God's revelation by aligning with the Nazi party, an act he called the "German-Christian compromise."[8] When he learned of a clandestine plot to overthrow Hitler, the avowed pacifist was faced with an ethical dilemma: Would he become part of the compromise, or would he join the fight? He decided that he could not in good conscience retreat, and for the rest of his life he would remain devoted to carrying out the tasks of the Resistance and of the Confessing Church. Doberstein writes that "Here he acted in accord with his fundamental view of ethics, that a Christian must accept his responsibility as a citizen of this world where God has placed him," a personal decision that would become one of the primary themes in his theological writings.[9] Arrested by the Gestapo in 1943 for participating in a plot to assassinate Hitler, Bonhoeffer continued to develop his theology from prison until his martyrdom two years later.[10]

In 1944, the last year of Bonhoeffer's life, he wrote a series of letters to his good friend Eberhard Bethge voicing his concerns about the church. It was Bonhoeffer's contempt for the German-Christian compromise and the church's withdrawal from ethical action that caused him to come to a jarring conclusion: "We are approaching a completely religionless age," he wrote to Bethge. "People as they are now simply cannot be religious anymore."[11] He was troubled by what he called a "world come of age," a world that no longer needed religion as a means of explaining reality. Instead, God "had been reduced to a *deus ex machina*," a last resort called upon when all human capabilities had been exhausted, a stopgap pushed to the margins of human experience.[12]

Religion, he surmised, had been disconnected from lived experience, rendering it irrelevant to the problems facing most people. This was evidenced by the fact that the church refused to stand up to the Third Reich. True Christianity had been replaced by a disembodied "God hypothesis."[13] Religion had come to mean "individualized piety, bourgeois privilege, and ghetto church."[14] The effects of religion, he wrote, make individuals "either provincials or secularists," either fleeing from the world into the Christian subculture or being wholly absorbed into the world.[15] Building on earlier work by Barth that contrasted revelation and religion, Bonhoeffer wrote:

> The religious path from human beings to God leads
> to the idol of our hearts which we have formed after
> our own image. Neither knowledge, nor morality, nor
> religion leads to God . . . If human beings and God are to
> come together, there can be but one path: God's path to
> human beings.[16]

Religion, he concluded, is the false idol of humankind's attempts to
reach "up" to God through our own efforts. This stands in contrast
to true revelation, which always originates with God reaching
"down" to humankind. Thus, neither mere knowledge about God
nor self-aggrandizing moralism is true Christianity, but only the
reality of God's grace through Christ.

Bonhoeffer wrote a letter to Bethge on April 30, 1944, that
would become the basis of what he called religionless Christianity.
"What is bothering me incessantly is the question what Christianity
really is, or indeed, who Christ really is for us today?" he wrote.[17]
"If religion is only the garb in which Christianity is clothed—and
this garb has looked very different in different ages—what then is
religionless Christianity?"[18]

Over the next year he would continue to write Bethge as
he wrestled with his "new theology."[19] He asked the provocative
question, "What if Christianity were not a religion at all?"[20] In an
attempt to answer the question, he created a world-centered ethic
for the church that pivoted away from inner preservation and
toward a concern for "being there for others."[21] A nonreligious
interpretation meant concrete ethical action by incarnating the
life, love, and resurrection power of Immanuel, God with us.[22] It
meant learning to take risks again rather than being preoccupied
with defending itself. It meant ceasing to be "heavily burdened by
difficult, traditional ideas" that made "no impact on the broader
masses."[23] This was religionless Christianity.

The God Hypothesis Versus Moralistic Therapeutic Deism
Bonhoeffer's questions have particular significance for my work, because they are grounded in the exploration of new cultural forms and symbols of the Christian faith that go beyond rote "religious" expressions of discipleship. Today, as in Bonhoeffer's day, what is needed is to construct a nonreligious interpretation of the Christian faith for a generation that no longer finds religion credible. What is the religious garb of today that needs to be shed? Based on my research, the answer is threefold. First is the imposter religion of today, Moralistic Therapeutic Deism. Second is the church's tendency to insulate and isolate from the world. Third is the Enlightenment encasement of Christian practices. This is the religious raiment that is encumbering the effective discipleship of millennials.

As previously noted, Christian Smith in his landmark book *Soul Searching: The Religious and Spiritual Lives of American Teenagers* describes "Moralistic Therapeutic Deism" (MTD) as a religion that views God as a distant creator who wants humans to be "nice" to one another and intervenes only to help them attain happiness and fulfillment.[24] Based on 3,300 interviews with American millennials, Smith identified five tenets of MTD: (1) "A God exists who created and orders the world and watches over human life on earth"; (2) "God wants people to be good, nice, and fair to each other, as taught in the Bible and by most world religions"; (3) "The central goal of life is to be happy and to feel good about oneself"; (4) "God does not need to be particularly involved in one's life except when he is needed to resolve a problem"; and (5) "Good people go to heaven when they die."[25] Smith points out that MTD is not just a millennial problem but is the belief system being modeled for millennials by older adults.[26]

Moralistic Therapeutic Deism bears a striking resemblance to the God hypothesis about which Bonhoeffer wrote. Both are steeped in a culture of autonomy and secularization: Bonhoeffer was concerned about what it meant to follow Christ in a "world come of age" that had pushed Jesus to the margins, while Smith

Supposition	Bonhoeffer's God Hypothesis	Smith's Moralistic Therapeutic Deism
Culture of autonomy/ secularization	"World come of age"	"The cultural triumph of liberal Protestantism"
God as remote	Religious relationship with a god who is formed after our own image	Belief in an impersonal higher power
God as a last resort	God as "*deus ex machina*"	God helps only when called upon
Resulting behavior	Isolating privatization of faith	Live by an individualized moral code

Table 5.1 Comparison of the God Hypothesis and MTD

called MTD "the cultural triumph of liberal Protestantism," writing that "liberal Protestantism's core values—individualism, pluralism, emancipation, tolerance, free critical inquiry, and the authority of human experience—have come to so permeate broader American culture that its own churches as organizations have difficulty surviving."[27]

Both are reflections of a church that, in terms of ethical living, looks no different from the world but has been absorbed into the cultural mainstream. Both MTD and the God hypothesis view God as a remote deity entreated only in times of personal duress as a last resort when human efforts have been exhausted.[28] The resulting behavior of both is an individualized, privatized faith that centers on either relieving personal pain or therapeutic self-improvement, with little impetus for missional living.

Bonhoeffer's solution to the God hypothesis was to revise Christian forms, symbols, and practices to render them "religionless" so that they could regain their ethical efficacy. By asking "Who is Christ for us today?" he invites us to think critically and reflexively about how we might remove the "religious garb" of both MTD and

the Enlightenment church and put on new cultural forms more
in line with millennials' postmodern epistemology.[29] The bottom
line is that, as we endeavor to disciple millennials, we must do the
difficult, uncomfortable work of changing. It is time to be missional;
it is time to be religionless.

In the following sections, aspects of Bonhoeffer's religionless
Christianity will be discussed in concert with my research findings.
Theme One, "Discipleship among millennials in missional
communities was facilitated by opportunities to become engaged
in ministry and mission in the world," will be discussed alongside
Bonhoeffer's concept of "holy worldliness." Theme Two, "Discipleship
among millennials was facilitated by authentic, caring, and loving
relationships," will be examined alongside Bonhoeffer's concept
of "being there for others." Theme Three, "Discipleship among
millennials in missional communities included a belief in the activity
of the Holy Spirit," will take Bonhoeffer's ideas and extend them to
create what I am calling "religionless pneumatology." My hope is
that, through theological reflection, a practical plan for the effective
discipleship of millennials in missional communities will come into
focus that can become normative for the church in the future.

THEME ONE: "HOLY WORLDLINESS"

A key theme of Bonhoeffer's religionless Christianity is the
demonstration of the life and love of Christ through "holy worldliness."[30]
A concept found throughout his writings, holy worldliness was
understood by Bonhoeffer as a complete dedication to being active in
the world, living out one's potential, and serving others.[31] Rather than
being cloistered away, the church must participate in the worldly tasks
of life in the community—not dominating but helping and serving.
It must tell people in every calling what a life with Christ is, what it
means to "be there for others."[32]

He reminded believers that they are the salt of the earth, the
light of the world, called by Jesus to be the visible representation
of Christ in every facet of society, the mundane and the banal, the

secular and the ordinary. Believers are not "too good for this world,"
he wrote in *The Cost of Discipleship*.[33] Followers of Jesus "must not
only think of heaven; they have an earthly task as well."[34] Jesus
entrusts his work on earth to them, and this is what it means to live
in Christ.

Millennials in my study often reflected the characteristics
of holy worldliness. As shown in my findings, they were eager to
engage in ministry in the church and mission in the community
immediately upon becoming involved with the faith community,
often through engaging with culture and using personal narratives.
This section will therefore proceed using Bonhoeffer's holy
worldliness in discourse with the subthemes previously highlighted
under the following headings: opportunities for the incarnational
engagement of culture, opportunities to proclaim the gospel
through testimony, and opportunities to be mobilized immediately
for ministry. The intention of this approach is to demonstrate
the need to involve millennials in discipleship efforts that stress
equipping them for ministry in the wider culture.

Opportunities for the Incarnational Engagement of Culture
Bonhoeffer wrote in *Ethics*:

> There is no part of the world, be it never so forlorn and
> never so godless, which is not accepted by God and
> reconciled with God in Jesus Christ. Whoever sets eyes
> on the body of Jesus Christ . . . can never again with
> clerical arrogance set himself apart from the world. The
> world belongs to Christ, and it is only in Christ that the
> world is what it is.[35]

Bonhoeffer considered it an act of religious arrogance to separate
oneself from the world. The world belongs to Christ, and we are his
ambassadors; therefore, the church is to be actively engaged with
the surrounding culture, going "out into the storm and the action,

trusting in God whose commandment you faithfully follow."[36] Urban Life Church was dedicated to training millennials of every calling to go out into the storm and action, as Pastor Jim explained:

> Part of my philosophy is that ministry happens outside the walls of the church building. This [the church building] is a place for worship and equipping and fellowship, yes, but the actual real, raw ministry happens outside the walls here. So, we would say that that happens in the marketplace . . . We want to prepare people to make an impact in the marketplace.

Pastor Jim was articulating the missional rhythm of the church: come in to be equipped and trained, and then go out beyond the walls to make disciples. The description "real, raw" connotes authenticity, riskiness, and even a sense of being unprotected. This is necessary in order to "make an impact." In fact, one of this church's stated missions was "developing followers of Jesus who influence and shape culture."

As explained in chapter 2, they created a conceptual framework called The Seven Cultural Streets to help implement this mission. Cultural streets are spheres of society where individuals are placed to do the ministry of Jesus. The biblical origin for the streets concept is Isaiah 58:12:

> Your people will rebuild the ancient ruins
>   and will raise up the age-old foundations;
> you will be called Repairer of Broken Walls,
>   Restorer of Streets with Dwellings.

The pastor shared in a sermon that the "last line, where it says restorer of streets . . . The terminology for cultural streets originated right there. That just means that you're called, and you're commissioned, and you are empowered by God to restore on that street." The streets are the places to which believers are called to "go and make disciples" and fulfill the Great Commission. Every person falls into at least one category and is placed there to bring spiritual restoration to the culture. The missional thrust of the streets concept echoes Bonhoeffer's concept of holy worldliness, which exhorts Christians to tell "men of every calling what it means to live in Christ." To exhibit holy worldliness does not mean to confuse Christian identity or maturity with separation from the world in monastic piety or even as a professional cleric but to go out into the world maintaining one's vocation or station in life.

The streets concept has its origins in the 1970s Christian youth movement promoted specifically by Bill Bright, founder of Campus Crusade for Christ, and Loren Cunningham, founder of Youth with a Mission.[37] The two leaders developed a vision for ministry called the seven "spheres of society," mission fields to which all believers, not just ordained clergy, can go as "sent ones" for Jesus to influence the culture with the gospel.[38] Cunningham was optimistic that millennials would find the concept appealing, saying that "we have the challenge for this generation that just fits perfectly, and I think it's like dry kindling ready to be set afire."[39] He considered millennials the "most exciting group" because of their sense of social justice, their technological proficiency, and their global mindset.[40] Urban Life Church was philosophically aligned with the seven spheres concept of Bright and Cunningham, as evidenced by their focus on equipping young people to become missionaries in their own cultures.

A millennial named Noah from Urban Life Church understood what it meant to go into the storm and the action of the world as a missionary, entering the culture and transforming it through personal relationships and shared experiences:

> A lot of that is like you hear all the time, you know, "We got to be in the world but not of it," but most people just [say], "Well, I'm just not going to be anywhere near the world; I'm not going to be anywhere near the bad stuff,"

... and I'm like, yeah, but that's where the people are, so that's where we have to go if we actually want to get people!

Noah's statement was profound in its simplicity: "[the world] is where the people are, so that's where we have to go." He viewed eschewing the "world" with its "bad stuff" as faulty missiology resulting in missed opportunities for making disciples.

Strip Club Church likewise emphasized actions that were consistent with Bonhoeffer's idea of holy worldliness; as Jennifer stated,

> they did an outreach at the porn convention, [and] I was like, wow, they get it, like they are doing something right ... It just clicked because I was, like, that is how ministry is supposed to be. I mean, here they're getting invited to come inside when there are a bunch of protestors outside claiming to be doing the same work.

Being "inside" the porn convention meant that she was entering into a specific cultural context that was different from her own. This is in line with Bonhoeffer, who stressed telling people of "every calling" about Christ, and the phrase is synonymous with Jesus's command in the Great Commission to go "into all the world" and make disciples. Jennifer pointed out that, meanwhile, Christians "claiming to do the same work" were "outside" the convention center expressing their faith through protest and separation rather than through the "worldliness" that lay inside.

The above discourse about the relationship between the church and cultural engagement is reminiscent of the famous work by H. Richard Niebuhr, *Christ and Culture*. Niebuhr constructed a fivefold typology of approaches to address what he called "The Enduring Problem" of church vis-à-vis culture: Christ against Culture, Christ of Culture, Christ above Culture, Christ and Culture in Paradox, and Christ the Transformer of Culture.[41] Each approach occupies a position along a continuum, ranging from the church's complete withdrawal from culture to complete immersion.

The philosophy of both fieldwork sites aligned most closely with Christ the Transformer of Culture. This view holds that, although corrupted by the fall, culture is redeemable through Christ. Believers are tasked with being agents of cultural transformation for the glory of God. This view has a "more positive and hopeful attitude toward culture"—in the words of Niebuhr, an attitude exhibited through the responses of my research interviewees.[42]

An enduring classic in Christian literature, Niebuhr's work nevertheless has recently been considered outdated by some theologians because Niebuhr wrote from the perspective of Christendom, the era in Western civilization in which Christianity had authority and influence in the public square.[43] The church, however, no longer has the voice it once did.[44] Craig A. Carter, in his work *Rethinking Christ and Culture: A Post-Christendom Perspective*, expresses his belief that this is not necessarily a negative development, because that which society has rejected is the Christianity of ruling elites and state churches; the Christianity of violent coercion and intolerance; the Christianity of power and privilege; the Christianity of racism, patriarchy, and colonialism; the Christianity of the Inquisition and the Holocaust.[45]

It was this type of Christianity that Bonhoeffer was reacting against with his religionless Christianity. The state church in Germany had capitulated to the Third Reich and was being manipulated to the point that the nation was being corrupted. With the mainstream church flowing in the same direction as Nazism and Hitler, Bonhoeffer was left asking how the Confessing Church was to respond to the culture.[46]

Theologians like D. A. Carson recommend a rethinking of Niebuhr for a post-Christendom, postmodern context.[47] The new paradigm would entail engaging in missions in Western culture but rejecting the Christianity of Christendom with its claims to domination in the public sphere.[48] Pastor Jim at Urban Life

Church articulated a similar approach, saying "Far too often I think Christians have it a little bit backward . . . We try to force an agenda on a culture . . . so the church always faces resistance." He went on to say, "That's just not our angle"; rather,

> the goal is training and equipping for evangelism and discipleship while they're out there making a difference and they're shaping culture and they're impacting culture, so . . . it's about getting involved in people's lives where you are leading them . . . to Jesus because when you begin to impact the culture-makers, the people who create culture here in this neighborhood, then that's when the cultural shift happens . . . Since we're here in the middle of downtown where culture is created, we just make friends with the culture-makers and impact their lives personally.

Discipleship in missional communities entails equipping millennials to live in the world and carry out their vocational calling while creating relational connection with individuals in the culture. It is through this one-on-one contact that lasting impact is made for the kingdom of God.

The church today is left with the same conundrum as the church of Bonhoeffer's day: how to respond faithfully to the culture. The missional-incarnational impulse is predicated on the notion that, just as God sent his Son into the world, Christians are to be sent as missionary people.[49] The intention is more than an evangelistic activity that seeks to extract people from their culture and incorporate them into a Christian subculture; rather, it is the action of becoming absorbed into the community to which one is called. It is a ministry of presence in the culture where relationships are paramount.[50] Alan and Deb Hirsch state that mission and discipleship are so linked that

> for way too long discipleship has been limited to issues relating to our own personal morality and worked out in

the context of the four walls of the church with its privatized religion. In doing this, we have severely neglected our biblical mandate to go and "make disciples" . . . The fact is you can't be a disciple without being a missionary: no mission, no discipleship. It's as simple as that.[51]

The missional impulse, hence, naturally results in making disciples outside the four walls of the church. By neglecting to follow Jesus into the world and instead staying cloistered in our Christian subculture, the church has severely truncated the discipleship mandate. To engage in discipleship, one must engage in mission. Both Bonhoeffer and the respondents in my research came to the same conclusion: everyone in every sector of society is to go into the world, being who they are created to be because the world belongs to Christ. In doing so, the church can overcome what both Bonhoeffer and many today consider the act of religious arrogance of separating from the "storm and the action" of the world. By not separating, we engage in holy worldliness.

Opportunities to Proclaim the Gospel through Testimony
One of Bonhoeffer's questions to Bethge was, "What does a church, a congregation, a sermon, a liturgy, a Christian life, mean in a religionless world?"[52] He saw a need to translate theological forms and practices for a contemporary world as part of the ethics of holy worldliness. Similarly, the church today is asking "What does a church look like in a postmodern world?" in order to translate discipleship methods for a new epistemological era. Perhaps the answer to the question lies with the telling of personal narratives as a discipleship practice, for recent research indicates that narrative is a useful method of discipleship for emerging adults.[53] My research was in agreement with this research and found that the testimonies of millennials could be religionless "sermons" to their peers.

The concept of narrative as testimony begins in Scripture.[54] The entire Old Testament recounts the Israelites' shared experience of God. Acts is full of accounts of the early church testifying about their faith and witnessing to others so that the newborn church could grow and thrive. The apostle Paul dedicated his whole life and ministry to sharing his testimony about Christ, as he said in Acts 20:24: "However, I consider my life worth nothing to me; my only aim is to finish the race and complete the task the Lord Jesus has given me—the task of testifying to the good news of God's grace."

Theologians throughout Christian history have likewise told their faith stories: Augustine's account of his conversion in the garden, Luther's description of discovering the doctrine of *sola fide* while studying Romans, Wesley's testimony of having his "heart strangely warmed" by the assurance of his salvation.[55] Missiologist Jeff Cloeter stresses the importance of this narrative tradition when ministering to millennials in his article "Millennials and Story":

> Christians are those who know God's story. Because of this, they recognize God's activity in their own personal stories. A Christian witness among the millennial generation necessitates a compelling narration of this intersection, between God's story and our own.[56]

Millennials value narratives as part of their postmodern worldview. Meanwhile, the church is largely stuck in its default mode of modernity, which for the most part prioritizes preaching truth statements over sharing stories. The result, as Cloeter writes, is that "sterile formulae fail to offer an appropriate response to a generation culturally attuned to communicating through the means of shared experience."[57] Dry presentations of doctrine fall on deaf ears. The net effect is that "Christians will continue to elicit all the stereotypical religious parodies unless we can be good storytellers."[58] These parodies are standard doctrinal statements that, while true to the Christian message, are culturally tone-deaf.

If the church at large is not adept at communicating through narrative, whether it's Scripture as narrative or personal faith stories, then they are not modeling the practice for younger generations. Kenda Creasy Dean writes that one of the main findings of the NSYR study (see Introduction) was that most young Americans are "*incredibly inarticulate* about their faith, their religious beliefs and practices, and its meaning or place in their lives" (emphasis original).[59] Why? "Smith hypothesizes that youth were inarticulate in matters of faith because no one had taught them how to talk about their faith or provided opportunities to practice talking about it."[60] Author David John Seel, writing about millennials' postmodern worldview, recommends the following:

> For churches to effectively reach [millennials], they need to provide authentic experiences of following Jesus into the arenas of their deepest longings, giving them an opportunity to connect their personal story with a larger narrative of meaning couched in a relationally humble . . . posture . . . The Bible needs to be used in a manner that emphasizes story—its narrative arc—rather than the Bible as a book or merely a compilation of proof texts.[61]

Communicating the Bible as a collection of stories about the lived experience of individuals will resonate with millennials much more than presenting it as simply a set of religious dogmas. Further, Seel draws attention to the fact that Christianity fundamentally is a relationship, not a religion, by stressing that the priority of churches should be humbly addressing the felt needs of millennials in this process. "Truth" first and foremost is the person of Jesus, not a correct set of beliefs. The more the church can learn to connect with millennials in relationship through the telling of stories, the more they will be modeling the practice, resulting in effective discipleship.

The implication for millennial discipleship is threefold: first, in order to create a relational bridge, ministry leaders in missional communities need to approach one-on-one discipling with personal narratives rather than programmatic didactic curricula when reaching out to young adults. Second, Scripture should be communicated as a story rather than a set of proof texts, whether in interpersonal relationships or in expository preaching. Third, millennials should be coached on how to formulate their own testimony using cultural language that is authentic and relatable to their cohorts. As the "sermon," the proclamation of the redemptive work of Christ, is recast in a new light using personal narrative, the church will be able to recapture the imagination, and the impetus for discipleship, among millennials.

Opportunities to Be Mobilized Immediately for Ministry

Integral to Bonhoeffer's holy worldliness concept is the notion that humans should follow God out of their strengths, not their weaknesses. Bonhoeffer had observed a German church that had pushed God to the margins of life, reducing him to a *deus ex machina* who was called upon only in times of crisis or distress.[62] As a result the church, in Bonhoeffer's estimation, had capitalized on this notion by exploiting people in their weaknesses. Bonhoeffer believed that, rather than existing in the margins, God should be "at the center" of life, addressing humans in their strengths as mature, responsible, and autonomous individuals.[63] He wrote, "I should like to speak of God not on the boundaries but at the center, not in weakness but in strength, thus not in death and guilt but in human life and human goodness."[64] Given this reorientation, Bonhoeffer suggests that holy worldliness results in relating to God out of our strength and blessings.

My findings reflected this concept in the way that volunteers were recruited and discipled. Strengths and abilities were identified and nurtured. Millennials were dispatched for service immediately, rather than being made to wait for a standard of maturity to be met or, in its most radical expression, even a profession of faith. This is what Bonhoeffer meant by "holy worldliness," the ability to move unencumbered by religious "trappings" into the world for the sake of others.

Historically, there has been a bifurcated view of evangelism and discipleship.[65] As Maddix and Akkerman write, "Evangelism in many circles has stressed belief before belonging . . . One must accept the gospel before becoming assimilated into the church. Missional engagement reverses the trend, stressing belonging first . . . trusting that belief will follow."[66] This approach broadens the view of discipleship, making it more holistic and inclusive.[67] It has been described as "missional discipleship," which "hinges on practice more than upholding a particular body of ideas or propositions."[68]

Based on the reactions from millennials at both sites, it appeared that engaging them for service without regard to their spiritual maturity level made them feel validated; for example, Gabby felt that Urban Life "empowered" her, and this was of "huge" importance to her because her previous experience at church had left her feeling like a "seat filler" or "just another body." She felt that Urban Life valued her enough to invest in her spiritual growth and development. Allison from Strip Club Church was grateful that she was considered a "leader" with "a voice," even as she struggled with being on a self-described emotional "roller coaster" of temptation to go back into the strip club lifestyle and walk away from her faith. Lauren at Strip Club Church felt validated that the ministry would start a discipleship group at her request, even as she was still stripping and not even sure she considered herself a Christian any longer. Thus, mobilizing millennials immediately for ministry, regardless of their level of experience or spiritual maturity, led to retention of participation in both missional communities in my fieldwork and opened doors for ongoing discipleship.

Bonhoeffer's notion of holy worldliness can be synthesized with my research findings in the following way: holy worldliness means entering into the world using vocational activity and expression to engage others out of one's strengths and abilities, regardless of spiritual maturity or even preparatory training. It is translating the tenets and truth of Christianity into the postmodern cultural vernacular using personal narrative and testimony. Millennials and their leaders can build relational capital with those in the world, thereby making inroads into the culture with the truth of Jesus, who exists for the world. The church, therefore, should provide guidance to young adults on identifying the sphere of society to which they are called, based on passion and ability, and training on how to share their testimony with others in their sphere; and it should dispatch them as soon as they desire so they can receive "on the job" discipleship as they go and make disciples themselves.

THEME TWO: "BEING THERE FOR OTHERS"

"Our relationship to God is no 'religious' relationship to some highest, most powerful, and best being imaginable—that is no transcendence," Bonhoeffer wrote. "Instead, our relationship to God is a new life in 'being there for others' through participation in the being of Jesus."[69] Bonhoeffer's discipleship places great emphasis on the social-ethical dimension.[70] As Jesus was "the man for others," so the believer is called to live beyond herself and in relationship to the world out of love for God and others.[71] "Real faith," what Bonhoeffer called "costly grace," means answering the call to discipleship and following Christ into the world.[72] Instead of love being merely a doctrine to believe, it is an ethic to live out.

From a biblical standpoint, love is one of the great themes of Christian discipleship.[73] Jesus spoke of love often during his earthly ministry, naming love for God and others as the two greatest commandments (Matt. 22:37–40). He identified love as the distinguishing mark of his disciples, saying, "Everyone will know that you are my disciples, if you love one another" (John 13:35). Love continued to occupy a prominent place in the epistles. For example, Paul identified love as the crowning attribute of the believer, and John associated love with the very nature of God (1 Cor. 13; 1 John 4:8).

Indeed, Bonhoeffer wrote that "What love is, only Christ tells in his Word. Contrary to all my own opinions and convictions, Jesus

Christ will tell me what love toward the brethren really is. Therefore, spiritual love is bound solely to the Word of Jesus."[74] This is spiritual love as Jesus described in the Word—Jesus who came not to judge but to save (John 12:47), who called his disciples "friends" (John 15:15), and who loved with unconditional love (Rom 5:8).

The millennials in my study were passionate about being there for others—and others being there for them. As love was expressed nonjudgmentally, in authentic friendship that challenged even as it accepted, and with concrete agapic action, they were receptive to ongoing discipleship within a community of faith. The following sections will discuss how "being there for others" corresponded with the three subthemes of "love instead of judgment," "philia love," and "agape love."

Love Instead of Judgment

The topic of love versus judgment was present throughout my fieldwork. This is perhaps not surprising, given the plethora of prior research that shows millennials think the church and Christians are "judgmental," "hypocritical," and "negative."[75] The findings of this study confirmed this earlier research, suggesting that this is precisely the millennial generation's perception of the church. If Christian discipleship is the church's "capacity to lovingly embody and transmit the life of Jesus through the lives of his followers," as Hirsch and Hirsch write, then the findings are disheartening.[76]

Bonhoeffer wrote, "Judging others makes us blind, whereas love is illuminating. By judging others, we blind ourselves to our own evil and to the grace which others are just as entitled to as we are."[77] Judgment leads to comparison. This is the peril of religion of which Bonhoeffer wrote, in which the individual tries to create a path to God through righteous acts rather than embracing God's path to humankind through faith in the redemptive work of Christ. This naturally leads to an us/them mentality, to retreating from the world rather than being there for others. Bonhoeffer wrote that when the church operates according to religion, it becomes a ghetto church, separated from the world for the sake of its own preservation.

Sociologists have a name for this phenomenon: "tribal altruism." The famous sociologist Pitirim Sorokin, who founded the Department of Sociology at Harvard University and the Harvard Research Center for Creative Altruism, coined the term in his book *The Ways and Power of Love*.[78] His work focuses on the difference between love and judgment, and he expounds upon what he calls a "universal law" about love:

> If unselfish love does not extend to all humanity, if it is confined within a group—a given family, tribe, nation, race, religion, political party, union, caste, social class or any part of humanity—such an in-group altruism tends to generate a corresponding "out-group" antagonism. The more intense and exclusive the solidarity among the "in-group" members, the more inevitable are clashes between that group and the rest of humanity. Herein lies the tragedy of tribal altruism which is not extended to all humanity and to every person. The group's exclusive love makes members of the group indifferent or even aggressive towards other groups and outsiders.[79]

Sorokin contends that tribal altruism is at play when an organization extends love only to its own kind, leading to indifference toward others, at best, and possibly even to hostility or aggression when left unchecked. Based on my research, it seems that tribal altruism is unfortunately alive and well in the contemporary church. Lest this seems like an unfair assessment, consider the following examples from my fieldwork.

Liz from Strip Club Church provided an example of the contrast between tribal altruism and being there for others. She described the first time she approached the drag show club: "I never thought we would get into this club because . . . the first time there was a church standing outside with bullhorns telling them they were going to hell, and they needed to get saved." In contrast to the actions of the church protestors, Liz chose to go inside the club to show what she described as "selfless love," using the "Jesus Loves" products:

> I just walked in. I had my Jesus Loves Drag Queens tumblers and I just asked to talk to the manager, and I said, "Look, I know y'all have had a bad experience," and I pulled out a tumbler and I said, "We just want to give these to the queens." And he said, "Oh, yeah, sure. No problem." It was just that easy.

It is moving to hear how receptive the manager was to Liz's overtures of love. It was as though Liz had the boldness to cross an invisible line that separated the "Christians" from the "non-Christians," the church from the mission field.

A similar example came from Annette, who talked about her days in the porn industry:

> At the porn conventions, there would be picketers outside. They had the same message [as the Strip Club Church women], right? The message is Jesus. But the way that they presented it had no impact on my life, because when I would walk in it was like, "Turn and burn!" etc. And like, yeah, I get it, but that's not the way you present the gospel; that's not who Jesus is.

"Who Jesus is," according to Annette, is an embodiment of love and not judgment. The judging "had no impact" on her, while the loving actions of the Strip Club Church were what created the path for discipleship. Being there for others, thus, goes beyond tribal altruism and follows Christ into the world to exhibit his love.

What Sorokin provided from a sociological perspective, Hirsch and Hirsch expressed in ecclesiological terms:

Church culture in North America is a vestige of the original [Christian] movement, an institutional expression of religion that is in part a civil religion and in part a club where religious people can hang out with other people whose politics, worldview, and lifestyle match theirs.[80]

Selfless love has been confined to the Christian subculture, they conclude, and its "circle-the-wagons" mentality has created an in-group / out-group dynamic and resulted, perhaps unwittingly, in the judgment of the out-group.

Bonhoeffer offers a strong response to these examples of tribal altruism:

The church can defend its own space not by fighting for him [Jesus Christ], but rather for the salvation of the world. Otherwise, the church becomes a "religious community" that fights for its own concerns and ceases to be the church of God in the world.[81]

Bonhoeffer stressed that Jesus does not need us to fight for him; he needs us to fight for others to know him. That is the difference between being separatist and missional. Tribal altruism is the antithesis of being there for others. It is an expression of privatized religion, not religionless Christianity.

What, then, is the antidote to the problem of tribal altruism in the church? It is the idea of being there for others, of extending grace so that we are not blinded by our own religious moralism that seeks to compare ourselves with others. According to Bonhoeffer, love provides insight and clarity about the magnitude of grace and the depth and breadth of Christ to all people. It is a missional ethic, being the church for others with Christlike love rather than judgmental moralism. Elaine from Strip Club Church expressed this beautifully:

We've kind of muddied the name of Jesus, and nobody really wants it. So, we are going to have to step out and

show what Jesus really looked like and what Jesus really
did . . . and try and counteract what the church has
done to people when it shunned them, when it hated
on them.

Elaine's conclusion was the same as Bonhoeffer's: show others what
love looks like through being there for them in nonjudgmental
actions, just as Jesus did.

Melissa with Strip Club Church expressed that the attitude
Jesus wants is to "just keep loving them with my love," elaborating,
"I feel that Jesus, he was our example . . . serving [people] when they
don't deserve to be served with love and compassion and grace, just
like Jesus did for us. I think that is the most impactful thing." To
love "just like Jesus did" is to live out the missional-incarnational
impulse. Just as Jesus entered the world through the incarnation,
believers are called to be little Jesuses, entering other cultures to
incarnate his love.

The above examples appear to be a fleshing out of a
Christological recalibration that Frost and Hirsch have asserted is
needed in order to live out effectively the *missio Dei* in the West.[82]
They write, "We believe that the fundamental correction for the
church" as we enter the twenty-first century is "a Christological
one that will in turn revolutionize our missiology as well as our
ecclesiology."[83] As the church returns to the life and love of Jesus as
the calibrating standard, it will be able to revise its methodologies
and practices. Using Jesus as the model, it is possible to see how
incarnational, radical love will be increasingly part of the church of
the future.

Zscheile, writing similarly from a missiological perspective,
says that spiritual formation includes "compassionate identification"
with humanity, exhibiting the love of Christ "on the cultural and
social terms of those to whom we are sent (as did the incarnation),
not primarily on the missionaries' terms."[84] That is precisely what
Jesus did. He came to earth to live among us so that we would

know what Love Incarnate looks, sounds, and acts like. What is needed is a reactivation of the *participatio Christi*, a dedication to following Jesus into the world as missionaries of his love.[85] In order to effectively disciple millennials, the church must be willing to overcome its perception of being judgmental and exclusive through missional-incarnational engagement, through being there for others. This is religionless Christianity.

Philia Love

Philia is deepened by authenticity and a willingness to be vulnerable, something Bonhoeffer viewed as a mark of true discipleship of Jesus. Bonhoeffer believed that, as believers abandon religious individual piety in favor of "being the church for others," the result will be a Christian community operating in "authenticity, trust, faithfulness."[86] It was exactly this type of vulnerable community that gave millennials in my fieldwork a sense of belonging, leading to a long-term commitment to the church body. Respondents often used either the word "authentic" or "real" to describe their discipleship relationships. Emily at Strip Club Church used the terms "real" and "raw" to describe her friendships with the dancers, and Gabby at Urban Life Church used the adjective "vulnerable" to describe her Christian relationships, explaining,

> You know, we're not just friends who are along for the ride. Like, we're friends who push each other to be more, who stretch each other, who challenge each other, and I need that . . . not friends who always tell me "Oh, you're doing fine."

They were not interested in a facade of Christianity. They wanted true, deep philia so that they could grow and change and be transformed by the power of Jesus.

Writing from the perspective of the missional movement, Hirsch and Hirsch stress the importance of authentic relationships marked by philia as part of missional discipleship, saying,

Reframing mission and evangelism around discipleship makes space for long-term, authentically loving relationships with the various people in our lives. This in turn will give credibility to our message and space for real and meaningful friendships—something we're not always known for.[87]

What Hirsch and Hirsch recognize about today's church—a reputation for not relating to others in genuine philia—is similar to what Bonhoeffer recognized in the church of his own time. Bonhoeffer considered the church "heavily burdened by difficult, traditional ideas" to the point that it was making "no impact on the broader masses."[88] If Hirsch and Hirsch are correct, then authentically loving relationships based on Bonhoeffer's notion that the church exists for others might have the power to heal the negative reputation the American church currently holds with much of the larger culture.

Bonhoeffer wrote about being the church for others with future generations in mind. In a letter to his nephew in 1944, he wrote, "After all, the most important question for the future is how we are going to find a basis for living together with other people, what spiritual realities and rules we honor as foundations for a meaningful life."[89] Bonhoeffer was concerned about how being there for others could set the stage for the church of tomorrow. He viewed his theology as one of taking responsibility to mold history for the next generation. By recovering the meaning of the gospel for a new historical context, he hoped to set the stage for younger generations to embrace Christ.[90]

The church during his time was at a crossroads: Would it live as a place of authentic community that had the power to renew and heal, or continue as a religious silo disconnected from the incarnational reality of Christ?[91] This question holds equal importance for us today as we consider how we are to disciple emerging generations in a time of congregational decline. Andrew Root, in his work

Bonhoeffer as Youth Worker, addresses these concerns. Drawing from Bonhoeffer's experiences in youth ministry, Root stresses the importance of focusing on the lived experience of Christianity vis-à-vis abstract doctrine divorced from praxis. Root writes,

> Bonhoeffer helps us see that a youth minister is not someone who heaves theology onto young people, getting them to know stuff, but is rather a minister of the gospel that stands near the concrete humanity of young people, sharing in their experience, helping them wrestle with God's action in and through their concrete lives.[92]

In his own ministry to young adults, writes Root, Bonhoeffer would "attend to the experiential" instead of "beating [one] over the head with theology."[93] Bonhoeffer called this tendency to prioritize doctrine over concrete action being "pedagogically doctrinaire" and made the claim that this approach is antithetical to authentic faith expressed through being there for others.[94] In Bonhoeffer's opinion, prioritizing doctrine over human lives is a mistake.[95] Instead, we should create the right context for "place-sharing" (*Stellvertretung*), where millennials can wrestle and grow together.[96] As with Seel's point discussed in the previous section, Root stresses the participation of the leaders themselves in this process, doing young adult ministry through "the stories of our own faith life" with "a calm disposition."[97] Bonhoeffer viewed the concrete and lived experience approach to youth ministry as the place where the revelation of God could be clearly seen through Christlike action.

By drawing on Bonhoeffer's themes, Root has sought to foster a vision of young adult ministry that moves away from the prevailing American approach of viewing it in purely utilitarian terms as "technology needed to solve the problems of adolescent religious apathy" and toward a more theological-relational approach that reflects "on the action of God in the lives of young people" in concrete reality.[98] This ethical orientation is quintessential Bonhoeffer. In fact, Root names Bonhoeffer as the "forefather" of the theological turn to young adult ministry because of Bonhoeffer's insistence that ministry must be conducted in the concreteness of everyday life.[99]

I wholeheartedly agree with Root's assessment, but, based on my findings, I would take his point a step further. Because of Bonhoeffer's religionless Christianity concept, I believe he is the forefather of an *epistemological* turn to young adult ministry, as well. By advocating "being there for others," he invites us to think critically and reflexively about how we might remove the "religious garb" of the Enlightenment church and put on new cultural forms more in line with millennials' postmodern worldview. The effective discipleship of millennials will be accomplished by the church shedding its tendency to be pedagogically doctrinaire and instead engaging them in authentic, vulnerable relationships that connect with their lived experience.

Agape Love

As stated earlier, the Greek word *agape* is defined as "affection or benevolence; charity; love."[100] It is unconditional and self-sacrificing.[101] Agape is the "law of love" in the New Testament, the phrase appearing 258 times.[102] Bonhoeffer was referring to this type of love when he wrote,

> God loves human beings. God loves the world. Not an ideal human, but human beings as they are, not an ideal world, but the real world. What we find repulsive in their opposition to God, what we shrink back from with pain and hostility, namely, real human beings, the real world, this is for God the ground of unfathomable love.[103]

Love, like other theological concepts for Bonhoeffer, is never disembodied. Love must be demonstrated in the realness of life, through concrete action. "The only fruitful relation to human beings—particularly to the weak among them—is love," wrote Bonhoeffer, going on, "that is, the will to enter into and to keep community with them."[104] Believing in love as a theological doctrine is not enough. It must be lived out. Just as Jesus Christ is the one who "is there for others," the church must look beyond its own preservation and be open to agapic action, especially to help those who are suffering and in need.

What does it mean to love a "real human being," as Bonhoeffer put it? Agape is unconditional acceptance based on the biblical principle of the *imago Dei*. Theologian Millard Erickson wrote, "God made the human in God's own image and likeness . . . The concept is critical because the image of God is what makes humans human. Our understanding of the image will affect how we treat our fellow humans and how we minister to them."[105]

The substantive view—dominant throughout Christian history and theology—holds that the "image" is a "definite characteristic or quality" within the human makeup. The locus is within the human as a "resident quality or capacity."[106] The conclusion is that the *imago Dei* is present in every person to the same degree. It is not dependent on any variable, such as behavior; it is a static, ontological quality.[107] Erickson explains that "the universality of the image means that there is dignity to being human."[108] Keeping this truth in the foreground of our ministry will result in treating people with dignity, respect, and unconditional love as we engage them in mission.

Hirsch and Hirsch propose that we must see people as objects of God's love even before seeing them as fallen, sinful human beings in need of salvation.[109] Yes, humankind needs redemption through Christ, but

> this is a secondary truth that only builds on the primary truth, which is that all humans carry the *imago Dei*. On this liberating truth rests a more genuinely biblical understanding of human beings. This truth also provides

the disciple with a more compassionate (and humane) basis for mission and ministry.[110]

The image of God is the basis for the agapic ethic. Therefore, "we should not be disdainful of any human," for, as theologian Philip Mercer notes, "agape is neither capricious nor exclusive."[111] Liz with Strip Club Church elaborated on how important it is to treat everyone—whether drag queens, strip club dancers, bartenders, or owners—with respect. "We don't want to offend anybody," she explains. "We're in their house . . . We are their guests, so we need to respect their rules." An important part of agape, then, is treating people with unconditional acceptance based on the image of God inherent in every human.

This analysis conceptually aligns with theologian and philosopher Soren Kierkegaard's notion of agape as presented in his *Works of Love*.[112] Kierkegaard bases his reflections on Matthew 22:39: "Love your neighbor as yourself." The neighbor is "every human being."[113] He argues that, in order to love the neighbor, it is necessary to remove any sense of dissimilarity and realize that, at the core, everyone is the same, "unconditionally like each other."[114]

Kierkegaard poetically likens humans to papers bearing watermarks:

> Take many sheets of paper, write something different on each one; then no one will be like another. But then again take each single sheet; do not let yourself be confused by the diverse inscriptions, hold it up to the light, and you will see a common watermark on all of them. In the same way, the neighbor is the common watermark, but you see it by means of eternity's light when it shines through the dissimilarity.[115]

Every millennial in the sex industry and at Urban Life Church had "diverse inscriptions" written on them, whether it was their family background, their sexual orientation, their ethnicity, their sins, their previous spiritual experiences . . . ad infinitum. It was the task of the Urban Life Church and Strip Club Church to take the time to look past the dissimilarities and hold these individuals "up to the light" by treating them with unconditional love so they could see the inherent value they have in God's eyes. Indeed, Kierkegaard writes that "when you love your neighbor, you are like God"; therefore, it is through acts of unconditional love that God can be made known.[116]

By contrast, to be "confused by the diverse descriptions" is to focus on the dissimilarities between individuals and to "forget what it is to love the neighbor."[117] This is an especially egregious act when perpetrated by Christians who consider themselves better than others; instead of being "outward focused," Christians avoid contact with others they deem beneath them in order to remain "unstained by the world."[118] Kierkegaard calls this "distinguished corruption," whereby the Christian behaves in an "un-Christian" manner by desiring to "deny kinship" with all humanity and shrinking back from the opportunities to love.[119]

In Kierkegaardian terms, the millennials in my research were shown agape in that the ministries turned outward. They did not capitulate to "distinguished corruption" but chose to relate to all types of people in all sorts of conditions with a God's-eye view of the common watermark of humanity. To Kierkegaard, and to Jesus, this was what it meant to love the neighbor unconditionally. Thus, agape in discipleship is demonstrated by seeing the millennial first and foremost not as a sinner who needs fixing but as a person of great inherent worth and value; this is the "gold" of which Morgan spoke in chapter one.

In addition to unconditional acceptance, agape is love in action. It is, as Don Browning wrote, "defined in many Protestant sources as entailing primarily impartial, self-sacrificial action on behalf of the other and without regard for oneself."[120] Agape is primarily an act of the will, not based on sentiment.[121] C. S. Lewis made the following observations about agape: "Love in the Christian sense does not mean an emotion. It is a state not

of feelings but of the will; that state of the will which we have
naturally about ourselves and must learn to have about other
people."[122] Agape is a social action, not merely a feeling. It offers
help and benefits to others within a relationship.

Jennifer with Strip Club Church made the connection
between unconditional love and social action, recalling,

> There was this one [girl] in particular. She had been in
> the industry for years and years, and [Strip Club Church]
> just loved on her unconditionally and she ended up not
> going back . . . I did a lot of relationship building with
> her, but [others] did a lot of heavy lifting with her. She
> has kids and so they helped her a lot financially; they
> helped her a lot materialistically.

Jennifer makes an important point, which is that sometimes love is
demonstrated by providing for material needs.

Julia, another member of the Strip Club Church, made the
point even more forcefully than Jennifer:

> It feels wrong on so many levels—morally, legally,
> ethically—to be a witness, to see these women progressing
> in their addiction using all these illegal substances . . .
> that are so hurtful to their bodies . . . and knowing where
> it's going to end them up in a few years . . . Knowing what
> it's doing to them and only being witness to it, and only
> coming in and smiling and handing out gifts and saying,
> "We love you, we're here for you, hope you're doing okay,
> have a great night, call us if you ever need anything,"
> handing them a card and gift—it feels so wrong.

She explained that to say "We love you" while simultaneously being
"a witness" to "the trauma they are experiencing" but not taking
action, "feels so wrong." Julia was echoing the words of the apostle
John in 1 John 3:18: "Dear children, let us not love [*agapao*] with

words or speech but with actions and in truth." She believed that
sometimes "loving them where they're at" was not sufficient; agape
requires action.

Bonhoeffer wrote that God is not a God of religion but "a
suffering God," a point he considered so crucial that he called it
"the starting point for our 'worldly interpretation'" of religionless
Christianity.[123] Thus, at times demonstrating agape means suffering
alongside others. For example, Barbie of Strip Club Church spoke
of how "your heart can get hurt" when you involve yourselves in
the lives of others, such as the tragic shooting at a strip club of two
men whom she and her husband had befriended. Julia similarly
spoke about her suffering as she observed dancers experiencing
"mental breakdown from huge amounts of trauma," such as rape,
sex trafficking, and addiction. "It broke me," she said. "It was heart-
wrenching . . . I cried and cried." Sometimes suffering simply means
venturing out of one's comfort zone and into the ministry venues,
such as when Gillian said she was "nervous" and "scared about
going back" into the club where she used to strip.

Agape love is the love of Jesus. He was God with Us, Immanuel,
which meant that he ventured into all nooks and crannies of
society to love everyone. In fact, Jesus was audacious in his love for
others during his ministry on earth. He acted boldly and in daring
violation of decorum in order to reach people—all people—with
his love. The Pharisees were constantly bemused and befuddled by
his disregard for the religious law as he did things like healing on
the Sabbath and consorting with "tax collectors and sinners" (Mark
3:1–6; 2:13–17). His response to their accusation was that "all the
Law and the Prophets hang on" the greatest commandments: to
love God and others (Matt. 22:40).

Jesus also loved with great compassion. He served others
tirelessly, receiving all who approached him, whether sick or
demonized, oppressed or poor. His capacity for empathy was immense,
sometimes even moving him to tears on behalf of others. As Jesus's
disciples, believers are to demonstrate the same bold, compassionate

love today. Those who are "predestined to be conformed to his image" and to do "even greater things" than he did are called to live by the commandment to love. Agape, as Noah at Urban Life Church put it, means to "do hard things" as we follow Jesus.

Being there for others, therefore, means being willing to see the *imago Dei* in every millennial and engaging in agapic action to convey to them their inherent worth. When the church is open to the world, especially to the oppressed and suffering, there is a shift in the way of being "church." Thus, religionless Christianity becomes a theology that has fundamental reorientation to the world.[124]

THEME THREE: "RELIGIONLESS PNEUMATOLOGY"

Bonhoeffer's theology is decidedly Christocentric. That is not to say, however, that he did not hold a Trinitarian view of God that included the person and work of the Holy Spirit. Clifford Greene, a preeminent Bonhoeffer scholar, asserts that "the doctrine of the Trinity is the unquestioned presupposition of Bonhoeffer's theology."[125] In *Discipleship*, he focuses on the Spirit's work in the church and gives perhaps the most comprehensive treatment of the Holy Spirit among his writings:

> The Holy Spirit is Christ himself dwelling in the hearts of believers (2 Cor 3:17; Rom 8:9–11, 14ff; Eph 3:16f.) . . . The Holy Spirit gives us a true understanding of Christ's nature (1 Cor 2:10) and of his will; the Holy Spirit reaches us and reminds us of all that Christ has said to us (Jn 14:26); the Holy Spirit guides us into all truth (Jn 16:13), so that we may not be lacking in the knowledge of Christ, and may understand the gifts bestowed on us by God (1 Cor 2:12; Eph 1:9). The Holy Spirit does not create uncertainty in us, but certainty and clarity. We are thus enabled to walk in the Spirit (Gal 5:16, 18, 25; Rom 8:1, 4), taking confident steps.[126]

Bonhoeffer believed that the work of the Holy Spirit is expressed concretely through the church community, giving witness to the presence of Christ.[127] It is the Holy Spirit who works sanctification in the believer, possessing and sealing those who belong to Christ.[128] The above discourse demonstrates that Bonhoeffer's theology, while Christocentric, was steadfastly Trinitarian.[129]

Bonhoeffer's paradigm of religionless Christianity, however, does not contain a pneumatological component. He was unable to fully develop his treatise because his life was tragically cut short, so we will never know how or whether he intended to include the Holy Spirit in his writings. We are tasked with picking up where he left off. Following his train of thought in which he wonders "What do a church, a community, a sermon, a liturgy, a Christian life mean in a religionless world? How do we speak of God—without religion?" we might ask, "What does the Holy Spirit mean in a religionless world? How do we speak of the Holy Spirit without religion?" Bonhoeffer wrote that he was "bothered" by the question of "who Christ really is for us today."[130] We may similarly ask, "Who is the Holy Spirit for us today?" I believe my findings answer this question and provide what can be termed a "religionless pneumatology."

In my study, the Spirit was regarded as playing a prominent role in helping volunteers engage missionally with millennials, so that discipleship connections could be made in innovative, authentic, and lasting ways. As a result, millennials (1) considered themselves recipients of the prevenient action of the Holy Spirit, (2) believed that they received discernment from the Holy Spirit, and (3) believed that they experienced the presence of the Holy Spirit. Each of these subthemes will be explored in the following sections. Reflecting theologically on Bonhoeffer's pneumatology and religionless Christianity, along with my results and pertinent secondary sources, will aid in the discovery of what "ought to be going on" with the discipleship of millennials in missional communities.

Belief in the Prevenient Action of the Holy Spirit in Missional Advance
A prominent theme emerging from my research was that the Holy
Spirit was viewed as working preveniently to bring the dechurched
back into Christian community, where they could receive discipleship.
Annette was praying alone on a plane when she "felt the Holy Spirit
come over her with great conviction," leading her to start going to
church with her grandparents and take steps to leave the adult film
industry. Emily said she remembered feeling that God was "stirring
in me" to leave the strip club and start going to church more regularly.
Melissa was lying alone in a hospital bed when she said the Holy
Spirit spoke to her heart, "commissioning" her for ministry, saying,
"I have rescued you from the darkness, and now I'm going to start
equipping you to go back into the darkness to rescue others in my
name." In each of these examples, the Holy Spirit was credited with
calling millennials back to the community of faith.

For the purposes of this section, I have borrowed the term
prevenient from soteriology and applied it to the process of discipleship.
Prevenient grace in Reformed soteriology is the preparatory, enabling
grace that goes before the sinner to bring conviction or reproof,
leading to salvation.[131] Both Calvinism and Arminianism recognize
the Holy Spirit as the initiator of prevenient grace.[132] In light of my
findings, I have transmuted the concept so that the word "prevenient"
is released from the confines of a soteriological context and applied to
the action of the Holy Spirit in restoring the dechurched believer to a
relationship with Christ and the church.

This lexical transmutation is needed in order to make room
for this new phenomenon of dechurched believers. Recent research
reveals that there are a vast number of Christian millennials in the
United States who have dropped out of congregations. A study
published in 2019 by Kinnaman and Matlock, *Faith for Exiles*,
reveals that, among today's 18–29-year-olds who grew up Christian,
22 percent are "ex-Christians" (the study gave them the moniker
"Prodigals") who are "individuals who do not currently identify as
Christian despite having attended a Protestant or Catholic church

or having considered themselves to be a Christian as a child or teen."[133] Another 30 percent are "unchurched"—those "who identify as Christian but have not attended church during the past month" (referred to as "Nomads"). Most Nomads have not attended church for six months or longer.[134] These statistics mean that over half—52 percent—of emerging adults who grew up Christian do not attend church. The upshot is that it is possible that many millennials whom the Holy Spirit is leading to missional communities have at one time been a part of the Christian faith.

As a result, "outreach" toward millennials becomes not so much evangelism of nonbelievers as missional discipleship of the unchurched and dechurched. Thus, instead of a traditional missiological paradigm of evangelism-leading-to-justification, what is needed is a missional model of discipleship-leading-to-sanctification. The Holy Spirit, in my fieldwork, was already "out there" in the world working on the hearts of believers in prayerful solitude. Many responded to the overtures of the Spirit, such as Annette in her Bible reading or Emily in her prayers. There were those like Noah and Amy who had been "burned" in the past by church leadership and had stopped attending before reengaging with the community of the Spirit at Urban Life Church. There were pastors' daughters I met in the strip clubs who had walked away from their faith and had just begun to reach out to the missional volunteers. There was the drag queen disowned by his Christian father who had found Christian community with Strip Club Church. These are the Nomads and the Prodigals whom the Spirit was preparing to be discipled. We might call this action "repatriation": as the Spirit repatriates exiled millennials back into the community of faith, missional communities can be ready to receive them and build them up through discipleship.

The notion of the Holy Spirit working in the hearts of others in preparation for reentering the church is in line with missional theology, which teaches that God is at work in the world beyond the church.[135] Hirsch links the Holy Spirit with the *missio Dei*: "There is no way to God, let alone to the dynamics of missional movements, without the *prior* work of the Spirit in making it all possible" (emphasis mine).[136] The prevenient action of the Holy Spirit provides the context for mission to take place. The missional community's task, then, is to listen and obey in order to build on what the Holy Spirit is already doing among the dechurched millennials. This makes for a more effective discipling process because the Holy Spirit knows who is prepared to hear and receive. As Newbigin states,

> Because the Spirit himself is sovereign over the mission, the church can only be the attentive servant. In sober truth the Spirit is himself the witness who goes before the church in its missionary journey. The church's witness is secondary and derivative. The church is witness insofar as it follows obediently where the Spirit leads.[137]

The active agent in mission is the Spirit of God. He himself is the witness. In *The Open Secret*, Newbigin calls attention to the fact that missional advance, essentially, is the direct result of the church's "obedient participation in that action of the Spirit" that allows the cultural interpretation of the gospel to take place.[138] Discipleship is much more fruitful, therefore, when the church is listening to the Holy Spirit because the church reinforces what the Spirit is already proclaiming.

Missional pneumatology diverges from Bonhoeffer's significantly. Bonhoeffer never separated the work of the Spirit from that of the church. In *Sanctorum Communio*, Bonhoeffer stressed that it is the Holy Spirit who gathers the church, maintains it, and "is at work *only within it*" (emphasis mine).[139] He was wary of "immediate" activity without intermediaries, arguing that the Spirit speaks only through the Scriptures, the sacraments, and the confessions, and therefore never apart from the church community.[140] This stands in direct contrast to Newbigin's belief that the church is "secondary and derivative" to the Spirit.

Based on my findings, my pneumatology is in line with missional theology. The *missio Dei* means that God is on mission not just to make new converts but also to pursue, reclaim, and repatriate his prodigal children through the preparatory action of the Spirit. As the church is attentive to the Spirit's leading and obedient to his direction, it can become an effective witness to the dechurched millennials in its midst. In summary based on my findings, a religionless Christianity of the Holy Spirit includes the prevenient action of the Spirit going ahead of the church and acting on the hearts of dechurched millennials in preparation for their repatriation back into the faith community where they can be discipled.

Belief in Discernment through the Holy Spirit

A prominent pneumatological theme that emerged from the data was a reliance on the Holy Spirit for discernment. Discernment in this context may be best understood as "attentiveness to God's presence and movement" in missional settings.[141] My research revealed that discerning the will, direction, and movement of the Spirit facilitated the establishing and deepening of discipleship relationships in missional communities. Obediently following a "nudge" from the Holy Spirit about whom to approach while out in the mission field often resulted in an encounter with millennials who were ready to receive a word of Scripture, hear a testimony, or accept an invitation for mentoring. The practice of prayer, both individually and corporately, was a vital means of discerning the Spirit's movements.

The New Testament speaks about the centrality of Spirit-given discernment in Christian discipleship and mission.[142] A passage that particularly elucidates this activity of the Holy Spirit recounts the story of Philip and the Ethiopian in Acts 8.[143] In this pericope Philip had, upon the direction of the Lord, gone to a certain desert road. There he encountered an Ethiopian man sitting in his chariot. Verse 29 tells us that the Spirit told Philip to "go to that chariot and stay near it." As Philip approached, he heard the man reading aloud from the book of Isaiah. By "coincidence" he was reading chapter 53, a prophetic passage about Christ as the suffering servant.

"Do you understand what you are reading?" Philip asked (v. 30). "How can I," the man replied, "unless someone explains it to me?" (v. 31). At that Philip climbed up into the chariot and "told him the good news about Jesus" (v. 35.) The man believed, was baptized, and "went on his way rejoicing" (v. 39). The Spirit had orchestrated the entire encounter between a man who was ready to hear the gospel and a believer who listened to and obeyed the Spirit's direction.

This dynamic provides a biblical example of the type of encounters reported by the millennials and the volunteers who discerned the Spirit's movement. Katherine spoke of the woman at Urban Life Church whom the Spirit "told" to sit by her. Gillian said that the Holy Spirit would "highlight" girls she was to speak to in the clubs. Julia, Liz, and Charlotte all spoke of "listening" to the Holy Spirit while they were in the clubs so he could "guide" them to whom they were to minister.

Respondents used phrases such as "being nudged" or "a tug at my heart" or the Holy Spirit's "prompting" to describe this felt knowledge leading them to a particular course of action. My purpose is not to authenticate the veracity of their claims of hearing from God, as I consider that to be unprovable. What is significant is that they *believed* they were discerning the voice of the Holy Spirit and were open to the possibility that the Holy Spirit would indeed speak to them. Time and time again, interview respondents would speak of their reliance on the direction of the Holy Spirit to indicate to whom they were to talk and what to say when they were among their missional constituents.[144]

Discerning the Spirit is considered by missional theologians as a crucial aspect of the missional movement. Missiologist Gary Tyra writes, "At the heart of the missional ministry impulse is a pneumatological question: what is the Holy Spirit up to in this or that ministry location, and might/should we cooperate with him?"[145] Similarly, Craig Van Gelder writes about the centrality of discernment in God's ongoing renewal of the church:

The church experiences this constant renewal only by developing discipline in discerning the leading of the Spirit. Through such discernment, the church becomes the primary means through which God answers its prayer that "thy kingdom come, thy will be done on earth as it is in heaven."[146]

The Spirit created and is still recreating the church as each generation hears the gospel anew. When this activity of the Spirit is rightly discerned, the church can join him where he is already at work.

Despite this positive assessment, Van Gelder recommends that missional theologians continue to "develop a missional ecclesiology that takes into account the continued work of the Spirit in leading and teaching the church."[147] Karina Kremenski of the missional organization Missio Alliance concurs, believing that some confusion and ambiguity still exists surrounding the praxis of discerning the work of the Holy Spirit despite these positive pneumatological developments in missional theology. She cites Van Gelder and Zscheile, who argue that, although there is a well-developed theology of God and Jesus, there exists an "inadequate explanation" of the activity of the Holy Spirit. She concludes that there is a crucial need for a better understanding of discernment in the missional church, of being "skilled at noticing" when the Spirit "reveals, compels and pushes" people to respond to his leading.[148]

Bonhoeffer's understanding of discernment helps shed light on what is needed in missional theology. Bonhoeffer called discernment *Prüfung*, "probing" or "examining" the will of God, which involves all the human faculties: "the heart, the understanding, observation, and experience."[149] When the reality of Christ is rightly discerned within the reality of the cultural context at hand, the result is that the church "is able to give the right word at the right hour."[150] By this Bonhoeffer meant that his question "Who is Jesus Christ for us today?" can be answered through faithful interpretation of the will of God through the power of the Holy Spirit for a particular historical and cultural context.[151]

Ever the ethicist, Bonhoeffer connects right discerning with right doing. As believers partake of "the reality of God" and "the reality of the world" at the same time, the "concreteness" of ethical action can be rightly discerned in every situation, so that the church's faithful witness can have maximum impact and relevance.[152] As the believer ventures beyond the cloister of the church and into the world in missional witness, discernment can draw the believer into "the risky courage of faithfulness," as Dahill eloquently puts it.[153]

In *Life Together*, Bonhoeffer juxtaposed what happens to a Christian community when discernment is not used. A community led by the Spirit will be governed by and surrendered to the Holy Spirit. By contrast, a community led by human effort will govern using "psychological techniques and methods," the result being "to dethrone the Holy Spirit, to relegate him to remote unreality."[154] No matter how pure the motive, if human construction is employed over the wisdom of the Spirit, the community begins to drift away from its spiritual center.[155] The consequence is factionalism, as Bonhoeffer explains: "When the way of intellectual or spiritual selection is taken, the human element always insinuates itself and robs the fellowship of its spiritual power and effectiveness for the Church, drives it into sectarianism."[156] This process of which Bonhoeffer writes is operational today; nowhere is sectarianism more evident than in the area of pneumatology.[157] The antidote is prioritizing spiritual discernment over human analysis, so that sectarianism can be superseded by reuniting the one holy catholic church.

What is needed, considering the above discussion, is a missional pneumatology that is nonsectarian in its praxis of discernment. This is exactly what my fieldwork revealed. The millennials in my study were wary of denominationalism in general and of pneumatological sectarianism. Pastor Jim reported, "One of the things we found right up front . . . is [that] people would say 'Well, what denomination are you?' because they are very suspicious of denominations . . . Talking to people it was unanimous: they are suspicious of denominations because of dogmatism and heavy traditions." "Most people," he went on to say, are satisfied that Urban Life "believes in the Bible, believes in Jesus, . . . God in three persons," and that they are "not going to get a bunch of rules and traditions we don't care about." His conclusion was that millennials "trust it" when the activity of the Spirit is presented in this way.

Zach confirmed Pastor Jim's assessment, saying, "Urban Life really encourages interactions with the Spirit . . . and they don't do it in a weird way that's off-putting." He elaborated by articulating his disdain for cessationist-continualist sectarianism, using his own nonreligious language. At one extreme, he was wary of Pentecostal stereotypes:

> I've heard of different churches that are like, you know, not to make fun of them because I know they had their heart behind it and wanted to seek out God . . . but that are like, "We are going to go dancing with poisonous snakes or . . ." You can pick any example, right?[158]

At the same time, Zach complained about the other extreme, cessationism: "I've been with churches [where] I say, 'Hey, look, the Spirit did this,' and I've had churches say to me, they're like, 'Yeah, sure . . . Yeah, I don't know about that.' They're very apprehensive." He was disappointed that his subjective spiritual experiences had not been validated, for in his view he had "experienced a lot of how God uses the Spirit to communicate directly with us, to interact in our lives." His appraisal of Urban Life was that they neither "downplay" the activity of the Holy Spirit nor present it in an "off-putting" way.

A millennial leader named Charlotte explained the importance of shedding sectarian religious language when teaching about

discernment. She said she understood that the Holy Spirit "can sound
really weird" to "the unchurched and dechurched." Using Christian
"lingo," she explained, "doesn't work in our downtown church, and
it doesn't work very well with a lot of millennials, frankly." She said
Urban Life understood that and was "strategic" in "not using, like,
churchy religious vocabulary . . . but [was] slowly . . . building on the
Holy Spirit" and the art of "listening" to him.

The key theme that can be deduced from these accounts is
that the millennials in my fieldwork were open to learning more
about the practice of discernment when it was not encased in
sectarian pneumatology. Thus, the development of a religionless
pneumatology is one that rises above denominational dogma and
theological camps. Bonhoeffer wrote, "When the Bible speaks of
following Jesus, it is proclaiming a discipleship which will liberate
it from all man-made dogmas."[159] What "ought to be going on," in
Osmerian terms, is that the church needs to develop a religionless
pneumatology that transcends sectarianism and rediscovers unity
in the Spirit in the domestic mission field.

Meredith from Strip Club Church stated it powerfully:

> This is my aggravation about mission work in the United
> States . . . If I'm called to be a [foreign] missionary . . . we
> [the church] would be asking about how you are seeing
> God. Where are you seeing God manifest? Over here we
> don't even expect that. So, I pray that we would become
> those expectant God-fearing servers that boldly go into
> these places when we feel called and expect to see God
> and *expect to hear Him* . . . to walk in that kind of faith.
> (Emphasis mine)

Meredith makes an important point: before one can discern the
Holy Spirit, one must expect that he is moving and speaking in the
first place, must resist the urge to consign him to "remote unreality"
(as Bonhoeffer wrote) rather than giving him a central place in

Christian community and mission. My fieldwork helps to develop more fully the praxis of discernment in missional communities that so many theologians say is needed. When missional pneumatology can overcome sectarianism, it will be religionless pneumatology.

Belief in the Presence of the Holy Spirit
Experiencing or "feeling" the presence of the Spirit was a common theme among interviewees. Millennials at both sites reported feeling a "calm," being "touched" with emotion that brought them to tears, or feeling "happy" or "joyful."[160] These feelings went beyond emotive expressions; they connoted the immanent presence of the Holy Spirit operating in the heart of the individual. The implication was that the Holy Spirit is a *person* who can be *experienced*. Their descriptions were reminiscent of what Tozer called a "conscious awareness of his presence."[161] It was this conscious awareness of God's presence that often accompanied a millennial's encounter with the missional ministries in my study, whether in worship, prayer, or pedagogical settings, resulting in inner healing and a sense of peace.

Classical biblical orthodoxy believes in the existence of the Holy Spirit as the Third Person of the Trinity and therefore hypostatically distinct and coequal with the Father and the Son (Matt 28:19; 1 Cor 12; 2 Cor 13:14; 1 Pet 1:2).[162] As a person and not an impersonal force, he possesses cognitive, affective, and volitional faculties (John 14:26; 1 Cor 12:11; Eph 4:30).[163] The Holy Spirit was present and working at creation, throughout the Old Testament, during the ministry of Jesus, and within the New Testament church.[164] It is the power of the Holy Spirit that changes hearts through the conviction of sin (John 16:8–11) and regeneration (John 3:5–8), and enables effective ministry (John 14:12; 16:7; Rom 15:19) and evangelism (Acts 1:8).[165]

Further, the Holy Spirit works sanctification in the life of the believer, a process that can be described as "the continued transformation of moral and spiritual character so that the believer's life actually comes to mirror the standing he or she already has in God's sight."[166] The Holy Spirit bestows spiritual gifts on believers

(Rom 12:6–8; 1 Cor 12:4–11; Eph 4:11; 1 Pet 4:11) for the purpose of edification of the body of Christ and empowerment for ministry.[167] Evangelicalism, the position from which I am writing, rests upon this foundation of the mutuality of the Word and the Spirit: the Spirit inspired the Word, and the Word teaches us about the Spirit.[168]

Bonhoeffer affirmed the personhood of the Holy Spirit in his sermon for Whitsunday in 1940, preaching that "The Holy Spirit is the living God, not some inert concept."[169] To Bonhoeffer, the Spirit was not a "remote unreality" but a person, actively teaching his people and leading them into the light of truth. He is present among the gathered ecclesia, working for its edification and growth.[170] That being said, Bonhoeffer was part of a theological undertaking that sought to restrict the Holy Spirit to narrow expression within the church gathered in order to distinguish the biblical Spirit from that of the free-thought spiritualism that had emerged from Enlightenment philosophers.[171] In order to differentiate itself from liberal deism, the church felt forced to emphasize that the One Holy Spirit was, as Jürgen Moltmann described, "bound to the ecclesiastical institution for mediating grace, and to the preaching of the official 'pastors and teachers.'"[172] A Spirit that was experienced personally was deemed "unholy" and "enthusiastic," bearing the marks of fanaticism and emotionality.[173]

Bonhoeffer wrote in the same vein that "God's own self as Holy Spirit" gathers and maintains the church community but is at work "only within it" through specific ecclesiastical "forms and functions," such as preaching, the sacraments of the Eucharist and baptism, and pastoral care.[174] Hence, reliance on the Spirit meant reliance on the community in which he is present and operating. Bonhoeffer was concerned with preserving the transcendent divinity of the Holy Spirit, so he too had a "distaste towards approaches deemed 'enthusiastic.'"[175]

Thus, it was the free thinking of the Enlightenment that led to a restricted doctrine of the Holy Spirit as the church reacted against a liberated consciousness that embraced a universal deist spirituality. Moltmann argues that such narrowing of the Spirit's expression impoverishes the congregation: "Men and women are not taken seriously," he writes, "if they are only supposed to be 'in the Spirit' when they are recipients of the church's ministerial acts and its proclamation."[176] Moltmann goes on to validate the inner, personal encounter with the Holy Spirit, saying that it is the Spirit in mutual relationship with the Word that provides spiritual vitality and personal dignity as the believer discovers their life in Christ.[177]

Moltmann asserts that, as a result of this neoorthodoxy, there was a "forgetfulness of the Spirit" for much of the twentieth century.[178] The Holy Spirit was so overlooked in theology that he was referred to as the "unknown person of the Godhead."[179] The eventual acknowledgment of the omission, concurrent with the rise of the charismatic/Pentecostal movement and the Eastern Orthodox emphasis on the deity of the Spirit, has resulted in a spate of writings on the work of the Holy Spirit in recent decades.[180]

However, despite this renewed attention to the work of the Spirit, theological works on the personhood of the Spirit remain modest.[181] Sinclair Ferguson puts it this way: "The assertion that the Holy Spirit, once forgotten, is forgotten no more needs rephrasing. For while his *work* has been recognized, the Spirit himself remains to many Christians an anonymous, faceless aspect of divine being."[182] Thus, although theology is progressing out of the restrictive pneumatology of the Enlightenment, further work needs to be done. Here again is evidence that, in theology generally, and pneumatology specifically, there is a post-Enlightenment hangover that needs to be addressed considering the turn to postmodernism and the corollary aspects of ministering to the millennial generation.

The neglect of the personhood of the Holy Spirit has extended to recent literature on young adult discipleship. Kinnaman and Matlock's book *Faith for Exiles* makes no reference to a relationship with the Holy Spirit in its discussion of the discipleship of millennials, despite their research findings that among young adults "there is a firm conviction about the supernatural dimension of life," including a belief that "the Holy Spirit leads me each day."[183] Seel's book on millennials and evangelicalism contains a chapter titled "Spirit" that verges on being a misnomer because the Holy Spirit is given a mere mention within a broader discussion on evangelism.[184] Setran and Kiesling's work is more comprehensive in its pneumatology, with a section dedicated to "practicing the presence of God," which rightly concludes that the purpose of Christian practices is to engage with the Holy Spirit; however, the bulk of the section emphasizes the practices, while the personhood of the Holy Spirit remains underdeveloped.[185]

A notable exception to this paucity is an insightful article by PC(USA) pastor Michael Langford in *Theology Today* titled "A Spirit-Driven Discipleship: A Pneumatology of Youth Ministry." Langford attributes the failures in youth ministry to the "loss of pneumatological consciousness" borne out of the imposter religion MTD.[186] The "deism" component of MTD believes in a God who is transcendent but "balks" at the idea of his immanence. The proliferation of MTD in churches has left a malformed view of the Holy Spirit as impersonal and remote. Langford goes so far as to say that "the ethos in our churches in the West has largely disregarded the spiritual presence of God."[187] Millennials are either accepting MTD as true Christianity or leaving the church.

In order to counteract the pseudo-Christian beliefs of Moralistic Therapeutic Deism, Langford advocates for a holistic discipleship of young adults that stresses the importance of God's presence.[188] In my research, Pastor Jim articulated a similar emphasis. When asked what role the Holy Spirit plays in discipleship, he said that it begins with this spiritual vitality in the Spirit's presence: "We want people . . . to come into this atmosphere if they feel spiritually drained and then the Holy Spirit just reenergizes them." Langford points out that "the understanding of God's present immanence in the existence of the universe is precisely the understanding of God as Holy Spirit."[189] The God of MTD, thus, cannot be the Holy Spirit because he is not immanent.[190]

Langford stressed that the experience of God's presence is accessible easily to all. Unlike Bonhoeffer, he espouses the belief that "'Presence' is not isolated to emotional experiences, institutional structures, or charismatic leaders. Rather, that God is Holy Spirit means that the divine presence is one that may be apprehended wherever we are."[191]

The presence of the Spirit is constant, manifold, and sometimes unexpected. Noah at Urban Life Church described what happens when millennials unexpectedly encountered the Spirit: "On a Sunday so many people walk in and are, like, 'I have never been to a church like this,' and I'm, like, 'That's the presence of God! Like, it's awesome, isn't it?'" Noah served as a greeter at the Sunday morning service, so he had the benefit of seeing newcomers' first reactions to discerning God's presence. He was able to validate their subjective spiritual experience and help them understand that what they were "feeling" was the immanence of the Spirit. In this way, millennials should be encouraged and discipled to apprehend the presence of God whenever and wherever they need him so that they can grow in their faith, becoming more faithful followers of Jesus Christ through the inner witness and transforming, reenergizing power of the Spirit in their lives.

In order to regain a proper framework for the discipleship of young adults, the church must recover a "sense of God as Holy Spirit"—what Ferguson called the "personal-existential" dimension of Pentecost that is an ongoing part of the Holy Spirit's ministry.[192] This will reverse MTD and restore a truer understanding of his immanent presence. If MTD is the imposter religion of today, then a religionless pneumatology is one that reverses the false notion of God as a remote deity and recovers a sense of the personhood of the Holy Spirit. Millennials are intuitive, right-brained, and relational and thus hardwired for a relationship with the person of the Spirit. As the Holy Spirit is liberated from a theology of cold, remote utilitarianism and rendered "religionless" by recapturing the recognition of him as immanent and personal, the church can effectively disciple its millennial members.

Supposition	Bonhoeffer's God Hypothesis	Smith's Moralistic Therapeutic Deism	Research Findings	Religious relationship with a god who is formed after our own image
Culture of autonomy/ secularization	"World come of age"	"The cultural triumph of liberal Protestantism"	The millennial mission field	*"Metanoia"* of the church
God as remote	Religious relationship with a god who is formed after our own image	Belief in an impersonal higher power	Spirit-led discipleship	Religionless pneumatology
God as a last resort	God as *"deus ex machina"*	God helps only when called upon	Missional discipleship	"Holy worldliness"
Resulting behavior	Isolating privatization of faith	Live by an individualized moral code	Loving discipleship	"Being there for others"

Table 5.2 comparison of the God Hypothesis and MTD, offering religionless Christianity as an appropriate corrective

Religionless Christianity as a Common Corrective

Considering the above discussion on all three of my findings, it is possible to see with greater clarity the way Bonhoeffer's God hypothesis and Smith's MTD point to a set of common correctives found in religionless Christianity, as the far-right column indicates in Table 5.2, above.

Instead of a view of God as remote, he is understood to be immanently present in the world. Instead of a view of God as a last resort in a moment of crisis, he is found at the center of life in all its strength and goodness. Instead of retreating into an inner world of vague piety, the church is mobilized for loving service to others. In this way, Christianity is elevated out of its philosophical and ethical ghetto and once again picks up its missional mantle. It emerges from the quiet shadows of inert privatization and resumes its role as being "the church for others."

Bonhoeffer hoped that these correctives would result in the transformation of the church, a hope that we can apply to our own current ecclesiastical conditions as we seek to disciple millennials along missional-incarnational lines. In today's context, as in Bonhoeffer's, the task is to ensure that the faith being handed down to the next generations is true, authentic Christianity, not a set of heterodoxies that has insidiously made its way into the minds and hearts of believers. This was the task of undoing religion in Bonhoeffer's day, and it is the same task needed for interaction with millennials and MTD today. In this way, his religionless-Christianity framework provides a helpful blueprint as we wrestle with the topic of the effective discipleship of millennials in preparation for the church of the future.

CONCLUSION

This chapter has sought to answer the question of the normative task in the pastoral cycle: "What ought to be going on?" In order to understand more clearly the praxis of discipling millennials in missional communities, this study developed a theological framework based on the generative themes in critical correlation with Christian Scripture, tradition, and relevant literature on practical theology. Dietrich Bonhoeffer's theology of religionless Christianity was employed as a critical lens through which the findings could be theologically interpreted.

The first theme, "Discipleship among millennials in missional communities was facilitated by opportunities to become engaged in ministry and mission in the world," was interpreted using Bonhoeffer's concept of "holy worldliness." I argued that missional communities provide millennials with an opportunity to discover their sphere of influence, create a personal testimony, and be mobilized immediately.

The second theme, "Discipleship among millennials was facilitated by authentic, caring, and loving relationships," was explored using Bonhoeffer's notion of "being there for others." It was argued that loving others without judgment, being authentic in one's Christian friendships, and demonstrating the unconditional love of Jesus are all expressions of a church that exists for others.

The third theme, "Discipleship among millennials in missional communities included a belief in the activity of the Holy Spirit," used Bonhoeffer's pneumatology as a framework. I argued that millennials sought the Holy Spirit for guidance in their ministry through the practice of discernment, and I developed an (admittedly primordial) "religionless pneumatology" that includes a post-sectarian approach with an emphasis on the personhood of the Spirit.

Bonhoeffer asked the question "Who is Christ for today?" within his own cultural context. By identifying universal theological themes, I attempted to answer that same question for the American church today. Further, I have argued that there are conceptual parallels between the "God hypothesis" of Bonhoeffer's day and Moralistic Therapeutic Deism. Both are reflections of a church whose appearance bears little distinction from the world around it, but instead has been absorbed into the cultural mainstream. The resulting behavior of both Bonhoeffer's "God hypothesis" and MTD is an isolating privatization of faith, where religion is lived out as an individualized moral code, a bespoke set of beliefs and values tailored to the individual.

By extension, the church, instead of being there for others, loses its missional edge. Rather than living incarnationally as the hands, feet, and love of Jesus to a suffering world, the church settles for a "cheap grace" that abandons the discipleship of others in order to "live and let live."[193] The missional-incarnational impulse is truncated, and costly grace is left unspent. My intention is that the normative task undertaken in this chapter will result in transforming practice, which is the topic of the next chapter. What "ought to be going on," therefore, is that the church should be open to sorting through those things that are central tenets of Christian faith and tradition necessary for the transmission of Christianity to the next generation. Those things that are religious "trappings" should, like outdated "garb," be discarded in favor of more contextualized forms and symbols of the faith. I hope this book will in part answer Bonhoeffer's question, "What does a church . . . mean in a religionless world?" with missional ecclesiology and postmodern epistemology, a new theology resulting in a fundamentally different way of being the church.

CHAPTER 6

PRACTICAL DISCIPLESHIP

INTRODUCTION

This book has explored the discipleship of millennials in missional communities through an in-depth study of emerging adults and their leaders. By using ethnography as both method and methodology, I have been able to determine specific themes related to my research question. The themes that were noted came under three key areas: "Discipleship among millennials in missional communities was facilitated by opportunities to become engaged in ministry and mission to the world"; "Discipleship among millennials in missional communities was facilitated by authentic, caring, and loving relationships"; and "Discipleship of millennials in missional communities included a belief in the activity of the Holy Spirit."

These themes were examined theologically through the lens of Bonhoeffer's religionless Christianity. The goal of the theological reflection was to begin to identify "what ought to be going on" with discipleship among this cohort in this context. My conclusion is that Bonhoeffer's concept of religionless Christianity has prescriptive value as we help millennials follow Christ in today's cultural, ecclesiological, and epistemological milieu through contextualizing and translating core tenets of the faith.

Bonhoeffer's ideas have important implications in our own time for the discipleship of young people in the American

149

postmodern, post-Christian culture. The implementation of religionless Christianity in today's cultural context, and specifically in missional settings, requires a set of practices that considers this unique time in American history, while retaining the ancient and orthodox tenets of the faith. This penultimate chapter explores the nexus between the innovative and the traditional by offering three practices that correspond to the three research findings in my study. Bonhoeffer famously asked the question, "What does it mean to follow Christ today?" We are asking the same question of our own time, and implicit in it is the search for practices that retain Christian tradition and yet make room for bold revision.

This chapter addresses the fourth question in Osmer's pastoral cycle, "How might we respond in ways that are faithful and effective?" Consideration will be given to specific practices that may be employed based on the three key research themes. The first section deals with the relationship between discipleship and Christian practices in order to provide a conceptual context. The remainder of the chapter is arranged according to theme, each with recommended corresponding practices: testimony, hospitality, and discernment.

THE RELATIONSHIP BETWEEN DISCIPLESHIP AND PRACTICE

Dorothy C. Bass and Craig Dykstra define Christian practices as "things Christian people do together over time to address fundamental human needs in response to and in the light of God's active presence for the life of the world."[1] Taken together as a composite whole, Christian practices make up a "way of life abundant" for the believer.[2] Bass and Dykstra emphasize that Christian practices are theological and normative. Theologically speaking, practices are conducted in a world created and sustained by a God who is reconciling all things through Christ and has invited humankind to be participants in his reconciling work. Normatively speaking, Christian practices are a reflection of God's "good, pleasing, and perfect will" for us, and the expectation is for us to respond and faithfully incarnate his will through our actions for the good of humankind.[3] Lived out, Christian practices are "shared patterns of activity in and through which life together takes shape over time in response to and in the light of God as known in Jesus Christ."[4] The practices of individual believers are woven together with those of others in the community of faith as they live out the gospel, forming a way of life.

Disciples of Jesus are formed "to a significant degree by engaging in religious practices."[5] Some practices are done on a regular basis, creating a pattern and rhythm to the Christian life and contributing to the discipleship of the individual by becoming an ingrained part of their character through repetition and habit. Other practices are engaged in less often, thus taking the individual out of the normal routine and into areas of discomfort or stretching. The early church, as the prototypical example, had times of regular practices, such as the Lord's Supper, teaching, fellowship, and communal worship (see Acts 2). At other times, they were stretched to new limits, such as with the sending out of apostles to establish new churches (see, for instance, Acts 8 and 13). Such a combination of quotidian and exceptional activities can have a profound and lasting effect on the spiritual formation of the Christian disciple.[6] Discipleship, then, becomes a way of life expressed in regular and irregular practices as acts of gratefulness for God's goodness and presence.[7]

In their book *Practicing Our Faith*, Dykstra and Bass list twelve practices that constitute the rubric of the way of life abundant: honoring the body; hospitality; household economics; saying yes and saying no; keeping Sabbath; discernment; testimony; shaping communities; forgiveness; healing; dying well; and singing our lives to God.[8] This list is not intended to be exhaustive; rather, the scope is intentionally limited in order to represent fundamental human needs that can be addressed through these practices. Three of these practices—hospitality, discernment, and testimony—correspond suitably with my three research findings.

Although in my fieldwork I encountered the majority of the twelve practices, and although discipleship is not limited to these twelve, I have chosen the three that were given the greatest emphasis and provided the maximum impact for the millennials in my study. The three practices and the corresponding findings are as follows: (1) testimony: "engaged in ministry and mission to the world"; (2) hospitality: "authentic, caring, and loving relationships"; and (3) discernment: "the activity of the Holy Spirit." Each of these will be discussed in the following sections.

TESTIMONY

One of the key findings in my research was that millennials were eager to tell their faith stories as part of the process of outreach and discipleship. As a spiritual practice, this is known as testimony. Thomas Hoyt Jr., in *Practicing Our Faith*, describes testimony as the act of speaking truthfully about what one has seen or experienced. The testimony is given by a witness to the community for consideration for the purpose of edification.[9] Hoyt writes that testimony "is a deeply shared practice" that is possible "only in a community that recognizes that falsehood is strong, but that yearns nonetheless to know what is true and good."[10]

Hoyt implies that testimony is best practiced within the gathered church community where fellow believers can discern its veracity. I would argue that this takes a narrow view of the utility of testimony, neglecting the powerful missional impact that sharing one's story can have. For example, in my research, the *Jesus Loves Strippers Bible* was called the "Stories Edition" because it contained the personal faith stories of former strippers woven in with the book of Luke. Jamie's story testified of the effectiveness of Strip Club Church. She wrote,

> I stayed in the industry for three years feeling hopeless, numb, and wanting to die . . . until God came in to [sic] that strip club and changed my life. He surrounded me

with some of the most amazing friends who have shown me the healthy love I desired so much . . . If he can do all this for me, then I know he can do it for you.

Jamie was able to tell her story through the vehicle of the *Jesus Loves Strippers Bible*. The text was designed intentionally for those in the sex industry who might not be part of a faith community, contesting Hoyt's assumption of the gathered local church as the locus of bearing witness.

This idea of bearing witness is a significant dimension of testimony found in Scripture. The Old Testament Hebrew word for witness is *Eid*, and its New Testament Greek counterpart is *martus*. The verb forms, *'uwd* and *martureo*, according to Strong's concordance, mean "to bear witness, i.e. to affirm that one has seen or heard or experienced something, or that he knows it because taught by divine revelation or inspiration."[11]

There is an observable pattern in Scripture whereby God desires to raise up a group of people who see and experience him and who can then represent him—who can *'uwd* and *martureo*—to the rest of the world.[12] This pattern begins in Exodus 7–15 when the Israelites witness God as the great deliverer from Egypt, accompanied by miraculous demonstrations of his power and presence. God raises up Moses and appoints the Israelites to "bear witness" to the rest of the nations about what they have experienced.

The Hebrew people, however, rebel against Yahweh and start worshipping a god of their own making. Thus, God uses Moses and gives the Torah as an *'uwd*. The Israelite nation follows the law for a time but eventually begins to worship other gods and fails to bear witness to the neighboring peoples. God raises up prophets from among them, who, like Moses, can bear witness and warn Israel about what will happen if they continue to turn away from God (2 Kgs 17:13).

In the New Testament Jesus Christ, the Ultimate Witness, comes to the people to give the good news that the kingdom of God was among them (Luke 4:17–21). After the resurrection, Jesus sends out his disciples to bear witness to the nations about the power of the gospel through the missional proliferation of the early church. Thus, the word "witness" is present throughout the Bible. The pattern has continued down through history even to our current time—God continues to raise up witnesses to turn people back to him.

Each of these witnesses—Moses and the Torah, the prophets, Jesus Christ, the disciples, and the early church—was commissioned to testify about the reality of God's presence, love, and power during a time when the larger culture, even the previously faithful, were not following God. We might ask, then: who is God raising up as his witnesses to *martureo* to those who have forgotten, rejected, or perhaps never known about the God of the Bible? This is where my research finding that millennials were eager to tell their stories holds great promise.

Theologian Eugene Peterson noted that in today's churches information is more important than story. However, as he contended, "We don't live our lives by information"; life is lived in relationship with one another and with God.[13] Annette from Strip Club Church put it this way: "Preaching doesn't change lives. Discipleship changes lives." Presenting Christianity as an interweaving of God's story with ours can be a powerful means of witnessing, shifting the Christian faith from mere doctrinal abstractions to personally relatable and compelling accounts of a relational God.

It is my contention that Urban Life Church was successful in this attempt. They held a training session called "Creating Your Testimony" designed to help individuals make a cultural impact. They described the personal narrative as "Your Influence Vehicle" and provided a five-step outline on how to prepare one's story:

1. The "Lead In." The first step entails understanding the setting in which you are communicating your story in order to establish common ground.

2. Before. The second step is to talk about what your life was like before you knew Jesus. This step involves addressing a felt need of the hearer based on the common ground previously established.
3. How. The third step is to tell your story about how you found Jesus.
4. After. The fourth step is to talk about what happened after you found Jesus: What was it like after you gave your life to Jesus?
5. Their next step. The fifth step is their next step, the hearer's reaction to your story. Based on their response, you might offer to pray for them, invite them to church, etc.

Urban Life Church successfully drew a correlation between testimony and missional discipleship. They emphasized that the purpose of training members to share their testimony was to equip them to do the work of discipling others outside the walls of the church. They defined discipleship as a commitment to the spiritual growth and welfare of a person, both before and after conversion. They recommended several practices for discipling others: model your walk with Jesus; provide for practical needs, not just spiritual needs; share biblical truth; and baptize them. In this way, millennials were equipped and dispatched to "go" and fulfill the Great Commission.

I believe this training template could be used effectively in various missional environments. For example, it would have been a valuable resource for the volunteers of the Strip Club Church, where testimony was prominently featured as a means of discipleship, yet some struggled to establish common ground or to recognize the merits of their own story. Jennifer, for example, shared her anxiety about going into the clubs: "For a while when I first started going out, I felt like, 'Well, who am I? Like, I have no point of reference with these ladies; I'm not going to be able to relate.'"

If she'd had access to the "Creating Your Testimony" materials ahead of time, she might have been better prepared for, and less anxious about, relating to the dancers. It is clear that such training could translate across various contexts, becoming generalizable and normative among millennial-focused missional communities. I argue that in a world in which millennials consider expository pulpit preaching irrelevant and obsolete, training them to share their testimonies with their peers is a highly effective means of fostering their discipleship as followers of Jesus Christ.

HOSPITALITY

The practice of hospitality is linked to the second research finding: "Discipleship among millennials in missional communities was facilitated by authentic, caring, and loving relationships." Christian hospitality means creating a space that welcomes the stranger.[14] To welcome the stranger means to acknowledge the *imago Dei* in him or her and to view them as having inherent worth and value. To treat others with dignity is to act in unconditional love, the agapic ethic discussed in the previous chapter. The New Testament word for hospitality, *philoxenia*, can be translated as "a love for the guest or stranger."[15] The root word, *philo*, is related to the other type of love previously discussed, friendship love or *phileo*, while *xenia* means "the stranger." Christian hospitality is thus given full expression when it welcomes the stranger in unconditional love and friendship and makes space for them in the community of faith.

Christian hospitality is a biblical practice found in both the Old and New Testaments. Deuteronomy instructs the Israelites: "You are to love those who are foreigners, for you yourselves were foreigners in Egypt" (Deut. 10:19). Foreigners and aliens were to be given the same rights and respect as the Hebrews. In the New Testament, we see Jesus welcoming all who approached him: prostitutes and tax collectors, the infirm, and little children (for example, Matt. 19; Luke 5; 7). The early church practiced hospitality primarily in their homes, as was the Greek and Hebrew custom.

As the Christian community gathered, sharing meals, welcoming the sojourner, and providing for the material needs of the poor, it reflected the gracious and hospitable character of the God whom they followed.[16]

Hospitality crosses relational boundaries to the "others" in our lives, even those who are marginalized or rejected. The practice thus has a missional, and even a daring, quality. Christine D. Pohl elaborates in *Making Room: Recovering Hospitality as a Christian Tradition*:

> Although we often think of hospitality as a tame and pleasant practice, Christian hospitality has always had a subversive, countercultural dimension . . . Especially when the larger society disregards or dishonors certain persons, small acts of respect and welcome are potent far beyond themselves. They point to a different system of valuing and an alternate model of relationships.[17]

The institutional shift in the culture, however, over time has had an impact on the ministry of hospitality by taming it, depersonalizing it, and relegating it to religious and social services. Now we have soup kitchens, retirement homes, welfare offices, day care centers, and halfway houses, all with their institutional specializations, professional staff, and programmatic emphases. Even within the church, hospitality has become increasingly depersonalized, with greeting teams and hospitality committees rather than the interpersonal, organic form expressed by the early church.[18] In fact, Bass and Dykstra point out that today strangers are sometimes even treated with hostility by Christians.[19]

Henri Nouwen describes hospitality and hostility as existing at opposite poles. In his book *Reaching Out: The Three Movements of the Spiritual Life*, hospitality is conveyed as one of the most important practices of living "a life in the Spirit of Jesus Christ."[20] An authentic spiritual life entails a movement from hostility to hospitality, which deals with "reaching out to our fellow human beings."[21] He reminds the reader that the world is often a hostile place, fraught with suspicion, aggression, and defensiveness, and asserts that it is the job of the church to create a "free and fearless space where brotherhood and sisterhood can be formed and fully experienced."[22]

Nouwen rightly observes that the church, ideally, should be a place where one can know and be known through transparency, authenticity, and acceptance, reflecting the nature of Christ to one another. I agree with Bass and Dykstra and argue that, unfortunately, it is the church who has become suspicious, fearful, and defensive, sometimes even acting aggressively. The first step, therefore, is for the church to overcome its fear and hostility of "the other" so it can reach out in hospitable love to those living in the surrounding culture.

An excellent illustration of the difference between hostility and hospitality was the ministry of the Strip Club Church at sex-industry expos. Strip Club Church traveled to these large convention venues all over the U.S. where sex-industry vendors set up booths to showcase their goods and services. The ministry would set up a booth of its own, staffed by volunteers who offered Bibles and T-shirts advertising the love of Jesus and providing a space for Christian hospitality.

Former sex workers, such as Annette from my fieldwork, reported that when they attended these expos, they were sometimes met by protesters outside the venues carrying picket signs reading "Turn or Burn" and aggressively yelling about the need to repent of their sin. The protesters' hostility stood in stark contrast to the hospitality offered at the Strip Club Church booth inside the convention center.

Nouwen elaborates that the space created through hospitality should be a "free and friendly space," offering friendship with no conditions. The individual does not have to change or conform in order to be treated hospitably. They simply can enter in freedom and move from being an enemy to being a friend.

Figure 6.1 Banner Designating Room Set Aside for Strippers at Sex Industry Expo

Again, this was exemplified quite well by the Strip Club Church at the sex-industry expos. In addition to the booth on the main floor, they also had a separate, more private space in one of the adjacent conference rooms designated as the "Hotties Room," where strippers could escape the freneticism of the larger expo and find food, rest, and solitude. Figure 6.1 depicts a photo of the banner inviting women inside.

Nouwen stresses that, although hospitality is offered without demands for conformity, the hope is that the guest will experience a free and friendly space where transformation can take place. The desire is to create a space for the Spirit to move in those *kairos* moments where people's hearts can be changed. Nouwen says it eloquently, and it is worth quoting his words in their entirety:

> Hospitality is not to change people, but to offer them space where change can take place . . . It is not to bring men and women over to our side, but to offer freedom not disturbed by dividing lines. It is not to lead our

neighbor into a corner where there are no alternatives
left, but to open a wide spectrum of options for choice
and commitment . . . [Hospitality should create] a
friendly emptiness where strangers can enter and
discover themselves as created free.[23]

Receptivity, then, is a core concept in hospitality. The guest must
feel received unconditionally, affirmed in her gifts, and validated in
her being. Simply reaching out without demonstrating receptivity
can be harmful, exploitative, or manipulative.

Nouwen writes that, once the stranger has been received,
accepted, and validated in her worth and gifts, the receptivity must
be balanced with confrontation. He describes this confrontation
as setting "boundaries" or "limits" that help define our position as
Christians. Christian hospitality means providing an "unambiguous
presence" in relation to others, being clear about who we are, what we
believe, whom we worship, and why.[24] It is a matter of integrity not
to remain neutral but to let others see us in all our transparency and
authenticity. The hope is that articulating our worldview will allow
others to think reflexively about their own beliefs and opinions.

The main question is in what manner we will make our
unambiguous presence known. Will it be with words of love and
validation, or with hostility and fear? Strip Club Church confronted
others with the love of Jesus using T-shirts, Bibles, safe spaces, and
welcoming conversation. In stark contrast, the Christians outside
confronted with words of intolerance and hatred of those "others"
in their midst from whom they had a differing worldview. Every
Christian is faced with the same choice.

Thus, Christian hospitality requires a balance between
receptivity and confrontation. Nouwen describes this balancing
act: "Receptivity without confrontation leads to bland neutrality
that serves nobody. Confrontation without receptivity leads to
an oppressive aggression which hurts everybody."[25] Another way
to state this dynamic is Paul's exhortation to the Ephesians to

"speak the truth in love" (Eph. 4:15). Love without truth is empty sentimentality, whereas truth without love is intolerant bigotry. To be out of balance is to be like those Paul warned against in 1 Corinthians 13:1: believers without love who are "only a resounding gong or a clanging cymbal." Such shrillness only causes the hearer to cover their ears to drown out the noise.

It is perhaps because of the church's fearfulness that hospitality has lost some of its missional edge and instead has become a practice that is safe, tame, and insular. Hospitality too often has come to mean a polite dinner gathering or social event, either in one's home or in the church building among other "members." If we take seriously Nouwen's call to embrace authentic Christian spirituality, then we need to recapture the more radical nature of true hospitality and welcome the stranger.

Pohl's recommendation is to reclaim the household as a key place for hospitality and link it to the larger institution of the church so that both can be recovered as "key settings for hospitality."[26] Based on my research findings, however, I would recast this vision in light of missional theology and the emergence of Christian communities in third-place settings. True, there are missional churches springing up everywhere that meet in homes, but this is not the only place where hospitality can occur.[27] The example of the sex-industry convention demonstrates that hospitality can be missional as believers travel cross-culturally into various cultural contexts.

Annette's story proves that disciples can be made outside the walls of the institutional church, finding Christian community, and being guided to replicate the discipleship process within their own familiar cultural contexts. If the church wants to disciple dechurched millennials, it is imperative that missional outposts of hospitality be established as places to earn their trust, demonstrate acceptance, and lovingly but intentionally confront them with the irresistible grace of Jesus.

Another important consideration is how missional communities might reframe Christian hospitality in order to view themselves not only as hosts to millennials but also as guests in their culture. Swinton has suggested such a "rethinking" of hospitality in the church.[28] He writes that the church often approaches others with a set of assumptions that include caring for and making room for others—duties of a host. This is well and good; however, when the church reverses its role and instead sees itself as guest, it has a chance to listen to and understand others in new ways, to learn "beautiful things" not otherwise noticed.[29]

The ultimate purpose of such a frame shift, writes Swinton, is to establish co-equality through friendship.[30] He uses Jesus as the exemplar, noting that his ministry included both giving and receiving hospitality. Swinton calls this "incarnational hospitality" and notes that "God was with a totally different group of people doing something quite different: offering friendship and acceptance and revealing the kingdom in and through that friendship."[31] Friendship—the *philéō* love spoken about in my findings—is based on commonality and relational equality, as opposed to the notion of the Christian paid professional who enters into a relationship with the presumption of helping, fixing, or controlling another based on a spiritual hierarchy. Swinton advises the church to "slow down and take the time to listen to and take seriously" the experiences of others so that trust and respect may be established and the kingdom of God may be received.[32]

By contrast, problems arise when the church adopts the posture of host only. Willie James Jennings writes about the negative results of a one-sided view of hospitality in his important work *The Christian Imagination*, in which he explores the historical perspective of the origins of race during the missionary expansion of the colonial period:

> Christian theological imagination was woven into processes of colonial dominance. Other peoples and their ways of life had to adapt, become fluid, even morph into the colonial order of things . . . Indeed, it is as though

Christianity, wherever it went in the modern colonies, inverted its sense of hospitality. It claimed to be the host, the owner of the spaces it entered, and demanded native peoples enter its cultural logics, its ways of being in the world, and its conceptualities.[33]

By inverting its hospitality, the expanding church regarded itself as the host of its subjugated peoples, forcing them into inculcation of the colonized order. The result was what Jennings terms a "diseased social imagination" in Western Christianity that has persisted even to this day, a world in which theology has been untethered from place and people and exists in a supersessionist state.[34] Like Swinton, he believes that the solution is found in relational connection based on intimacy with others and creating "spaces of communion" with God and others.[35] In this way, Christian imagination can be rescued from its disembodied state and once again find its place concretely "anywhere and everywhere the disciples of Jesus live together," unifying cultures, people groups, and ethnicities.[36]

Swinton's and Jennings's works were written about dissimilar topics—Swinton about a practical theology of mental health and Jennings about Christian colonialism and race relations—but their concepts of hospitality can be extrapolated and applied to millennials in missional communities. Synthesizing their ideas, a missional construct of hospitality to millennials would include incarnational hospitality, whereby the church assumes the posture of guest with the intent to listen and understand. The resulting environment of shared communion would foster the "authentic, loving, and caring relationships" that were so important to millennials in my findings (see Theme 2).

Further, I propose that shifting our understanding of hospitality from the perspective of host to that of guest would avoid the danger of falling into epistemological colonization of millennials whereby the evangelical church assumes the superiority of Enlightenment-based discipleship methods rather than considering millennials' postmodern worldview. Indeed, if millennials are the first fully postmodern generation, then the rest of us are merely guests in their world. The church can learn from these epistemological natives as it seeks to love, listen to, and understand them.

Developing an effective praxis of missional hospitality thus will require learning how to not only take the posture of host but also to assume that of guest so that discipleship can truly be contextualized, not just in a spatial/geographical sense but also in a philosophical/epistemological one. Not to do so runs the risk of establishing missional communities without regard to the forms, language, and symbols of the host culture, thereby continuing the colonizing tendencies of the Christian imagination that disregards context.

DISCERNMENT

A third key finding in my research was that millennials relied on the Holy Spirit to help them discern when, where, and with whom to conduct discipleship. Discernment is the practice of recognizing God's leading, his voice, his presence, and his will for a given situation, person, event, or church. Quite simply, discernment is "figuring out what to do" by listening to the Holy Spirit, understanding where he is working, and then participating.[37] God is a speaking God. He is not a remote, impersonal force but a person who is immanently present and desires to be in loving relationship with his creation. He has a will and desires to make it known. This is accomplished through the person of the Holy Spirit.

If practicing discernment aids in knowing God's will, then it also aids in knowing his timing, for the two are inextricably linked. Henri Nouwen is a source of wisdom on this practice, as well. In his book, *Discernment: Reading the Times of Daily Life,* he discusses Thomas Merton's differentiation between *kairos* time and *chronos* time and its importance in the context of discernment.[38] *Chronos* time is "clock time" measured in hours, minutes, and seconds, while *kairos* time is eternal; things occur when the situation is spiritually ready for fulfillment, according to a divine opportunity full of purpose and meaning. Such a time is one of spiritual ripeness, when opportunities may be seized.[39] Discernment, Nouwen concludes, is about knowing the right time.

We see the power of *kairos* in the story of the beggar in Acts 3:6–10. A man crippled from birth was brought each day to the temple gate called Beautiful. One day Peter and John were going up to the temple at the time of prayer and saw the man. "Then Peter said, 'Silver or gold I do not have, but what I have I give you. In the name of Jesus Christ of Nazareth, walk.' Taking him by the right hand, he helped him up, and instantly the man's feet and ankles became strong. He jumped to his feet and began to walk" (v. 6–8).

If this man had been begging at the same gate for years, it is likely that Jesus passed him many times. Why did Jesus not stop and heal him earlier? The answer may be found in the *kairos* concept. The people of Jerusalem recognized the healed man as the one who always sat at the gate, so his healing caused such a disturbance that a great crowd assembled. Peter preached to the crowd and, as a result, the number of believers grew from two thousand to about five thousand (Acts 4:4). The *kairos* moment was needed so that the maximum kingdom impact could be achieved. Interestingly, the word for beautiful in this passage, *Hōraian*, is derived from the root word *hora*, which means "belonging to the right hour or season."[40] What does this have to do with discernment? Discernment is about understanding the right hour or season for action so that the maximum impact can be achieved for the kingdom of God.

There were moments in my fieldwork when I experienced the difference between *chronos* and *kairos*. When I did not adequately prepare my heart to discern the Lord's direction before going out into ministry, I would either miss opportunities or try to force a spiritual encounter out of a sense of duty. I remember one such occasion when I was determined to "do the Lord's work" by initiating conversation with one of the dancers. Reacting to my misdirected, undiscerning attempt to make a connection, one girl said to me, "You're freaking me out!" and walked away.

Other attempts, when I was more sensitive to the Spirit's leading, resulted in fruit. For example, one night I walked into a dressing room and was prayerfully asking for discernment. I gravitated to one girl, named Juanita, I had seen before. She saw me and exclaimed, "Oh good! You're here!" before explaining that she was in the middle of a family crisis. I asked, "Can I pray for you?" and, instead of my "freaking her out," she responded, "Yes, I would love that."

Here is what I wrote in my fieldwork journal: "She was sobbing, so eager for me to pray. We went into the bathroom, held hands, and [I] prayed. I felt the Holy Spirit's presence as I prayed. She seemed grateful, and I loved it because I felt useful and connected. And yes, she was topless!"[41] Being sensitive to the Spirit's leading provided an opportunity for me to be present in a *kairos* moment, an intersection of human need and the presence of God.

The above example involved the discernment by an individual, but discernment can be a communal act as well. Corporate discernment takes place when a group of people wishes to make decisions within the context of God's will and activity within the church or society. Christian communities in various times and places have developed their own forms of communal discernment. David F. White of Emory University has written about Christian discernment among youth and suggests that four prominent models of discernment contain different practices worth exploring: Ignatian contemplation, Quaker communal discernment, Latin American Christian Base Communities, and Protestant biblical reflection.[42] I will give a brief description of each, followed by a discussion of their merits vis-à-vis my research question.

Ignatian Contemplation. Ignatian discernment always has as its goal the enhancement of one's understanding about how to participate in the work of God.[43] This is true whether engaging in individual or in communal discernment. Rogers suggests three critical considerations for practicing this form of discernment: "a passionate commitment to follow God," "an attitude of indifference toward all other drives and desires," and "a deep sensitivity to the ways and being of God."[44] Communal Ignatian discernment is punctuated by individual times of prayer, and decisions are made by a majority consensus, accompanied by a pervasive feeling of peace among the group—even dissenters.[45]

Quaker Communal Discernment. Quakers have a distinctive formal process of communal discernment based on "decision making by consensus."[46] The process entails a time of silence (prayerful listening) followed by a time of discussion and dissent, which is repeated until full consensus is achieved.[47] The assumption is that every member is a repository of the Holy Spirit and thus has something to offer. The goal is to attain unity among the members; unity is not necessarily unanimity but what the Quakers call "concord," a shared goal of engaging, discerning, and following the will of God in their midst.[48] The Quakers call these discernment meetings Meeting for Worship in which Business Is Conducted, highlighting their conviction that discernment is an act of worship conducted by believers with the Spirit of God as an active participant.[49]

Christian Base Communities. A Christian Base Community (*Comunidades Eclesiales de Base*–CEB) is a small, grassroots group of Catholic believers, usually twelve to twenty people, comprised of the poor, marginalized, and oppressed, primarily in Latin America.[50] They gather to study the Bible, pray, and discern how they might engage politically in their setting. A key practice of Christian Base Communities is conscientization. First introduced by philosopher Paul Friere, conscientization is the process of empowering the marginalized by "raising their consciousness" of their conditions in order to inspire them to make changes. It entails understanding the reality of their situation, discerning how it aligns with God's will, and then evaluating options for transformation. There is often an overarching understanding that this guidance is facilitated by the Holy Spirit's presence among them.[51]

Protestant Biblical Reflection. Protestant biblical reflection is predicated on the idea that the Christian Scriptures are best understood through a combination of human reason and illumination by the Spirit. Theologian Millard Erickson explains that "illumination by the Holy Spirit helps the Scripture reader or hearer understand the Bible" but that "when we come to determine the message's meaning" and "assess its truth, we must utilize the power of reasoning."[52] John Calvin described this combination as wearing "spectacles of faith" that allow the truth of Scripture to be seen with clarity.[53] Bonhoeffer similarly spoke of the "clear gaze" provided by Scripture by which we can view the world.[54] And Bonhoeffer described a practice of discernment that combines listening to the Word and scrutinizing current events and ideas. The church, he argued, needed to learn to "read the Bible in an entirely new way" so that it could take responsibility for its place in the world.[55]

What value can be gleaned from these forms of discernment that can inform praxis among millennials in missional communities? I argue that there are merits of each approach that, when combined, could become an effective model for discernment. Both the Quaker and the Christian Base Community models, for example, stress equality and the importance of giving a voice to the voiceless. This could be helpful in young adult ministry, because White argues that young adults are often marginalized by the church, segregated from the rest of the congregation and ascribed "questionable value" as to the spiritual contribution they can make.[56] His assertion is consistent with the attitude expressed by some in my research, such as Zach, who observed that

> sometimes in big churches . . . there is a divide [between] the older generation and the young generation. You know, millennials, you'll hear, typically want to be valued in their input. Past churches I've been at—there's an age gap, [so] it's easy to not be involved or to be in a place where you don't feel relevant.

White argues that the church needs to invite young people to engage in corporate discernment so that their gifts can be activated and their voices heard.

The concept of conscientization could have application with millennials in missional communities, as well. Asking the Spirit's help to raise their consciousness to see the reality of their situations and inspiring them to make changes that lead to personal and societal transformation corresponds with the propensity of emerging adults to be drawn to social justice issues. It is possible to envision this application to the Seven Cultural Streets model of discipleship at Urban Life Church, where conscientization could lead to cultural transformation in business, education, or the arts, for example. It is also possible to envision application to those at Strip Club Church who need to be healed from trauma, such as sexual abuse and exploitation. Guiding women through the process of prayerfully discerning the reality of their situation and determining options for change could lead to moments of powerful transformation, both in terms of healing and as opportunities to hear the Spirit's call to vocational ministry.

It is problematic, however, that conscientization is rooted in the tenets of liberal theology, which minimizes the authority and normativity of Scripture.[57] This is where Protestant biblical reflection can be of value. Using Scripture as a plumb line between reason and the Spirit can aid in maintaining balance. Furthermore, we are to read Scripture with the intent of living it out in our current context without misapplying its principles, so reliance on the Spirit can help discern whether pioneering missional communities are going too far afield from the Christian tradition. Missional practitioners, thus, can assure that discernment remains grounded in the Word by committing to its normativity and authority.

Finally, both Quaker and Ignatian discernment approaches have a back-and-forth rhythm of individuals discerning in prayer and then coming together in community to verify. This method lends

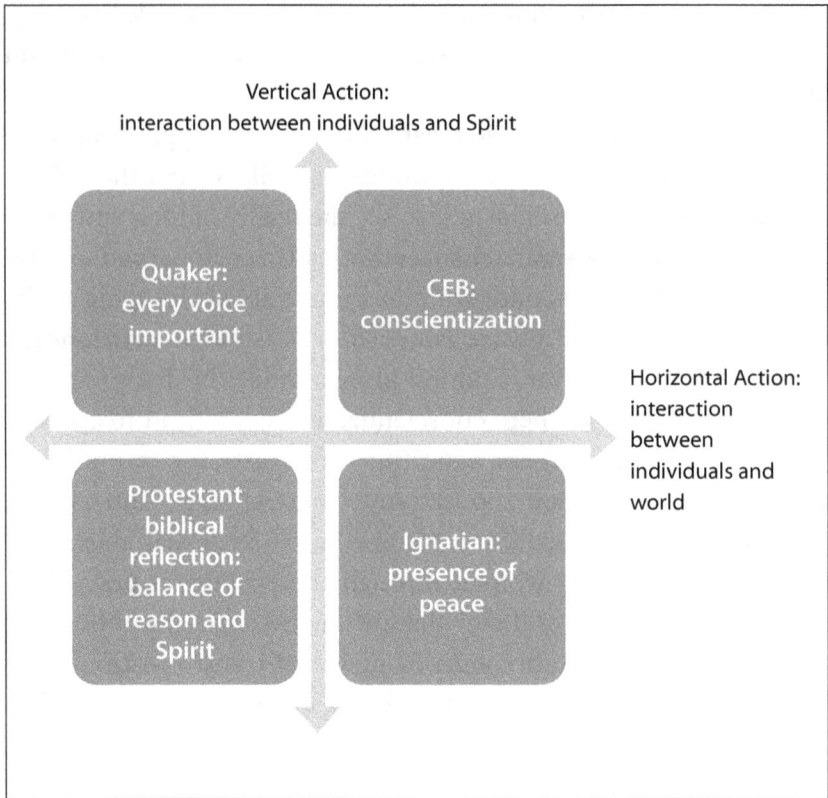

Figure 6.2 Discernment Matrix

itself to the highly relational, authentic bent of millennials. I saw this rhythm time and time again in my fieldwork. Both sites reported that they would seek God in prayer, discern a particular leading or directive, and then receive confirmation within the corporate body. Feelings of peace were often reported as accompanying these actions, a hallmark of Ignatian discernment.

Combining elements of each of the approaches creates a matrix of discernment that becomes a new model for millennials in missional communities. (See Figure 6.2, Discernment Matrix). There is overlap in some of the characteristic practices of each of the models; however, I have chosen to highlight those that are most prominent within each. The matrix includes four practices drawn from each of the models: the equality of the Quakers, the conscientization of the CEBs, the balance of reason and Spirit of the Protestants, and the presence of peace of the Ignatians. The vertical axis represents the action of seeking and receiving the guidance of the Holy Spirit, while the horizontal axis represents the action taken once God's will is discerned. In some ways, discernment is the umbrella practice over all the others. If the goal is to do things in God's strength, according to his will and his calling, and not our own, then discernment is at the core of every other practice. Considering this discussion, it is clear that the practice of discernment could be greatly beneficial to millennials as part of their missional discipleship.

CONCLUSION

This chapter has discussed the findings of my study, in concert with biblical texts and theological writings, in order to determine how the church might respond in faithful action. By correlating key themes with specific Christian practices, I have argued that the effective discipleship of millennials in missional communities might be accomplished through three key methods. First, helping young adults craft their testimonies could help them feel confident to engage in spiritual conversations outside the four walls of the church. The template provided by Urban Life Church shows promise in being an effective pedagogical tool for equipping millennials to incarnate the redemptive aspects of the gospel out in the world.

Second, engaging millennials in acts of hospitality demonstrates the unconditional love of Jesus and provides a place, both physically and conceptually, for them to be confronted with the compelling love of Jesus. Third, inviting young adults to participate in communal discernment, as well as encouraging individual contemplative discernment, could serve to help them determine God's will, timing, and calling. A matrix of communal discernment based on the four primary methods creates a model that encourages authenticity and community, gives them a voice within the faith community, and prepares them to consider how the Spirit might be calling them into Christian vocation.

My hope is that these practices could become normative for missional ecclesiological structures in the future. Ministry leaders and practitioners can respond to the crisis of young adults' disengagement from the American church through reinvigorating discipleship practices. By adopting missional, action-oriented discipleship practices that utilize millennials' epistemological emphasis on relationship and experiential meaning-making in fresh ways, they become relevant for a new church age.

CHAPTER 7

CONCLUSION

THE SITUATION: A REPRISE

Millennials are unique. The first fully postmodern generation, they are right-brained, intuitive, subjective, and highly relational. They see the world not in black and white but in shades of gray. Relationships are paramount. Truth is relative. Meaning is self-generated, and identity is in flux. Millennials are the first to occupy an entirely new life stage called emerging adulthood. The younger millennials are no longer youth but not quite adults, and they find themselves in a liminal state marked by infinite possibilities and unlimited options. Having delayed the requisite milestones used by previous generations to mark the transition into adulthood, such as marriage, family, and clear career paths, millennials are left with a dizzying array of life choices. The open-endedness of such an infinite universe of contingencies results in conflicting feelings of freedom and uncertainty. A time of exploration, emerging adulthood contains a high degree of self-focus and self-discovery. Some have branded this focus on self as full-blown narcissism hardwired into their psyches, while others are crossing their fingers that millennials will outgrow it as they continue to move into full adulthood.

Concurrent with these generational developments is the rise of the missional movement in the United States. The missional movement is a new way of "doing" church, a shift from the prevailing attractional-extractional model to a missional-incarnational one. The principal idea is that God is always on mission, bringing his kingdom to earth, and the ecclesia is invited to join him in his work. The *missio Dei* is the driving force, and contextualization is the driving ethos. It is about "taking church to the people, rather than bringing people to the church," as Alan Hirsch writes, and current research suggests that it is gaining significant traction in the United States.[1]

The problem is that the old institutional churches are losing millennials in droves. So precipitous is the decline that the term "dropout phenomenon" has been used to describe it. The church is by and large still entrenched in Enlightenment thinking and methods, centered on rationality, logic, and the transmission of information through teaching and preaching. This is neither right nor wrong; it just is. The Enlightenment-based thinking and ministry approaches reflect the leadership of the older generations: Generation X, baby boomers, and the Silent Generation. However, there has been a seismic epistemological turn to postmodernism, with millennials at the helm. The upshot is that millennials approach life and faith very differently from the rest of the church. Thus, within the American church today there is not just a generation gap but an epistemological gap. Attempting to shoehorn millennials into the existing church is proving futile.

A second problem is the proliferation of an imposter religion called Moralistic Therapeutic Deism. A watered-down version of Christianity that posits that an impersonal deity can be called upon in times of trouble but otherwise leaves people to their own devices as long as they are "nice" to one another, MTD has seeped deep into the American church. Millennials are often cited as the primary carriers of this spiritual malady, but, in reality, "patient zero" may be the older generations who are transmitting it to their children. The problem of MTD begs the question: do we even want to bring millennials back into such churches?

Meanwhile, there continues to be a persistent discipleship problem in American churches. It is possible that a combination of MTD and the Enlightenment-based focus on the transmission of information has led to the stifling of the discipleship process, particularly with millennials. Urban Life Church cleverly likened the problem to the Sea of Galilee and the Dead Sea. Both bodies of water have the same source: the Jordan River. The river flows through the Sea of Galilee and into the Dead Sea, which is its terminus. The Sea of Galilee is teeming with life, while the Dead Sea is just that: dead. It is possible that the discipleship problem in today's churches is due to a similar lack of flow: although believers may be receiving the fresh water of the Word and the Spirit, if they sit as mere passive recipients without an outlet, they become stagnant.[2]

My investigation developed out of these concerns regarding the recent "dropout phenomenon" of emerging adults from the American church and the need to address the discipleship crisis among this demographic.[3] How can the church promote the flow of discipleship, reverse the damage done by MTD, and provide a platform where millennials can live out their postmodern orientation in the midst of their emerging adulthood, all while remaining faithful to the core tenets and essential orthodoxy of Christian faith and tradition? This is a tall order. And this is where my research is located, and the gap I have intended to fill. This inquiry set out to investigate the effective discipleship of millennials in missional communities.

My central research question was "What does it mean for millennials to follow Christ today in missional communities?" The study answered the primary research question and satisfied the aims using the pastoral cycle put forth by Richard Osmer.[4] The pastoral cycle contains four critical tasks that were undertaken during research. The first is the descriptive-empirical task, which asks the question "What is going on?" in a research setting and involves gathering and examining information from that setting. I wanted to select settings that were most conducive to answering my research question; therefore, I selected two missional communities with 85 to 90 percent millennial membership.

The second task in the pastoral cycle is the interpretive task, which asks the question "Why is this going on?" to acquire deeper insights and understanding into the setting under study. It is during this phase that the researcher often draws from multiple disciplines. In order to complete the first two tasks and answer the corresponding questions, I employed the method and methodology of ethnography. For one year I immersed myself in the two missional communities and studied the discipleship methods, approaches, and practices used with the millennials among their populations. Participant observation, interviews, and document analysis were the primary methods of data collection. As is often the case with ethnographic research where one is involved in the "realness" of human lives, occasionally things got messy, with the threat of danger, the witnessing of illicit activities, and strained interpersonal dynamics taking place in the field. All of these contributed to the richness of the experience and a greater understanding of the cultural contexts being studied.

The third task in Osmer's pastoral cycle asks the question "What ought to be going on?" This stage of the cycle requires the researcher to reflect theologically on information gleaned from the field in order to guide the Christian community into faithful practice. To fulfill this task, I selected Dietrich Bonhoeffer's concept of religionless Christianity as the theological lens through which to view my research data. With its world-centered ethic, noninstitutional focus, and the resulting *metanoia* of the church, religionless Christianity made a robust dialectical partner with missional theology. Further, Bonhoeffer's premise of religionless Christianity as an antidote for the imposter religion of his day, called the God Hypothesis, was valuable in considering how to undo today's imposter religion, Moralistic Therapeutic Deism.

The fourth task in the pastoral cycle is the pragmatic task, which asks "How might we respond?" to what has been learned through the first two tasks by transforming future praxis within the Christian community. As a result of data collection through big ethnography at two missional sites with millennials and theologically interpreting the data, I was able to form conclusions and make recommendations for how the practices of the discipleship of millennials should be formed or reformed for the future.

SUMMARY AND DISCUSSION OF FINDINGS

Discipleship among Millennials in Missional Communities Was Facilitated by Opportunities to Become Engaged in Ministry and Mission in the World.

First, discipleship was facilitated by opportunities for the engagement of culture. Urban Life Church instituted an innovative discipleship framework called the Seven Cultural Streets, designed to help implement their mission of "developing followers of Jesus who influence and shape culture." The "streets" are spheres of society to which one is called to fulfill the Great Commission. The millennial congregants at Urban Life Church caught the vision of being culture molders in their respective streets and were dedicated to taking the church "beyond the four walls" and into their vocations. Strip Club Church also trained and equipped millennials to disciple others in their missional sphere of influence. Some of this training was conducted through formal pedagogical curricula, while at other times it was conducted more organically through relationships and modeling.

Second, millennials were enthusiastic about proclaiming their faith to others. The sharing of personal narratives was found to be a powerful means of discipleship. Both sites emphasized the importance of telling faith stories to legitimize the Christian faith. The personal testimonies allowed tenets and principles of Christianity to be translated into the cultural vernacular of the hearer, thus building a bridge between the church and the culture. This was especially effective because many millennials described having been "burned" by the church in the past and thus had a measure of mistrust for anything that sounded "churchy," as one millennial described it. For those in the sex industry who had endured trauma and abuse, personal narratives provided a peer-to-peer discipleship that circumvented the possibility of triggering feelings of exploitation by authority figures. These findings were a key to understanding how testimony is linked to the deinstitutionalization of missional churches, because narrative accounts acted as contextualized sermons in the field.

Third, millennials were ready to be mobilized for service immediately. Both sites made efforts to eliminate barriers to serving so that millennials could get involved as easily and quickly as possible. Urban Life even placed individuals in positions of service before they had made a profession of faith, describing this as "the pre-conversion part" of discipleship. Millennials were eager to get involved, thus receiving discipleship training as they served. Serving was a means to, and not a result of, spiritual maturity. This resulted in their feeling validated and affirmed rather than feeling the need to attain some external standard, or negotiating "hoops to jump through," in order to serve. This fulfilled my research aim to understand the pedagogical aspects of discipleship. Teaching took place "along the way" as leaders and mentors came alongside millennials to train them in the field.

Discipleship among Millennials Was Facilitated by Authentic, Caring, and Loving Relationships.

Millennials were open to forming discipleship relationships when they were approached with love instead of judgment. Many millennials are estranged from the church because they have deemed it too harsh and judgmental. Being missional, then, meant being among those millennials who are especially susceptible and vulnerable to feeling judged. This attitude was found to be particularly present among the dancers at the strip clubs, who considered themselves disenfranchised from mainstream society in general, and from Christians and the church specifically. Both sites in my study, however, included millennials who had felt shamed or hurt by the institutional or traditional church at one time, in one way or another. It was paramount for ministry leaders seeking to establish discipleship relationships to be sensitive to these feelings and ensure that they were initiating contact in love, not in judgment.

Millennials desired to form discipleship relationships based on philia, or friendship love. Philia is based on common interests and companionship. Most interviewees stressed the importance of authenticity in their Christian friendships. They wanted relationships in which they could feel free to be vulnerable, honest, and safe. In this way, they could be peer disciples to one another, "challenging" and "pushing" and "stretching" one another in their spiritual growth. As millennials learned to be vulnerable and authentic, they felt validated and were willing to commit to either the faith community or to one-on-one discipleship relationships.

Millennials were willing to enter a relationship with Christians when they felt the agape love of Jesus. Unconditional love shown toward millennials in missional settings went a long way in deconstructing the bias they held against the church. Many reported feelings of judgment and rejection from churches in their past and recounted that they had not been loved for themselves. Thus, agape was tied to celebrating the *imago Dei* in each person, expressed through words and actions that demonstrated dignity and respect. Trust was gained through demonstrations of agape, establishing a solid foundation on which to build a discipleship relationship. My findings were consistent with prior research, which found that most millennials have a positive view of the person of Jesus Christ, even as they consider the church to be "judgmental," "homophobic," and "negative."[5]

Volunteers equated serving others with incarnating the love of Jesus by following his example of loving others "right where they are." Millennials responded positively, even enthusiastically, to these expressions of love, setting the stage for further engagement in discipleship relationships. Overall, the theme of love was the most significant aspect of the relational dimension of discipleship. If love could be expressed and received, whether in friendship, in unconditional acceptance, or in the name of Jesus, assumptions of judgment dissipated and defenses were dropped, setting the stage for deeper spiritual growth.

Discipleship among Millennials in Missional Communities Included a Belief in the Activity of the Holy Spirit.
Millennials relied on discernment given through the Holy Spirit to aid them in discipleship. Attentiveness to God's movement and direction was imperative in these missional settings that were often full of adventure, danger, or unexpected activities. There was a great reliance on the Spirit's leading about whom to approach in conversation and what to say. Discernment took place both individually and corporately, most often by receiving guidance in prayer. Accurate discernment resulted in powerful moments of ministry in which a well-timed prayer, Scripture, or a word of encouragement opened the door to ongoing ministry.

The Holy Spirit prepared dechurched millennials for discipleship relationships through prevenient action. Millennials reported that they experienced the Spirit's conviction, leading, or answered prayer in preparation for reengaging with a faith community. This dynamic, when paired with the discernment of the ministry volunteers, resulted in a powerful experience that led to the assurance that God was leading the prodigal home. Former feelings of hostility or isolation melted away as millennials found a new home in their missional community.

Millennials relied on the Holy Spirit for inner healing. The presence of the Holy Spirit, sometimes referred to by informants as "the presence of God" or "the presence of Jesus," was experienced in a way that reversed battered self-esteem, healed childhood trauma, and loosened the chains of addiction. Millennials described "feeling" the Spirit's presence or experiencing fruit of the Spirit, such as peace and joy. The Holy Spirit softened hard hearts, compelling individuals to connect with others in the family of God.

RESULTING CONCLUSIONS

Many Christian millennials are in missional communities because they feel disregarded or hurt by the traditional churches they used to attend. Thus, the effective discipleship of millennials centers on reestablishing trust. It is important for missional practitioners to keep in mind that "outreach" among millennials is just as much about discipleship of the unchurched and dechurched believer as it is about evangelism of the nonbeliever. The Great Commission is not to be narrowly defined as going into the world to make disciples of those who need "saving"; instead, it is about the action of an ambassador going into all the world to encounter, befriend, and "repatriate" the exile who is already being wooed by the Holy Spirit in prayerful solitude.

This trust is earned slowly over time. Activities that fostered authentic relationships, such as small groups and one-on-one mentoring relationships, were effective in rebuilding trust. Millennials needed to know that they would be heard and accepted. Hospitality was a key practice, but it needed to be missional hospitality, outposts of friendship erected in the middle of culture. Establishing missional outposts of hospitality provided places, both physically and conceptually, for millennials to think reflexively about their own beliefs. A relational bridge based on love and acceptance can be built that can form a foundation for ongoing discipleship.

Millennials do not want to sit on the sidelines; they want to be mobilized to serve and help immediately upon becoming part of the family of faith. Serving becomes a means to, as opposed to being a result of, spiritual maturity. Missional practitioners will need to commit themselves to hands-on discipleship that walks alongside millennials in the mission field to help them grow and mature while they are serving. This approach considers their postmodern worldview by removing them from the classroom and placing them in live situations where they can learn kinesthetically and intuitively. For example, in my fieldwork they were mobilized for service often within their first week of attending. These communities were able to retain millennials because the millennials felt useful and wanted.

Establishing the practice of helping young adults craft their testimonies could help them feel confident to engage in spiritual conversations outside the four walls of the church. As churches wrestle with how to remain faithful to Christian theology and tradition in a postmodern world, the use of personal narratives can provide a means of transmitting the gospel in culturally relevant ways, using contextualized language, meanings, and cultural symbols.

The effective discipleship of millennials in missional settings relied heavily on the Holy Spirit. They often preferred to forgo a detailed plan or program; the Holy Spirit *was* the program. He was the road map. And millennials liked it that way. They felt comfortable being spontaneous, seeking the Holy Spirit's direction for the next move. They did not need a logical, planned agenda; they were happy to be on a wild adventure with God in the driver's seat. As a result, prayerful discernment was a very important practice among millennials. They sought the Lord for each next step as they served missionally, learning as they went.

The unique contribution of my research is that it constitutes a reimagining of discipleship methods and practices in postmodern terms within missional contexts. It is about "translating" the traditions of the Christian faith into postmodern forms and symbols to which millennials can relate. The personal narrative becomes a sermon. The third-place setting becomes the classroom. Intuiting the Holy Spirit becomes the curriculum. As conventional, Enlightenment-based approaches are reframed for a postmodern context, we begin to speak the millennials' epistemological language.

LIMITATIONS AND CONSIDERATIONS FOR FURTHER STUDY

This study has raised further questions that need to be explored in future research. For instance, how is sin to be addressed with young adults in missional settings? Great efforts were made to show unconditional love and acceptance of millennials by entering their worlds and speaking their cultural language. Time and time again they were assured that they were accepted the way they were, that Jesus loved them, and that the power of the Holy Spirit was available to them regardless of their choices. Where and when are issues of sin addressed? Ongoing confession and repentance of sin is a biblical commandment and one of the chief areas in the sanctification of the believer. Further research needs to be done on how to effectively confront sin so that greater spiritual maturity can take place, without jeopardizing the progress made in making millennials feel accepted and loved, but also without crossing the line to legalism or moralism.

A second consideration for further study is how the traditional, institutional church is to respond to the missional discipleship of millennials. Are there findings from my study that could be implemented from within the mainline churches that would bring millennials back into the fold, or are they gone for good? The incarnational approach to youth ministry developed by the parachurch ministries of the 1970s and 1980s, especially Young Life, was so successful in reaching young people that the denominational churches began modeling their youth programs after them. Are there similar ways that youth ministries at traditional churches could adopt some of the discipleship practices and methods of millennials in missional settings? Many traditional churches are in the process of developing church plants and satellite churches that are missional in orientation, but there is a gap within young adult ministry for this type of approach. This could be a critical topic for the future of the church.

SUMMARY

Much of the academic literature has focused on the deficiencies of millennials' faith. There is sufficient data to support this claim. However, if emerging adults reflect the attitudes and priorities of the American church at large, then perhaps the church needs to think reflexively about its own deficiencies, especially in the area of discipleship.[6] Perhaps the mission field, the liminal spaces, is where God is working to bring renewal and recalibration.

The scene is a bit like that of Moses at Mount Sinai in Exodus 32. He and his young aide, Joshua, ventured away from the Israelite camp to meet with God and receive a new set of instructions for the people. Upon their return to camp, they found the Israelites engaged in idolatry. Moses had been gone so long that the community had given up on him, saying, "We don't know what happened to him." (Ex. 32:1). Perhaps, in the same way, missional leaders and their millennial disciples have been meeting with God in remote places, receiving a new blueprint for the church. Will the church consider what they are bringing back from their adventure? Will the church allow some of its sacred cows—culturally bound forms, symbols, practices, and expressions—to be smashed? Or has the church given up on millennials, lamenting, "We don't know what has happened to them?" It is possible that the millennials may be carrying with them the "stone tablets" of the blueprint of the future of the church. It is time to take them seriously.

The remarkable thing about the Christian faith is its focus on redemption. God is continually "making everything new" as part of his ongoing restoration (Rev. 21:5). Throughout the ages, he has consistently extracted the gold from his people, pulling out the "riches stored in secret places" for the praise of his glory (Isa. 45:3). The eschatological reality is that God will continue to redeem the generations, for he has promised a bride "without stain or wrinkle or any other blemish" until the day of his return (Eph. 5:27). There are problems to be solved, to be sure. The current problems in discipleship, however, are temporal; they are simply growing pains as the church, his bride, adapts to new situations. His redemption remains a constant throughout the volatility of navigating change. What a privilege to participate in the equipping of his millennial disciples who will be tomorrow's faith leaders and ensure the transmission of the gospel and the discipleship of the faithful for ages to come.

BIBLIOGRAPHY

Alch, Mark L. "The Echo-Boom Generation: A Growing Force in American Society." *The Futurist* 34, no. 5 (September/October 2000): 42–46. Accessed March 18, 2020. https://search.proquest.com/docview/218599582?accountid=8155.

Alford, Chris. "Chris Alford: Worship (The Purpose of the Church)." *Alumni Blog, The Robert E. Webber Institute for Worship Studies* (December 31, 2004): 1–21. https://iws.edu/2004/12/chris-alford-worship-the-purpose-of-the-church/.

Andrews, Alan with Christopher Morton. "Introduction: The Journey of TACT." In *The Kingdom Life: A Practical Theology of Discipleship and Spiritual Formation.* Edited by Alan Andrews. Colorado Springs: NavPress, 2010.

Andrews, Christopher. "Sociological Imagination." In *The Blackwell Encyclopedia of Sociology.* Edited by G. Ritzer. Wiley Online Library. October 26, 2015. https://doi.org/10.1002/9781405165518.wbeoss205.

Armstrong, Chris. "The Rise, Frustration, and Revival of Evangelical Spiritual Ressourcement." *Journal of Spiritual Formation & Soul Care* 2, no. 1 (2009): 113–21. https://doi.org/10.1177/193979090900200107.

Arnett, Jeffrey Jensen. *Emerging Adulthood: The Winding Road from the Late Teens through the Twenties.* New York: Oxford University Press, 2006.

Arnett, Jeffrey Jensen and Lene Arnett Jensen. "A Congregation of One: Individualized Religious Beliefs among Emerging Adults."

Journal of Adolescent Research 17, no. 5 (September 2002): 451–67. https://doi.org/10.1177%2F0743558402175002.

Arnett, Jeffrey Jensen, Marion Kloep, Leo B. Hendry, and Jennifer L. Tanner. *Debating Emerging Adulthood: Stage or Process?* Oxford: Oxford University Press, 2011.

Arnett, Jeffrey Jensen, Kali H. Trzesniewski, and M. Brent Donnellan. "The Dangers of Generational Myth-Making: Rejoinder to Twenge." *Emerging Adulthood* 1, no. 1 (March 1, 2013): 17–20. http:// journals.sagepub.com/doi/abs/10.1177/2167696812466848.

Bader-Saye, Scott. "Improvising Church: An Introduction to the Emerging Church Conversation." *International Journal for the Study of the Christian Church* 6, no. 1 (2006): 12–23. https://doi. org/10.1080/14742250500484519.

Barna Group. *The Connected Generation: How Christian Leaders around the World Can Strengthen Faith and Well-Being Among 18–35-Year-Olds.* Ventura, Calif.: Barna Group, 2019.

————. "A New Chapter in Millennial Church Attendance." *Articles in Faith & Christianity.* August 4, 2022. https://www. barna.com/research/church-attendance-2022/?utm_source =Newsletter&utm_medium=email&utm_content=Barna +Update%3A+A+New+Chapter+in+Millennial+Church +Attendance&utm_campaign=2022-8-3_Church +Attendance+2022_BU.

Barnett, Victoria J. and Barbara Wojhoski, ed. *Dietrich Bonhoeffer Works.* Vol. 8. *Letters and Papers from Prison.* Minneapolis: Fortress Press, 2010.

Barrett, Lois. "Defining Missional Church." In *Evangelical, Ecumenical, and Anabaptist Missiologies in Conversation: Essays in Honor of Wilbert R. Shenk,* 177–83. Edited by James R. Krabill, Walter Sawatsky, and Charles E. Van Engen. Maryknoll: Orbis, 2006. https://www.mwc-cmm.org/sites/default/files/website_files/ miscom-fd-barrett_defining_missional_church.pdf.

Barton, Bernadette. *Stripped: More Stories from Exotic Dancers.* 2nd ed. New York: New York University Press, 2017.

Beard, Christopher. "Missional Discipleship: Discerning Spiritual-Formation Practices and Goals within the Missional Movement." *Missiology: An International Review* 43, no. 2 (2014): 175–94. https://doi.org/10.1177/0091829614563059.

Bebbington, David. "Evangelical Conversion, c. 1740–1850." *Scottish Bulletin of Evangelical Theology* 18, no. 2 (2000): 102–27.

_____. *Evangelicalism in Modern Britain: A History from the 1730s to the 1980s*. London and New York: Routledge, 1989.

Bedford, Nancy E. "Little Moves against Destructiveness: Theology and the Practice of Discernment." In *Practicing Theology: Beliefs and Practices in Christian Life*, 157–81. Edited by Miroslav Volf and Dorothy C. Bass. Grand Rapids: Eerdmans, 2001.

Behar, Ruth. *The Vulnerable Observer: Anthropology That Breaks Your Heart*. Boston: Beacon Press, 1996. https://www.academia.edu/24946657/Ruth_Behar_The_Vulnerable_Observer_Anthropology_That_Breaks_Your_Heart.

The Bible Project. "Witness." https://thebibleproject.com/explore/witness/.

Bjork, David E. *Every Believer a Disciple! Joining in God's Mission*. Cumbria, U.K.: Langham Global Library, 2015.

Bogdan, Robert and Sari Knopp Biklen. *Qualitative Research for Education: An Introduction to Theory and Methods*. 2nd ed. Allyn and Bacon, 1992.

Bonhoeffer, Dietrich. *The Cost of Discipleship*. Rev. ed. New York: Collier Books, 1963.

_____. *Creation and Fall/Temptation: Two Biblical Studies*. Translated by Kathleen Downham. London: SCM, 1959.

_____. *Dietrich Bonhoeffer Works*. Vol. 1. *Sanctorum Communio: A Theological Study of the Sociology of the Church*. Edited by Clifford J. Green. Translated by Reinhard Krauss and Nancy Lukens. Minneapolis: Fortress Press, 1998.

_____. *Dietrich Bonhoeffer Works*. Vol. 4. *Discipleship*. Edited by Geffrey B. Kelly and John D. Godsey. Translated by Barbara Green and Reinhard Krauss. Minneapolis: Fortress Press, 2003.

_____. *Dietrich Bonhoeffer Works*. Vol. 6. *Ethics*. Edited by Clifford J. Green. Translated by Reinhard Krauss, Charles C. West, and Douglas W. Scott. Minneapolis: Fortress Press, 2005.

_____. *Dietrich Bonhoeffer Works*. Vol. 8. *Letters and Papers from Prison*. Edited by John W. DeGruchy. Translated by Isabel Best, Lisa E. Dahill, Reinhard Krauss, and Nancy Lukens. Minneapolis: Fortress Press, 2010.

_____. *Dietrich Bonhoeffer Works*. Vol. 11. *Ecumenical, Academic, and Pastoral Work*. Edited by Victoria J. Barnett, Mark S. Brocker, and Michael B. Lukens. Translated by Anne Schmidt-Lange, with Isabel Best, Nicolas Humphrey, and Marion Pauck. Minneapolis: Fortress Press, 2012.

_____. *Discipleship*. Minneapolis: Fortress Press, 2003.

_____. *Ethics*. Translated by Reinhard Krauss. Minneapolis: Fortress Press, 2015.

_____. *Life Together*. New York: Harper and Row, 1954.

_____. "Sermon for Whitsunday, 1940." In *The Cost of Moral Leadership: The Spirituality of Dietrich Bonhoeffer*. Edited by Geffrey B. Kelly and F. Burton Nelson. Grand Rapids: Eerdmans, 2003.

Bradley-Geist, Jill C. and Julie B. Olson-Buchanan. "Helicopter Parents: An Examination of the Correlates of Over-Parenting of College Students." *Education + Training* 56, no. 4 (2014): 314–28. https://doi.org/10.1108/ET-10-2012-0096.

Bramer, Paul. "Guest Editorial: Introduction to the Special Focus: Spiritual Formation and Christian Education." *Christian Education Journal* 7, no 2 (2010): 334–49. https://doi.org/10.1177/073989131000700207.

Brewer, J. *Ethnography*. Buckingham, U.K.: Open University Press, 2000.

Brown, Ryan, Karolyn Budzek, and Michael Tamborski. "On the Meaning and Measure of Narcissism." *Personality and Social Psychology Bulletin* 35, no. 7 (June 1, 2009): 951–64. http://journals.sagepub.com/doi/abs/10.1177/0146167209335461.

Browning, Don S. "Altruism and Christian Love." *Zygon* 27, no. 4 (1992): 421–36. https://doi.org/10.1111/j.1467-9744.1992.tb01077.x.

Byrd, Nathan C. "Narrative Discipleship: Guiding Emerging Adults to 'Connect the Dots, of Life and Faith.'" *Christian Education Journal: Series 3* 8, no. 2 (2011): 244–62. Accessed August 13, 2020. https://doi.org/10.1177/073989131100800202.

Carson, D. A. *Christ and Culture Revisited.* Grand Rapids: Eerdmans, 2008.

———. *Showing the Spirit.* Grand Rapids: Baker, 1987.

Carter, Craig A. *Rethinking Christ and Culture: A Post-Christendom Perspective.* Grand Rapids: Brazos, 2006.

Clark, Jeff. "Philosophy, Understanding and the Consultation: A Fusion of Horizons." *The British Journal of General Practice* 58 (January 2008): 58–60. https://www.ncbi.nlm.nih.gov/pmc/articles/PMC2148246/.

Cloeter, Jeff. "On Millennials and Story." *Missio Apostolica: Journal of the Lutheran Society for Missiology* XXI, no. 1 (May 2013): 48–54. https://www.lsfm.global/our-journals/.

Codrington, Graeme. "Detailed Introduction to Generational Theory." *Tomorrow Today* (July 2008). https://workspacedesigncoza.files.wordpress.com/2017/04/tomorrowtoday_detailed_intro_to_generations.pdf.

Creswell, John W. *Qualitative Inquiry and Research Design: Choosing Among Five Approaches.* 2nd ed. London: Sage, 2007.

Cunningham, Loren. "Transcript of Interview of Loren Cunningham on Original 7 Mountains Vision." http://www.7culturalmountains.org/apps/articles/default.asp?articleid=40087&columnid=4347.

Dahill, Lisa. "Probing the Will of God: Bonhoeffer and Discernment." *Dialog: A Journal of Theology* 41, no. 1 (Spring 2002): 42–49. https://onlinelibrary.wiley.com/doi/epdf/10.1111/1540-6385.00098.

Daniel, Lillian. *Tell It Like It Is: Reclaiming the Practice of Testimony.* Lanham: Rowman and Littlefield, 2006.

Datt, Shruti. "Differences and Similarities in Grounded Theory and Ethnography." *Project Guru*, May 26, 2014. https://www. projectguru.in/grounded-theory-ethnography/.

Davies, C. A. *Reflexive Ethnography: A Guide to Researching Selves and Others*. 2nd ed. London: Routledge, 2008.

Dean, Kenda Creasy. *Almost Christian: What the Faith of Our Teenagers Is Telling the American Church*. Oxford: Oxford University Press, 2010.

Delamont, Sara. "Ethnography and Participant Observation." In *Qualitative Research Practice*, 205–17. Edited by Clive Seale, Giampietro Gobo, Jaber F. Gubrium, and David Silverman. London: Sage, 2004.

Demy, Timothy J. and Paul R. Shockley, ed. *Evangelical America: An Encyclopedia of Contemporary American Religious Culture*. Santa Barbara: ABC-CLIO, 2017.

Dimock, Michael. "Defining Generations: Where Millennials End and Generation Z Begins." Fact Tank: News in the Numbers. Pew Research Center. https://www.pewresearch.org/fact-tank/2019/01/17/where-millennials-end-and-generation-z-begins/.

Doberstein, John W. "Introduction." In Dietrich Bonhoeffer, *Life Together: A Discussion of Christian Fellowship*. San Francisco: HarperCollins, 1954.

Duncan, L. E. and G. S. Agronick. "The Intersection of Life Stage and Social Events: Personality and Life Outcomes." *Journal of Personality and Social Psychology* 69, no. 3 (1995): 558–68. https://psycnet.apa.org/doi/10.1037/0022-3514.69.3.558.

Dunn, Richard R. and Jana L. Sundene. *Shaping the Journey of Emerging Adults: Life-Giving Rhythms for Spiritual Transformation*. Downers Grove, Ill.: InterVarsity Press, 2012.

Dykstra, Craig and Dorothy C. Bass. "A Theological Understanding of Christian Practices." *Lifelong Faith* 2, no. 2 (Summer 2008): 3–18. https://www.lifelongfaith.com/uploads/5/1/6/4/5164069/lifelong_faith_journal_2.2.pdf.

Ellingston, Laura L. "'Then You Know How I Feel': Empathy, Identification, and Reflexivity in Fieldwork." *Qualitative Inquiry* 4, no. 4 (1998): 492–514. https://doi.org/10.1177/107780049800400405.

Elwood, Sarah A. and Deborah G. Martin. "'Placing' Interviews: Location and Scales of Power in Qualitative Research." *Professional Geographer* 52, no. 4 (November 2000): 649–57. https://doi.org/10.1080/0966369X.2017.1339022.

Emerson, R., I. Fretz, and L. L. Shaw. "Participant Observation and Fieldnotes." In *Handbook of Ethnography*, 352–68. Edited by Paul Atkinson, Amanda Coffey, Sara Delamont, John Lofland, and Lyn A. Lofland. London: Sage, 2001.

England, Kim. "Getting Personal: Reflexivity, Positionality and Feminist Research." *The Professional Geographer* 46, no. 1 (January 1994): 80–89. Accessed July 12, 2020. https://www.researchgate.net/publication/227706307_Getting_Personal_Reflexivity_Positionality_and_Feminist_Research.

Erikson, Erik H. *The Life Cycle Completed*. New York: Norton, 1998.

Erickson, Millard J. *Christian Theology*, 2nd ed. Grand Rapids: Baker, 1998.

————. "Christology from an Evangelical Perspective." *Review & Expositor* 88, no. 4 (December 1991): 379–97. https://doi.org/10.1177%2F003463739108800405.

Evans, Rachel Held. "Why Millennials Are Leaving the Church." CNN Belief Blog. July 27, 2013. http://religion.blogs.cnn.com/2013/07/27/why-millennials-are-leaving-the-church/.

Ferguson, Sinclair. *The Holy Spirit: Contours of Christian Theology*. Downers Grove, Ill.: InterVarsity Press, 1996.

Fitch, David E. *Faithful Presence: Seven Disciplines That Shape the Church for Mission*. Downers Grove, Ill.: InterVarsity Press, 2016.

————. "The Other Missional Conversation: Making Way for the Neo-Anabaptist Contribution to the Missional Movement in North America." *Missiology* 44, no. 4 (2016): 466–478. https://doi.org/10.1177/0091829616669180.

Fontana, Andrea and James H. Frey. "Interviewing." In *Handbook of Qualitative Research*. Edited by N. Denzin and Y. Lincoln. London: Sage, 1994.

Foster, Richard J. *Celebration of Discipline: The Path to Spiritual Growth*. New York: Harper Collins, 1988.

Foster, Richard with Kathryn A. Helmers. *Life with God: Reading the Bible for Spiritual Transformation*. San Francisco: Harper One, 2008.

Foster, Richard and James Bryan Smith, ed. *Devotional Classics: Selected Readings for Individuals and Groups*. San Francisco: Harper and Row, 1993.

Fox, Claire. *"I Find That Offensive!"* London: Biteback Publishing, 2016.

France, Alan and Steven Roberts. "The Problem of Social Generations: A Critique of the New Emerging Orthodoxy in Youth Studies." *Journal of Youth Studies* 18, no. 2 (2015): 215–30. https://doi.org/10.1080/13676261.2014.944122.

Frost, Michael. *Exiles: Living Missionally in a Post-Christian Culture*. Grand Rapids.: Baker, 2006.

Frost, Michael and Alan Hirsch. *ReJesus: A Wild Messiah for a Missional Church*. Grand Rapids: Baker, 2009.

————. *The Shaping of Things to Come: Innovation and Mission for the 21st Century Church*. Peabody, Mass.: Hendrickson, 2003.

Fuller Youth Institute. The Sticky Faith Research. https://fulleryouthinstitute.org/stickyfaith/research.

Gangel, Kenneth O. and James C. Wilhoit, ed. *The Christian Educator's Handbook on Spiritual Formation*. Wheaton, Ill.: Victor Books, 1994.

Gibbs, Eddie. *Churchmorph: How Megatrends Are Reshaping Christian Communities*. Grand Rapids: Baker Academic, 2009.

Glesne, Corrine. "Rapport and Friendship in Ethnographic Research." *International Journal of Qualitative Studies in Education* 2, no. 1 (1989): 45–54. https://doi.org/10.1080/0951839890020105.

Graue, Elizabeth and Anne Karabon. "Standing at the Corner of Epistemology Ave, Theoretical Trail, Methodology Blvd, and Methods Street: The Intersections of Qualitative Research." In

Reviewing Qualitative Research in the Social Sciences: A Guide for Researchers and Reviewers, 11–20. Edited by Audrey A. Trainor and Elizabeth Graue. London: Routledge. http://ebookcentral. proquest.com/lib/abdn/detail.action?docID=1143680.

Guder, Darrell. *The Incarnation and the Church's Witness.* Eugene, Ore.: Wipf & Stock, 2005.

Guder, Darrell, ed. *Missional Church: A Vision for the Sending of the Church in North America.* Grand Rapids: Eerdmans, 1998.

Hernandez, Wil. *Henri Nouwen and Soul Care: A Ministry of Integration.* New York: Paulist Press, 2008.

Hillman, Os. *Change Agent: Engaging Your Passion to Be the One Who Makes a Difference.* Lake Mary, Fla.: Charisma House, 2011.

Hirsch, Alan. *The Forgotten Ways: Reactivating Apostolic Movements.* Grand Rapids: Brazos, 2016.

Hirsch, Alan and Debra Hirsch. *Untamed (Shapevine): Reactivating a Missional Form of Discipleship.* Grand Rapids: Baker, 2010.

Holmes, Christopher R. J. "The Holy Spirit." In *The Oxford Handbook of Dietrich Bonhoeffer*, 168–78. Edited by Michael Mawson and Philip G. Ziegler. New York: Oxford University Press, 2019.

Houston, James M. "The Future of Spiritual Formation." *Journal of Spiritual Formation & Soul Care* 4, no. 2 (2011): 131–39. http:// www.kairos2.com/Voc.Holi.03_Houston_Future.of.Spiritual. Formation_JSFSC.Fall2011.pdf.

_____. *Joyful Exiles: Life in Christ on the Dangerous Edge of Things.* Downers Grove, Ill.: InterVarsity Press, 2006.

Hoyt, Thomas, Jr. "Testimony." In *Practicing Our Faith: A Way of Life for a Searching People*, 89–101. 2nd ed. Edited by Dorothy C. Bass. San Francisco: Jossey-Bass, 2010.

International Missionary Council. "The Growing Church: The Madras Series." Papers Based on the Meeting of the International Missionary Council at Tambaram, Madras, India, December 12–29, 1938. Vol. 2. New York: International Missionary Council, 1938.

Iorio, Genario. *Sociology of Love: The Agapic Dimension of Societal Life.* Vernon Art and Science Inc., 2015. Kindle.

Jennings, Willie James. *The Christian Imagination: Theology and the Origins of Race*. New Haven: Yale University Press, 2011.

Jones, Hywel R. "The Doctrine of the Holy Spirit in 20th Century Ecumenism." *The Banner of Truth* (November 17, 2003). https://banneroftruth.org/us/resources/articles/2003/the-doctrine-of-the-holy-spirit-in-20th-century-ecumenism/.

Keller, Tim J. *Ministries of Mercy: The Call of the Jericho Road*. 2nd ed. Phillipsburg, N. J.: Presbyterian & Reformed Publishing House, 1997.

Kertzer, David I. "Generation as a Sociological Problem." *Annual Review of Sociology* 9 (August 1983): 125–49. https://doi.org/10.1146/annurev.so.09.080183.001013.

Kierkegaard, Søren. *Kierkegaard's Writings*. Vol. XVI. *Works of Love*. Edited by Howard V. Hong and Edna H. Hong. Princeton: Princeton University Press, 1995.

Kimball, Dan. *They Like Jesus but Not the Church: Insights from Emerging Generations*. Grand Rapids: Zondervan, 2007.

Kinnaman, David. *You Lost Me: Why Young Christians Are Leaving Church . . . and Rethinking Faith*. Grand Rapids: Baker, 2011.

Kinnaman, David and Gabe Lyons. *unChristian: What a New Generation Thinks about Christianity . . . and Why It Matters*. Grand Rapids: Baker, 2007.

Kinnaman, David and Mark Matlock. *Faith for Exiles: 5 Ways for a New Generation to Follow Jesus in Digital Babylon*. Grand Rapids: Baker, 2019.

Kirby, Sandra and Kate McKenna. *Methods from the Margins: Experience, Research, Social Change*. Toronto: Garamond Press, 1989.

Kowske, Brenda J., Rena Rasch, and Jack Wiley. "'Millennials' (Lack of) Attitude Problem: An Empirical Examination of Generational Effects on Work Attitudes." *Journal of Business and Psychology* 25, no. 2 (June 2010): 265–79. http://www.jstor.org/stable/40605785?seq=1&cid=pdf-reference#references_tab_contents.

Kremenski, Karina. "The Discipline of Discerning the Holy Spirit." Missio Alliance. August 20, 2013. https://www.missioalliance. org/the-discipline-of-discerning-the-holy-spirit/.

Kuyper, Abraham. *The Work of the Holy Spirit*. New York: Funk and Wagnalls Company, 1900.

Labaree, Robert. "Research Guides: Organizing Your Social Sciences Research Paper: Writing Field Notes." USC Libraries Research Guides. Last modified June 25, 2020 at 11:23 a.m. https:// libguides.usc.edu/writingguide/fieldnotes.

Lakies, Chad. "Candy Machine God, or, Going to Church without Going to Church: Millennials and the Future of the Christian Faith." *Missio Apostolica: Journal of the Lutheran Society for Missiology* XXI, no. 1 (May 2013): 14–30. https://www.lsfm.global/uploads/ files/MA-5-13_Final_Online.pdf.

Langford, Michael D. "Spirit-Driven Discipleship: A Pneumatology of Youth Ministry." *Theology Today* 71, no. 3 (2014): 323–36. https://doi.org/10.1177%2F0040573614542309.

Lareau, Annette and Jeffrey Shultz, ed. *Journeys through Ethnography: Realistic Accounts of Fieldwork*. New York: Routledge, 1996.

Law, David R. "Christian Discipleship in Kierkegaard, Hirsch, and Bonhoeffer." *The Downside Review* 120, no. 421 (October 2002): 293–306. https://journals.sagepub.com/ doi/10.1177/001258060212042105.

Leeper, Roy V. and Kathie A. Leeper. "Public Relations as 'Practice': Applying the Theory of Alasdair MacIntyre." *Public Relations Review* 27, no. 4, (2001): 461–73. https://doi.org/10.1016/S0363-8111(01)00101-1.

Lee-Treweek, Geraldine and Stephanie Linkogle, ed. *Danger in the Field: Risk and Ethics in Social Research*. London: Routledge, 2006.

Legard, R., J. Keegan, and K. Ward. "In-Depth Interviews." In *Qualitative Research Practice*, 139–68. Edited by J. Richie and J. Lewis. London: Sage, 2003.

Lewis, C. S. *The Four Loves*. London: Geoffrey Bles, 1960.

_____. *Mere Christianity*. New York: Harper and Row, 1952.

Love, Curtis R. and Cornelius J. P. Niemandt, "Led by the Spirit: Missional Communities and the Quakers on Communal Vocation Discernment." *Herv. Teol. Stud.* 70, no. 1 (January 2014): 1–9. http://www.scielo.org.za/scielo.php?script=sci_arttext&pid=S0259-94222014000100051&lng=en&nrm=iso.

Lovelace, Richard F. *Dynamics of Spiritual Life: An Evangelical Theology of Renewal.* Downers Grove, Ill.: InterVarsity Press, 1979.

Luis, Michael. "The Python Now Has Two Pigs: Boomers and Millennials." *Washington Realtors* (September 2015): 1–15. https://www.warealtor.org/docs/default-source/ga-resources/millennials_final.pdf?sfvrsn=0.

MacIlvaine, W. Rodman, III "What Is the Missional Church Movement?" *Bibliotheca Sacra* 167 (January–March 2010): 89–106. https://www.dts.edu/download/publications/bibliotheca/DTS-What%20Is%20the%20Missional%20Church%20Movement.pdf.

Maddix, Mark A. and Jay Richard Akkerman. *Missional Discipleship: Partners in God's Redemptive Mission.* Kansas City: Beacon Hill Press, 2013.

Malinowski, Bronislaw. *Argonauts of the Western Pacific: An Account of Native Enterprise and Adventure in the Archipelagoes of Melanesian New Guinea.* London: Routledge and Kegan Paul, 1922. https://archive.org/details/in.gov.ignca.15655/page/n59/mode/2up.

Mannheim, Karl. *The Problem of Generations.* London: Routledge, 1928.

————. "The Problem of Generations." In *Karl Mannheim: Essays.* Edited by Paul Kecskemeti. Abington-on-Thames: Routledge, 1972.

Manser, Martin H., Alister E. McGrath, J. I. Packer, and Donald J. Wiseman, ed. *Zondervan Dictionary of Bible Themes: An Accessible and Comprehensive Tool for Topical Studies.* Grand Rapids: Zondervan, 1999.

Mason, Mark. "Sample Size and Saturation in Ph.D Studies Using Qualitative Interviews." *Forum Qualitative Social Research* 11, no. 3 (September 2010): [63 paragraphs]. http://www.qualitative-research.net/index.php/fqs/article/view/1428/3027.

McKnight, Scot. *Kingdom Conspiracy: Returning to the Radical Mission of the Church*. Grand Rapids: Brazos, 2014.

McLeod, J. *Qualitative Research in Counselling and Psychotherapy*. London: Sage, 2001.

Mercer, Philip. *Sympathy and Ethics: A Study of the Relationship Between Sympathy and Morality with Special Reference to Hume's Treatise*. Oxford: Clarendon Press, 1972.

Michaud, Derek ed. "Dietrich Bonhoeffer." *Boston Collaborative Encyclopedia of Western Theology*. Accessed January 9, 2020. http://people.bu.edu/wwildman/bce/bonhoeffer.htm.

Mies, M. "Towards a Methodology for Feminist Research." In *Theories of Women's Studies*, 117–39. Edited by G. Bowles and R. D. Klein. London: Routledge Kegan Paul, 1983.

Mikoski, Gordon S. "Educating and Forming Disciples for the Reign of God: Reflections on Youth Pilgrimages to the Holy Land." In *For Life Abundant: Practical Theology, Theological Education, and Christian Ministry*, 329–52. Edited by Dorothy C. Bass and Craig Dykstra. Grand Rapids: Eerdmans, 2008.

Moltmann, Jürgen. *The Spirit of Life: A Universal Affirmation*. Minneapolis: Fortress, 1992.

Morden, Peter. *The Message of Discipleship: Authentic Followers of Jesus in Today's World*. London: InterVarsity Press, 2018. Kindle.

Moritz, Joshua M. "Beyond Strategy, Towards the Kingdom of God: The Post-Critical Reconstructionist Mission of the Emerging Church." *Dialog: A Journal of Theology* 47, no. 1 (Spring 2008): 27–36. https://doi.org/10.1111/j.1540-6385.2008.00365.x.

Moschella, Mary Clark. *Ethnography as Pastoral Practice: An Introduction*. Cleveland: Pilgrim Press, 2008.

Mulholland, M. Robert, Jr. *Invitation to a Journey: A Road Map for Spiritual Formation*. Expanded by Ruth Haley Barton. Downers Grove, Ill.: InterVarsity Press, 2016.

Neufeld, Tim. "Postmodern Models of Youth Ministry." *Direction, A Mennonite Brethren Forum* 31, no. 2 (Fall 2002): 194–205. https:// directionjournal.org/31/2/postmodern-models-of-youth-ministry.html.

Newbigin, Lesslie. "Can the West Be Converted?" *International Bulletin of Missionary Research* 11, no. 1 (January 1987): 2–7.

————. *The Open Secret: An Introduction to the Theology of Mission.* Rev. ed. Grand Rapids: Eerdmans, 1995.

————. *The Relevance of Trinitarian Doctrine for Today's Mission.* London: Edinburgh House Press, 1963.

Niebuhr, H. Richard. *Christ and Culture.* San Francisco: Harper Collins, 1951.

Nouwen, Henri. *Discernment: Reading the Signs of Daily Life.* New York: Harper One, 2013.

————. *Lifesigns: Intimacy, Fecundity, and Ecstasy in Christian Perspective.* New York: Doubleday, 1986.

————. *Making All Things New: An Invitation to the Spiritual Life.* San Francisco: Harper and Row, 1981.

————. *Reaching Out: The Three Movements of the Spiritual Life.* New York: Doubleday, 1975.

O'Hanlon, Gerry. "Theological Reflection." *The Furrow* 46, no. 4 (April 1995): 232–36. https://www.jstor.org/stable/27662898?seq=1#metadata_info_tab_contents.

O'Reilly, K. *Ethnographic Methods.* London: Routledge, 2005.

Oden, Patrick. "An Emerging Pneumatology: Jürgen Moltmann and the Emerging Church Conversation." *Journal of Pentecostal Theology* 18 , no. 2 (2009): 263–84. https://doi.org/10.1163/096673609X12469601162150.

Ogden, Greg. *Transforming Discipleship: Making Disciples a Few at a Time.* Downers Grove, Ill.: InterVarsity Press, 2016.

Oldenburg, Ray. *The Great Good Place: Cafes, Coffee Shops, Bookstores, Bars, Hair Salons, and Other Hangouts at the Heart of a Community.* New York: Marlowe and Company, 1999.

Olson, Roger. *Against Calvinism.* Grand Rapids: Zondervan Academic, 2011.

Orr, James. "Entry for 'LOVE.'" *International Standard Bible Encyclopedia* (1915 ed.). https://www.biblestudytools.com/encyclopedias/isbe/love.html.

Ortiz, Anna. "The Ethnographic Interview." In *Research in the College Context: Approaches and Methods*, 35–48. Edited by Frances K. Stage and Kathleen Manning. New York: Brunner-Routledge, 2003.

Osmer, Richard. *Practical Theology: An Introduction*. Grand Rapids: Eerdmans, 2008.

Pajo, Bora. *Introduction to Research Methods: A Hands-On Approach*. Los Angeles: Sage, 2018. https://us.sagepub.com/sites/default/files/upm-assets/83269_book_item_83269.pdf.

Parahoo, Kader. *Nursing Research, Principles, Process and Issues*. London: MacMillan Press, 1997.

Pattison, Stephen and Gordon Lynch. "Pastoral and Practical Theology." In *The Modern Theologians: An Introduction to Christian Theology since 1918*, 408–26. 3rd ed. Edited by David F. Ford with Rachel Muers. Malden, Mass.: Blackwell Publishing, 2005.

Peterson, Eugene. "Living into God's Story." https://static1.squarespace.com/static/55a6400fe4b0062f1359e218/t/581ef178d2b85747b9d-d2e7c/1478422904361/Living+into+God%27s+Story.pdf.

Pew Research Center. "Millennials in Adulthood: Detached from Institutions, Networked with Friends." March 2014. https://www.pewsocialtrends.org/2014/03/07/millennials-in-adulthood/#fn-18663-1.

Pineda, Ana Maria. "Hospitality." In *Practicing Our Faith: A Way of Life for a Searching People*, 29–42. 2nd ed. Edited by Dorothy C. Bass. San Francisco: Jossey-Bass, 2010.

Pinnacle Forum. "The Seven Mountains of Culture." https://pinnacleforum.com/about/.

Pitts, Margaret Jane and Michelle Miller-Day. "Upward Turning Points and Positive Rapport-Development Across Time in Researcher-Participant Relationships." *Qualitative Research* 7, no. 2 (May 2007): 177–201. https://doi.org/10.1177%2F1468794107071409.

Pohl, Christine D. *Making Room: Recovering Hospitality As a Christian Tradition*. Grand Rapids: Eerdmans, 1999.

Porter, Steven L. "Is the Spiritual Formation Movement Dead?" *Journal of Spiritual Formation and Soul Care* 8, no. 1 (2015): 843–61. http://www.jstor.org/stable/2090964?origin=JSTOR-pdf.

Prior, Lindsey. "Documents." In *Qualitative Research Practice*, 345–60. Edited by Clive Seale, Giampietro Gobo, Jaber F. Gubrium, and David Silverman. London: Sage, 2004. http://ebookcentral. proquest.com/lib/abdn/detail.action?docID=1138447.

Rainer, Thom S. and Jess W. Rainer. *The Millennials: Connecting to America's Largest Generation*. Nashville: B&H Publishing Group, 2011.

Raines, Claire. "Managing Millennials." Academia.edu (2002). https:// www.academia.edu/13219793/Managing_Millennials.

Rainwater, Conan. "Christian Base Communities in Peru: Lessons for North America." *Quest: A Journal of Undergraduate Research* 5 (2015): 81–94. https://dspace2.creighton.edu/xmlui/bitstream/ handle/10504/111837/Article_6.pdf?sequence=1&isAllowed=y

Rapley, Tim. "Interviews." In *Qualitative Research Practice*, 15–33. Edited by Clive Seale, Giampietro, Gobo, Jaber F. Gubrium, and David Silverman. London: Sage, 2004. https://ebookcentral.proquest.com/lib/abdn/reader.action? docID=1138447&ppg=1&query=qualitative%20research%20 practice.

Renovaré Institute for Christian Spiritual Formation. https://renovare. org/institute/overview.

Rogers, Frank, Jr. "Discernment." In *Practicing Our Faith: A Way of Life for a Searching People*, 103–16. Edited by Dorothy C. Bass. San Francisco: Jossey-Bass, 2010.

Root, Andrew. *Bonhoeffer as Youth Worker: A Theological Vision for Discipleship and Life Together*. Grand Rapids: Baker Academic, 2014.
_____. *Christopraxis: A Practical Theology of the Cross*. Minneapolis: Fortress Press, 2014.

Roxburgh, Alan J. "The Missional Church." *Theology Matters* 10, no. 4 (September/October 2004): 1–8. https://theologymatters.com/wp-content/uploads/2020/03/04Vol10-No4-TM.pdf.

_____. *The Sky Is Falling*. Eagle, Ida.: ACI.

Ryder, Norman B." The Cohort as a Concept in the Study of Social Change." *American Sociological Review* 30, no. 6, (December 1965): 843–61. https://www.jstor.org/stable/2090964.

Ryen, Ann. "Research Ethics and Qualitative Research." *Qualitative Research*. 4th ed. Edited by David Silverman. London: Sage, 2016.

Sanders, Teela. "Becoming an Ex-Sex Worker: Making Transitions Out of a Deviant Career." *Feminist Criminology* 2, no. 1 (January 2007): 74–95. https://doi.org/10.1177/1557085106294845.

Saldaña, Johnny. *The Coding Manual for Qualitative Researchers*. Los Angeles: Sage, 2016.

Savin-Baden, Maggi and Claire Howell Major. *Qualitative Research: The Essential Guide to Theory and Practice*. New York and London: Routledge, 2013.

Scharen, Christian. "Practices of Dispossession: The Shape of Discipleship in a Church Taken, Blessed, Broken, and Given." In *Cultivating Sent Communities: Missional Spiritual Formation*. Edited by Dwight J. Zscheile. Grand Rapids: Eerdmans, 2012.

Schmalzbauer, John. "Campus Ministry: A Statistical Portrait." *SSRC Web Forum* (December 2007). http://religion.ssrc.org/reforum/Schmalzbauer.pdf.

Schoon, Christopher James. *Cultivating an Evangelistic Character: Integrating Worship and Discipleship in the Missional Church Movement*. Eugene, Ore.: Wipf & Stock, 2018.

Seale, Clive, Giampietro Gobo, Jaber F. Gubrium, and David Silverman, ed. "Field Relations." In *Qualitative Research Practice*, 203–04. London: Sage, 2004. https://ebookcentral.proquest.com/lib/abdn/detail.action?docID=1138447.

Seel, David John. *The New Copernicans: Understanding the Millennial Contribution to the Church*. Nashville: Thomas Nelson, 2018.

Senter, Mark H. III. *Four Views of Youth Ministry and the Church.* Edited by Mark H. Senter III. Grand Rapids: Zondervan, 2001.

_____. "A History of Youth Ministry Education in the USA." *Journal of Adult Theological Education* 11, no. 1 (May 2014): 46–60. https://doi.org/10.1179/1740714114Z.00000000011.

_____. *When God Shows Up: A History of Protestant Youth Ministry in America.* Grand Rapids: Baker Academic, 2010.

Setran, David P. and Christ A. Kiesling. *Spiritual Formation in Emerging Adulthood: A Practical Theology for College and Young Adults Ministry.* Grand Rapids: Baker Books, 2013.

Sexton, Jason S. "Missional Theology's Missing Ingredient: The Necessity of Systematic Theology for Today's Mission." *Mission Studies* 32 (2015): 384–97. https://static1.squarespace.com/static/5998d28af5e231fe01b43226/t/599fbbf2a803bbdd82 7a5d68/1503640563605/Missional_Theology_s_Missing_Ingredient.pdf.

Shelley, Bruce L. *Church History in Plain Language.* 2nd ed. Dallas: Word, 1995.

Sheridan, Tim M. and Jurgens Hendriks. "The Missional Church Movement." *NGTT* 54, no. 3 & 4 (September and December 2013): 1–13. https://doi.org/10.5952/54-3-4-402.

Siegrist, Anthony. "Colonialism and Mission: 4 Lessons We Must Learn from History." *Missio Alliance* (December 6, 2018). https://www.missioalliance.org/colonialism-and-mission-4-lessons-we-can-learn-from-history/.

Silva, Jennifer M. "Slight Expectations: Making Sense of the 'Me Me Me' Generation." *Sociology Compass* 8, no. 12 (December 2014): 1388–97. http://onlinelibrary.wiley.com/doi/10.1111/soc4.12227/abstract.

Smith, Christian and Melina Denton Lundquist. *Soul Searching: The Religious and Spiritual Lives of American Teenagers.* New York: Oxford University Press, 2005.

Smith, Christian and Patricia Snell. *Souls in Transition: The Religious and Spiritual Lives of Emerging Adults.* New York: Oxford University Press, 2009.

Smith, Gordon. *Beginning Well: Christian Conversion and Authentic Transformation*. Downers Grove, Ill.: InterVarsity Press, 2001.

Smith, Kevin G. "Review of Richard Osmer, Practical Theology: An Introduction." *Conspectus: The Journal of the South African Theological Seminary* 10, no. 1 (2010): 99–113. https://www.sats.edu.za/wp-content/uploads/2020/02/Smith_ReviewOsmer.pdf.

Sorokin, Pitirim. *The Ways and Power of Love: Types, Factors, and Techniques*. Radnor, Pa.: Templeton Foundation Press, 2002.

Spradley, J. P. *The Ethnographic Interview*. New York: Harcourt Brace Jovanovich, 1979.

Stearns, Richard. *Unfinished: Filling the Hole in Our Gospel*. Nashville: Thomas Nelson, 2013.

Stern, Phyllis. "Eroding Grounded Theory." In *Critical Issues in Qualitative Research Methods*. Edited by Janice M. Morse. Los Angeles: Sage, 1994.

Stetzer, Ed. "Is Your Church Missional?" *On Mission*. Pastor's Edition (2006).

_____. "The Missional Nature of the Church and the Future of Southern Baptist Convention Churches." In *The Mission of Today's Church: Baptist Leaders Look at Modern Faith Issues*, 73–94. Edited by R. Stanton Norman. Nashville: B & H Academic, 2007. Kindle.

_____. "Monday Is for Missiology: Missional Voices." *The Exchange with Ed Stetzer* (blog), *Christianity Today* April 19, 2020. https://www.christianitytoday.com/edstetzer/2010/april/monday-is-for-missiology-missional-voices.html.

_____. *Planting Missional Churches: Planting a Church That's Biblically Sound and Reaching People in Culture*. Nashville: B & H Publishing Group, 2006.

Stott, John. *The Contemporary Christian: An Urgent Plea for Double Listening*. Leicester, U.K.: InterVarsity Press, 1992.

_____. *The Radical Disciple: Some Neglected Aspects of Our Calling*. Downers Grove, Ill.: InterVarsity Press, 2010.

Strauss, William and Neil Howe. *Generations: The History of America's Future, 1584 to 2069*. New York: Harper and Row, 1991.

Strong, James. *The New Strong's Exhaustive Concordance of the Bible.* Nashville: Thomas Nelson, 1990.

Swinton, John. "Time, Hospitality, and Belonging: Towards a Practical Theology of Mental Health." *Word & World* 35, no. 2 (Spring 2015): 171–81. https://wordandworld.luthersem.edu/issues.aspx? article_id=3849.

————. "'Where Is Your Church': Moving Toward a Hospitable and Sanctified Ethnography." In *Perspectives on Ecclesiology and Ethnography*, 71–92. Edited by Pete Ward. Grand Rapids: Eerdmans, 2012.

Swinton, John and Harriet Mowat. *Practical Theology and Qualitative Research.* London: SCM Press, 2013.

Taylor, John. *The Go-Between God: The Holy Spirit and the Christian Mission.* London: SCM Press, 1972.

Tozer, A. W. *The Pursuit of God: The Human Thirst for the Divine.* Camp Hill, Pa.: Christian Publications, 1993.

Tracy, Sarah J. "Qualitative Quality: Eight 'Big-Tent-Criteria for Excellent Qualitative Research'" *Qualitative Inquiry* 16, no. 10 (2010): 837–51. https://doi.org/10.1177%2F1077800410383121.

Trull, T. J., S. Jahng, R. L. Tomko, P. K. Wood, and K. J. Sher. "Revised NESARC Personality Disorder Diagnoses: Gender, Prevalence, and Comorbidity with Substance Dependence Disorders." *Journal of Personality Disorders* 24, no. 4 (August 2010): 412–26. https://europepmc.org/article/med/20695803.

Twenge, Jean. *Generation Me: Why Today's Young Americans Are More Confident, Assertive, Entitled—and More Miserable Than Ever Before.* New York: Free Press, 2006.

Twenge, Jean M., W. Keith Campbell, and Elise C. Freeman. "Generational Differences in Young Adults' Life Goals, Concern for Others, and Civic Orientation, 1966–2009." *Journal of Personality and Social Psychology* 102, no. 5 (2012): 1045–62. https://www.apa.org/pubs/journals/releases/psp-102-5-1045.pdf.

Twenge, Jean M., Sara Konrath, Joshua D. Foster, Keith W. Campbell, and Brad J. Bushman. "Egos Inflating Over Time: A Cross-

Temporal Meta-Analysis of the Narcissistic Personality Inventory." *Journal of Personality* 76, no. 4, (August 2008): 875–902. http://onlinelibrary.wiley.com/doi/10.1111/j.1467-6494.2008. 00507.x/abstract.

Tyra, Gary. *The Holy Spirit in Mission.* Downers Grove, Ill.: InterVarsity Press, 2011.

Van Gelder, Craig. "Rethinking Denominations and Denominationalism in Light of a Missional Ecclesiology." *Word and World* 25, no.1 (Winter 2005): 23–33. Accessed August 13, 2020. https://wordandworld.luthersem.edu/content/pdfs/25-1_ Denominations/25-1_VanGelder.pdf.

Van Gelder, Craig, and Dwight J. Zscheile. *The Missional Church in Perspective: Mapping Trends and Shaping the Conversation.* Grand Rapids: Baker Academic, 2011.

van Manen, Max. *Researching Lived Experience: Human Science for an Action Sensitive Pedagogy.* New York: State University of New York Press, 1990. https://ebookcentral.proquest.com/lib/abdn/ detail.action?docID=3408268.

Vanden Berg, Mary L. "Bonhoeffer's Discipleship: Theology for the Purpose of Christian Formation." *Calvin Theological Journal* 44 (2009): 333–50. https://www.calvin.edu/library/database/crcpi/ fulltext/ctj/2009-442-333.pdf.

Ward, Pete. *Introducing Practical Theology: Mission, Ministry, and the Life of the Church.* Grand Rapids: Baker Academic, 2017.

————. *Liquid Church.* Eugene, Ore.: Wipf & Stock, 2002.

Warren, Rick. "Your Testimony: Sharing Your Life Message." In *The Complete Evangelism Guidebook: Expert Advice on Reaching Others for Christ*, 61–65. 2nd ed. Edited by Scott Dawson. Grand Rapids: Baker, 2006.

Watson, David. *Discipleship.* London: Hodder & Stoughton, 1981.

White, David P. *Practicing Discernment with Youth: A Transformative Youth Ministry Approach.* Eugene, Ore.: Wipf & Stock, 2005.

Wilkins, Michael J. *Following the Master: Discipleship in the Steps of Jesus.* Grand Rapids: Zondervan, 1992.

Willard, Dallas. *The Divine Conspiracy: Rediscovering Our Hidden Life in God*. New York: Harper One, 1997.

————. *Renovation of the Heart: Putting on the Character of Christ*. Colorado Springs: NavPress, 2002.

————. *The Spirit of the Disciplines: Understanding How God Changes Lives*. San Francisco: Harper and Row, 1988.

Willig, Carla. *Introducing Qualitative Research in Psychology: Adventures in Theory and Method*. London: McGraw-Hill, 2001.

Wright, J. H. *The Mission of God*. Downers Grove, Ill.: InterVarsity Press, 2006.

Wright, N. T. *Simply Christian: Why Christianity Makes Sense*. San Francisco: Harper Collins, 2006.

Wüstenberg, Ralf K. *A Theology of Life: Dietrich Bonhoeffer's Religionless Christianity*. Grand Rapids: Eerdmans, 1998.

Wyn, Johanna and Dan Woodman. "Generation, Youth and Social Change in Australia." *Journal of Youth Studies* 9, no. 5 (2006): 495–514. https://doi.org/10.1080/13676260600805713.

Zscheile, Dwight. "A Missional Theology of Spiritual Formation." In *Cultivating Sent Communities: Missional Spiritual Formation*, 1–28. Edited by Dwight J. Zscheile. Grand Rapids: Eerdmans, 2012.

CHAPTER NOTES

CHAPTER 1

1.   I have employed the use of pseudonyms throughout the book, except in the case of Morgan. She was so pleased to be quoted that she preferred the use of her own name.

2.   A common enough problem that National Public Radio warned about in the article by Michel Martin: "'Millennials': Be Careful How We Use This Label," https://www.npr.org/2017/12/09/569413425/millennials-be-careful-how-we-use-this-label.

3.   Claire Fox, *"I Find That Offensive!"* (London: Biteback Publications, 2016), 57.

4.   Richard Osmer, *Practical Theology: An Introduction* (Grand Rapids: Eerdmans, 2008), 24.

5.   Osmer, *Practical Theology*, 24.

6.   John Swinton and Harriet Mowat, *Practical Theology and Qualitative Research* (London: SCM Press, 2013), 13.

7.   Swinton and Mowat, *Practical Theology*, 5.

8.   Jeffrey Jensen Arnett, *Emerging Adulthood: The Winding Road from the Late Teens through the Twenties* (New York: Oxford University Press, 2006), 3–4.

9.   Arnett, *Emerging Adulthood*, 6.

10.   David P. Setran and Chris A. Kiesling, *Spiritual Formation in Emerging Adulthood: A Practical Theology for College and Young Adults Ministry* (Grand Rapids: Baker, 2013), 2.

11.   Jean Twenge, *Generation Me: Why Today's Young Americans Are More Confident, Assertive, Entitled— and More Miserable Than Ever Before* (New York: Free Press, 2006), 92–106. Twenge has conducted extensive

research on this demographic, and her conclusion is that millennials are the most narcissistic generation in history. It is possible, however, that the rise in narcissism is not unique to millennials; sociologist Christopher Lasch had written in the 1970s about a larger, society-wide narcissistic turn in his work *The Culture of Narcissism: American Life in an Age of Diminishing Expectations* (New York: W. W. Norton and Company, Inc., 1979), xv.

12.   David John Seel, *The New Copernicans: Understanding the Millennial Contribution to the Church* (Nashville: Thomas Nelson, 2018), 20.

13.   Seel, *The New Copericans*, 11.

14.   Ibid., 5.

15.   Ibid., x.

16.   Ibid., 30.

17.   Ibid., 102.

18.   Richard R. Dunn and Jana L. Sundene, *Shaping the Journey of Emerging Adults: Life-Giving Rhythms for Spiritual Transformation* (Downers Grove, Ill.: InterVarsity Press, 2012), 127.

19.   Darrell Guder, ed., *Missional Church: A Vision for the Sending of the Church in North America* (Grand Rapids: Eerdmans, 1998), 4.

20.   Alan Hirsch, *The Forgotten Ways: Reactivating Apostolic Movements* (Grand Rapids: Brazos, 2016), 145.

21.   Alan J. Roxburgh, *The Sky Is Falling* (Eagle, Ida.: ACI), 12.

22.   Edward Stetzer, *Planting Missional Churches: Planting a Church That's Biblically Sound and Reaching People in Culture* (Nashville: B&H Publishing Group, 2006), 8–9; Eddie Gibbs, *Churchmorph: How Megatrends Are Reshaping Christian Communities* (Grand Rapids: Baker Academic, 2009), 18.

23.   Hirsch, *The Forgotten Ways*, 241–42, 144.

24.   Gibbs, *Churchmorph*, 191, 15. Others are gravitating toward more ancient liturgical forms, what Robert Webber termed the "ancient-future" expression. Robert E. Webber, *The Younger Evangelicals: Facing the Challenges of the New World* (Grand Rapids: Baker, 2002), 20. Perhaps both of these expressions, missional and ancient-future, are reactions against the polished, highly produced form of young adult ministry of the church growth movement in recent decades.

25.   Hirsch, *The Forgotten Ways*, 112.

26. Dallas Willard, *Spirit of the Disciplines: Understanding How God Changes Lives* (San Francisco: Harper and Row, 1988), 15–16; John Stott, *The Radical Disciple: Some Neglected Aspects of Our Calling* (Downers Grove, Ill.: InterVarsity Press, 2010), 38–39.

27. Dietrich Bonhoeffer, *The Cost of Discipleship*, rev. ed. (New York: Collier Books, 1963), 99; Greg Ogden, *Transforming Discipleship: Making Disciples a Few at a Time* (Downers Grove, Ill.: InterVarsity Press, 2016), 22.

28. Rachel Held Evans, "Why Millennials Are Leaving the Church," CNN Belief Blog, July 27, 2013, accessed June 24, 2020, http://religion.blogs.cnn.com/2013/07/27/why-millennials-are-leaving-the-church/.

29. David E. Bjork, *Every Believer a Disciple! Joining in God's Mission* (Cumbria, U.K.: Langham Global Library, 2015), 4.

30. Alan Andrews with Christopher Morton, "Introduction: The Journey of TACT," in *The Kingdom Life: A Practical Theology of Discipleship and Spiritual Formation*, ed. Alan Andrews (Colorado Springs: NavPress, 2010), 10.

31. Bjork, *Every Believer a Disciple!*, 196.

32. Thom S. Rainer and Jess W. Rainer, *The Millennials: Connecting to America's Largest Generation* (Nashville: B&H Publishing Group, 2011), 236.

33. David Kinnaman, *You Lost Me: Why Young Christians Are Leaving Church . . . and Rethinking Faith* (Grand Rapids: Baker, 2011), 19.

34. Rainer and Rainer, *The Millennials*, 122.

35. Christian Smith and Melina Denton Lundquist, *Soul Searching: The Religious and Spiritual Lives of American Teenagers* (New York: Oxford University Press, 2005), 72.

36. Smith and Lundquist, *Soul Searching*, 162–63.

37. Kenda Creasy Dean, *Almost Christian: What the Faith of Our Teenagers Is Telling the American Church* (New York: Oxford University Press, 2010), 16; Christian Smith and Patricia Snell, *Souls in Transition: The Religious and Spiritual Lives of Emerging Adults* (New York: Oxford University Press, 2009), 154.

38. Smith and Lundquist, *Soul Searching*, 166.

39. Ibid., 170.

40. Hirsch, *The Forgotten Ways*, 111–13.

41.   Ibid., 109; Alan Hirsch and Debra Hirsch, *Untamed (Shapevine): Reactivating a Missional Form of Discipleship* (Grand Rapids: Baker Publishing Group, 2010), 23; Christian Scharen, "Practices of Dispossession: The Shape of Discipleship in a Church Taken, Blessed, Broken, and Given," in *Cultivating Sent Communities: Missional Spiritual Formation*, ed. Dwight J. Zscheile (Grand Rapids: Eerdmans, 2012), 102.

42.   Dwight J. Zscheile, "A Missional Theology of Spiritual Formation," in *Cultivating Sent Communities: Missional Spiritual Formation*, ed. Dwight J. Zscheile (Grand Rapids: Eerdmans, 2012), 1.

43.   Dunn and Sundene, *Shaping the Journey of Emerging Adults*, 19.

44.   Seel, *The New Copernicans*, x.

45.   Michael Frost and Alan Hirsch, *The Shaping of Things to Come: Innovation and Mission for the 21st Century Church* (Peabody, Mass: Hendrickson, 2003), 30.

46.   Stetzer, *Planting Missional Churches*, 5.

47.   Mary Clark Moschella, *Ethnography as Pastoral Practice: An Introduction* (Cleveland: Pilgrim Press, 2008), 59.

48.   Statistics according to personal communication with church leadership.

49.   Pete Ward, *Introducing Practical Theology: Mission, Ministry and the Life of the Church* (Grand Rapids: Baker Academic, 2017), 98–100.

50.   Osmer, *Practical Theology*, 4.

51.   Ibid., 12.

52.   Ibid., 4.

53.   Ibid.

54.   Ibid., 8.

55.   Ibid., 4.

56.   Ibid., 10.

57.   Ward, *Introducing Practical Theology*, 100–102. Ward highlights two other criticisms of the pastoral cycle: its Marxist origins and its truncation of theology by confining it to one stage in the process.

58.   Osmer, *Practical Theology*, 22–23. Osmer based his work on the five-stage rubric of hermeneutical experience outlined by Gadamer: (1) preunderstanding; (2) being brought up short; (3) dialogical interplay; (4) fusion of horizons; and (5) application.

59.   Kevin G. Smith, "Review of Richard Osmer, Practical Theology: An Introduction," *Conspectus: The Journal of the South African Theological Seminary* 10, no. 1 (2010): 108.

60. Osmer, *Practical Theology*, 162.

61. Ibid., 22–23.

62. James P. Spradley, *The Ethnographic Interview* (1979; repr., Long Grove, Ill.: Waveland Press, 2016), 5.

63. Spradley, *The Ethnographic Interview*, 6.

64. Dietrich Bonhoeffer, *Letters and Papers from Prison*, ed. Eberhard Bethge (New York: Touchstone, 1997), 278.

65. Bonhoeffer, *Letters and Papers from Prison*, 280.

66. Ibid., 381.

67. Ibid., 361.

68. Ibid., 50.

69. Osmer, *Practical Theology*, 10, 175.

70. Michael Luis, "The Python Now Has Two Pigs: Boomers and Millennials," *Washington Realtors* (September 2015): 1, https://www.warealtor.org/docs/default-source/ga-resources/millennials_final.pdf?sfvrsn=0.

71. Setran and Kiesling, *Spiritual Formation in Emerging Adulthood*, 5.

72. See, for example, Setran and Kiesling, *Spiritual Formation in Emerging Adulthood*; Dunn and Sundene, *Shaping the Journey of Emerging Adults*; and Hirsch and Hirsch, *Untamed*.

73. There is new research that offers the possibility that they may indeed return. The Barna Group reports that church attendance was up across all generations, including millennials, during 2020 due to online options during the COVID-19 pandemic. Now that the pandemic is over, millennials are most likely to adopt a "hybrid" form of church attendance, both online and in person. Daniel Copeland, a researcher at Barna, concludes, "Should church leaders keep themselves open to something new, there are new opportunities in store for the health and the future of the church." "A New Chapter in Millennial Church Attendance," The Barna Group Inc., *Articles in Faith & Christianity*, August 4, 2022, https://www.barna.com/research/church-attendance-2022/?utm_source=Newsletter&utm_medium=email&utm_content=Barna+Update%3A+A+New+Chapter+in+Millennial+Church+Attendance&utm_campaign=2022-8-3_Church+Attendance+2022_BU.

CHAPTER 2

1.   Seel, *The New Copernicans*, x.
2.   Thom S. Rainer and Jess W. Rainer, *The Millennials: Connecting to America's Largest Generation* (Nashville: B&H Publishing Group, 2011), 236.
3.   Hirsch, *The Forgotten Ways*, 86–87.
4.   David Kinnaman, *You Lost Me: Why Young Christians Are Leaving Church . . . and Rethinking Faith* (Grand Rapids: Baker, 2011), 19.
5.   Osmer, *Practical Theology*, 31.
6.   Ibid., 33–34.
7.   Ibid., 34.
8.   I have borrowed the phrase "incarnational engagement of culture" from David Fitch in his article "4 Building Blocks for a Missional Ecclesiology" (Leading a Church into Mission): #2 The Incarnational Engagement with Culture, Missio Alliance, November 2, 2010, https://www.missioalliance.org/4-building-blocks-for-a-missional-ecclesiology-leading-a-church-into-mission-2-the-incarnational-engagement-w-culture/.
9.   The pastor did not cite the source of this research. It is possible he was citing Robert Redfield and Milton B. Singer, "The Cultural Role of Cities," *Economic Development and Cultural Change* 3, no. 1 (October 1954): 53–73, 70, https://doi.org/10.1086/449678.
10.   Hirsch, *The Forgotten Ways*, 137.
11.   Darrell Guder, *The Incarnation and the Church's Witness* (Eugene, Ore.: Wipf & Stock, 2005), xii.
12.   Hirsch, *The Forgotten Ways*, 140.
13.   Guder, *The Incarnation and the Church's Witness*, 3.
14.   Richard Stearns, *Unfinished: Filling the Whole in Our Gospel* (Nashville: Thomas Nelson, 2013), xx.
15.   Guder, *The Incarnation and the Church's Witness*, 39; See, for example, N. T. Wright, *Simply Christian: Why Christianity Makes Sense* (San Francisco: Harper Collins, 2006); Scot McKnight, *Kingdom Conspiracy: Returning to the Radical Mission of the Church* (Grand Rapids: Brazos, 2014); Tim J. Keller, *Ministries of Mercy: The Call of the Jericho Road*, 2nd ed. (Phillipsburg, N. J.: Presbyterian & Reformed Publishing House, 1997); and Stearns, *Unfinished*.

16. McKnight, *Kingdom Conspiracy*, 1; Wright, *Simply Christian*, xi.
17. Wright, *Simply Christian*, 3.
18. Stearns, *Unfinished*, xx.
19. Keller, *Ministries of Mercy*, 54.
20. Ibid., xi.
21. Dietrich Bonhoeffer, *The Cost of Discipleship*, revised edition (New York: Macmillan, 1963), 245.
22. Bonhoeffer, *Letters and Papers from Prison*, 383.
23. Ibid., 383.
24. Kenda Creasy Dean. *Almost Christian: What the Faith of Our Teenagers Is Telling the American Church*. Oxford: Oxford University Press, 2010, 23.
25. Dean, *Almost Christian*, 132.
26. Ibid.
27. Ibid., 133.
28. Hirsch and Hirsch, *Untamed (Shapevine)*, 248.
29. Anthony Siegrist, "Colonialism and Mission: 4 Lessons We Must Learn from History," *Missio Alliance*, December 6, 2018, https://www.missioalliance.org/colonialism-and-mission-4-lessons-we-can-learn-from-history/.
30. Dean, *Almost Christian*, 105.
31. Ibid., 133.
32. Jeff Cloeter, "On Millennials and Story," *Missio Apostolica: Journal of the Lutheran Society for Missiology* XXI, no. 1 (May 2013), 48, https://www.lsfm.global/our-journals/. See also Seel, *The New Copernicans*.
33. Cloeter, "On Millennials and Story," 48.
34. I am not necessarily implying that the women on this board were immature or "unsaved," as I have no way of knowing that, and it is not my place to judge. My point is that their service was based on a knowledge of the culture and not on their spiritual "status."
35. Hirsch, *The Forgotten Ways*, 132.
36. Ibid.
37. Ibid.
38. Ibid., 130.
39. Ibid., 128.
40. Ibid.
41. Ibid.
42. Dallas Willard, *The Divine Conspiracy: Rediscovering Our Hidden Life in God* (New York: Harper One, 1997), 305.

43. Willard, *The Divine Conspiracy*, 305.
44. Mark A. Maddix and Jay Richard Akkerman, *Missional Discipleship: Partners in God's Redemptive Mission* (Kansas City: Beacon Hill Press, 2013), 16.
45. Maddix and Akkerman, *Missional Discipleship*, 20.
46. Ibid.
47. Ibid., 16.

CHAPTER 3

1. James Orr, "Entry for 'LOVE,'" *International Standard Bible Encyclopedia* (1915 ed.), https://www.biblestudytools.com/encyclopedias/isbe/love.html.
2. This photo was taken from a follow-up email sent by Pastor Jim outlining the previous Sunday's sermon, which is why the time stamp reads 10:35 p.m. and is not from the Sunday morning service, as described.
3. Barna Group, *The Connected Generation: How Christian Leaders around the World Can Strengthen Faith and Well-Being Among 18–35-Year-Olds* (Ventura, Calif.: Barna Group, 2019), 6–7.
4. Barna Group, *The Connected Generation*, 46.
5. Ibid., 22.
6. Ibid., 24, 22.
7. Ibid.
8. Ibid., 22.
9. Ibid., 24.
10. Ibid.
11. Ibid., 22.
12. Strong's *Concordance of the Bible*, 5384: philos, accessed April 28, 2020, https://biblehub.com/greek/5384.htm.
13. C. S. Lewis, *The Four Loves* (London: Geoffrey Bles, 1960), 42, 69, 106, 133.
14. Lewis, *The Four Loves*, 44.
15. Ibid.
16. Erik H. Erikson, *The Life Cycle Completed* (New York: W. W. Norton, 1998), 1.
17. Erikson, *The Life Cycle Completed*, 71.
18. Ibid., 70.
19. Ibid.

20. Ibid.
21. Ibid.
22. Michael Frost, *Exiles: Living Missionally in a Post-Christian Culture* (Grand Rapids: Baker, 2006), 108.
23. Frost, *Exiles*, 123.
24. Strong's *Concordance of the Bible*, 7.
25. Don Browning, "Altruism and Christian Love," *Zygon* 27, no. 4 (December 1992), 421–36. https://doi.org/10.1111/j.1467-9744.1992.tb01077.x 422.
26. Lewis, *The Four Loves*, 177.
27. Ibid., 175.
28. I do not have specific names of individuals in these examples because these stories were taken from the Facebook page of Strip Club Church.
29. Liz said that she was still working on using the correct pronoun, sometimes forgetting to call Rosie Mystique "her" and accidentally calling her "him." I refer to Rosie with masculine pronouns for the sake of continuity.
30. Thom S. Rainer and Jess W. Rainer, *The Millennials: Connecting to America's Largest Generation* (Nashville: B&H Publishing Group, 2011), 244. Interestingly, this same study revealed that 70% consider the American church to be irrelevant.
31. Dan Kimball, *They Like Jesus but Not the Church: Insights from Emerging Generations* (Grand Rapids: Zondervan, 2007), 67.
32. Kimball, *They Like Jesus but Not the Church*, 234.
33. Ibid.
34. Ibid., 236.
35. Zscheile, "A Missional Theology of Spiritual Formation," 19–20.

CHAPTER 4

1. In retrospect, looking at the data, I acknowledge the possibility of the prominence of the Holy Spirit because of the interview questions. For example, it has already been noted that millennials have a difficult time articulating their faith, so it is possible that they were using the language I provided them about the Holy Spirit. Of course, this could be said about other concepts as well, such as "faith" and "discipleship."
2. Osmer, *Practical Theology*, loc. 303. Kindle.

3. Ibid., loc. 1763.

4. Millard Erickson, *Christian Theology*, 2nd ed. (Grand Rapids: Baker, 1998), 933. The term "prevenient" is usually associated with soteriology and God's prevenient grace. Generally understood, in Wesleyan (Arminian) terms prevenient grace is "God's grace given to all humans indiscriminately" so that all may be capable of receiving salvation. I have chosen to use the term "prevenient" to describe a nuanced activity: the anticipatory action of God calling individuals back to the body of Christ. My purpose here is not to adjudicate the salvation status of the respondents but to elucidate the belief in the work of the Spirit in bringing back the dechurched to the community of faith.

5. Lesslie Newbigin, *The Relevance of Trinitarian Doctrine for Today's Mission* (London: Edinburgh House Press, 1963), 71.

6. Newbigin, *The Relevance of Trinitarian Doctrine*, 71.

7. Ibid.

8. Ibid.

9. Ibid.

10. Guder, *Missional Church*, 3.

11. Ibid., 4.

12. Ibid.

13. Ibid.

14. Ibid., 5.

15. Alan Hirsch, *The Forgotten Ways: Reactivating Apostolic Movements* (Grand Rapids: Brazos Press, 2016), 84.

16. David E. Fitch, *Faithful Presence: Seven Disciplines That Shape the Church for Mission* (Downers Grove, Ill.: InterVarsity Press, 2016), 39.

17. Hirsch, *The Forgotten Ways*, 138.

18. John Taylor, *The Go-Between God: The Holy Spirit and the Christian Mission* (London: SCM Press, 1972), 17.

19. Taylor, *The Go-Between God*, 17.

20. Ibid., 18.

21. Ibid., 3.

22. Ibid.

23. Ibid., 4. See John 20:21–22.

24. Dietrich Bonhoeffer, *Life Together: A Discussion of Christian Fellowship* (San Francisco: Harper and Row, 1954), 31.

25. Bonhoeffer, *Life Together*, 37.

26. Ibid., 39.
27. Taylor, *The Go-Between God*, 3. See Acts 1:4–5.
28. Hirsch and Hirsch, *Untamed (Shapevine)*, 97.
29. This chapter uses the terms "presence of God," "presence of Jesus" (or "Christ"), and "presence of the Holy Spirit" (or "Spirit") interchangeably, based on the triune understanding of the Godhead.
30. Teela Sanders, "Becoming an Ex-Sex Worker: Making Transitions Out of a Deviant Career," *Feminist Criminology* 2, no. 1 (January 2007): 87, https://doi.org/10.1177/1557085106294845.
31. David Watson, *Discipleship* (London: Hodder & Stoughton, 2014), 87–88. Watson lists four functions: spiritual birth, spiritual growth, spiritual gifts, and spiritual power.
32. Watson, *Discipleship*, 92.
33. Ibid.
34. Ibid.
35. Ibid.
36. Ibid., 94.
37. Ibid.
38. Ibid., 94–95.
39. Ibid., 94. See Galatians 5:22.
40. Ibid., 94.
41. Ibid., 87.
42. Ibid.

CHAPTER 5

1. Osmer, *Practical Theology*, 133.
2. Ibid., 4.
3. John Swinton and Harriet Mowat, *Practical Theology and Qualitative Research* (London: SCM Press, 2006), 12.
4. Dietrich Bonhoeffer, *Dietrich Bonhoeffer Works*, vol. 8, *Letters and Papers from Prison*, ed. John W. DeGruchy, trans. Isabel Best, Lisa E. Dahill, Reinhard Krauss, and Nancy Lukens (Minneapolis: Fortress Press, 2010), 363.
5. Bonhoeffer, *Works*, 8, *Letters and Papers from Prison*, 373.
6. Ibid., 24.

7.   Derek Michaud, ed., "Dietrich Bonhoeffer," *Boston Collaborative Encyclopedia of Western Theology*, accessed January 9, 2020, http://people.bu.edu/wwildman/bce/bonhoeffer.htm.

8.   John W. Doberstein, "Introduction," in *Life Together: A Discussion of Christian Fellowship* by Dietrich Bonhoeffer (San Francisco: Harper Collins, 1954), 10; Michaud, "Dietrich Bonhoeffer," 4.

9.   Doberstein, "Introduction," 10.

10.   Ibid., 13.

11.   Bonhoeffer, *Works*, 8, *Letters and Papers from Prison*, 362.

12.   Ibid., 479.

13.   Ibid.

14.   Ibid., 24. These are the words of John W. DeGruchy.

15.   Ralf K. Wüstenberg, *A Theology of Life: Dietrich Bonhoeffer's Religionless Christianity* (Grand Rapids: Eerdmans, 1998), 8.

16.   Wüstenberg, *A Theology of Life*, 3.

17.   Bonhoeffer, *Works*, 8, *Letters and Papers from Prison*, 362.

18.   Ibid., 22.

19.   Ibid., 490.

20.   Ibid., 501.

21.   Ibid., 25.

22.   Ibid., 27.

23.   Ibid., 363.

24.   Smith and Lundquist, *Soul Searching*, 162–63.

25.   Dean, *Almost Christian*, 16; Smith and Snell, *Souls in Transition*, 154.

26.   Smith and Lundquist, *Soul Searching*, 166.

27.   Ibid., 23; Smith and Snell, *Souls in Transition*, 287.

28.   Bonhoeffer, *Works*, 8, *Letters and Papers from Prison*, 24.

29.   Ibid., 363.

30.   Ibid., 355.

31.   Dietrich Bonhoeffer, *Ethics*, trans. Reinhard Krauss (Minneapolis: Fortress Press, 2015), 307.

32.   Bonhoeffer, *Works*, 8, *Letters and Papers from Prison*, 503.

33.   Bonhoeffer, *The Cost of Discipleship*, 129.

34.   Ibid., 130.

35.   Bonhoeffer, *Ethics*, 204.

36. Bonhoeffer, *Works*, 8, *Letters and Papers from Prison*, 513. Some translations read, "Dare to quit anxious faltering and enter the storm of events, carried alone by your faith and by God's good commandments."

37. Pinnacle Forum, "The Seven Mountains of Culture," accessed July 3, 2019, https://pinnacleforum.com/about/.

38. Pinnacle Forum, "The Seven Mountains of Culture"; Os Hillman, *Change Agent: Engaging Your Passion to Be the One Who Makes a Difference* (Lake Mary, Fla.: Charisma House, 2011), 9. In this same interview, Cunningham shared that Frances Schaeffer, founder of the L'Abri Institute, had the same idea around the same time period.

39. Loren Cunningham, "Transcript of Interview of Loren Cunningham on Original 7 Mountains Vision," 7 Cultural Mountains, accessed July 4, 2019, http://www.7culturalmountains.org/apps/articles/default.asp?articleid=40087&columnid=4347.

40. Cunningham, "Interview of Loren Cunningham."

41. H. Richard Niebuhr, *Christ and Culture* (San Francisco: Harper Collins, 1951), 43, 1.

42. Niebuhr, *Christ and Culture*, 191.

43. Craig A. Carter, *Rethinking Christ and Culture: A Post-Christendom Perspective* (Grand Rapids: Brazos, 2006), 14.

44. Carter, *Rethinking Christ and Culture*, 19.

45. Ibid.

46. Bonhoeffer, *Works*, 4, *Discipleship*, 2.

47. D. A. Carson, *Christ and Culture Revisited* (Grand Rapids: Eerdmans, 2008), 7.

48. Carter, *Rethinking Christ and Culture*, 25.

49. Ibid.

50. Ibid, 140.

51. Hirsch and Hirsch, *Untamed (Shapevine)*, 29.

52. Bonhoeffer, *Works*, 8, *Letters and Papers from Prison*, 364.

53. Nathan C. Byrd III, "Narrative Discipleship: Guiding Emerging Adults to 'Connect the Dots of Life and Faith,'" *Christian Education Journal: Series 3* 8, no. 2 (2011): 244.

54. Lillian Daniel, *Tell It Like It Is: Reclaiming the Practice of Testimony* (Lanham: Rowman and Littlefield, 2006), xv.

55. Bruce L. Shelley, *Church History in Plain Language*, 2nd ed. (Dallas: Word, 1995), 126–27, 239, 335.

56. Jeff Cloeter, "On Millennials and Story," Missio Apostolica: Journal of the Lutheran Society for Missiology XXI, no. 1 (May 2013): 48–49, https://www.lsfm.global/our-journals/.

57. Cloeter, "On Millennials and Story," 48.

58. Ibid., 49.

59. Dean, *Almost Christian*, 203.

60. Ibid., 204.

61. Seel, *The New Copernicans*, 186.

62. Literally, "the God from the machine." Bonhoeffer, *Works*, 8, *Letters and Papers from Prison*, 366, fn.

63. Bonhoeffer, *Works*, 8, *Letters and Papers from Prison*, 24.

64. Ibid., 366–67.

65. Maddix and Akkerman, *Missional Discipleship*, 16.

66. Ibid., 20.

67. Ibid., 16.

68. Ibid., 20.

69. Bonhoeffer, *Letters and Papers from Prison*, 501.

70. David Law, "Christian Discipleship in Kierkegaard, Hirsch, and Bonhoeffer," *The Downside Review* 120, no. 421 (October 2002): 301, https://journals.sagepub.com/doi/10.1177/001258060212042105.

71. Law, "Christian Discipleship," 303.

72. Bonhoeffer, Cost of Discipleship, 45.

73. Peter Morden, *The Message of Discipleship: Authentic Followers of Jesus in Today's World* (London: InterVarsity Press, 2018), loc. 3671. Kindle.

74. Bonhoeffer, *Life Together*, 35.

75. Kimball, *They Like Jesus but Not the Church*, 96, 115.

76. Hirsch and Hirsch, *Untamed (Shapevine)*, 13.

77. Bonhoeffer, *The Cost of Discipleship*, 205.

78. Pitirim A. Sorokin, *The Ways and Power of Love: Types, Factors, and Techniques* (Radnor, Pa.: Templeton Foundation Press, 2002), 459.

79. Gennaro Iorio, *Sociology of Love: The Agapic Dimension of Societal Life* (Vernon Art and Science Inc., 2015), 65, Kindle.

80. Hirsch and Hirsch, *Untamed (Shapevine)*, 23.

81. Dietrich Bonhoeffer, *Ethics*, ed. Clifford J. Green, vol. 6, Dietrich Bonhoeffer Works (Minneapolis: Fortress Press, 2005), 64.

82. Michael Frost and Alan Hirsch, *ReJesus: A Wild Messiah for a Missional Church* (Grand Rapids: Baker, 2009), 6.

83. Frost and Hirsch, *ReJesus*, 114.

84. Zscheile, "A Missional Theology of Spiritual Formation," 19–20.

85. Ibid., 24.

86. Bonhoeffer, *Works*, 8, *Letters and Papers from Prison*, 503.

87. Hirsch and Hirsch, *Untamed (Shapevine)*, 151.

88. Bonhoeffer, *Works*, 8, *Letters and Papers from Prison*, 500.

89. Ibid., 27.

90. Ibid., 50.

91. Ibid., 28.

92. Andrew Root, *Bonhoeffer as Youth Worker: A Theological Vision for Discipleship and Life Together* (Grand Rapids: Baker Academic, 2014), 71.

93. Root, *Bonhoeffer as Youth Worker*, 46.

94. Dietrich Bonhoeffer, *Dietrich Bonhoeffer Works*, vol. 11, *Ecumenical, Academic, and Pastoral Work*, ed. Victoria J. Barnett, Mark S. Brocker, and Michael B. Lukens, trans. Anne Schmidt-Lange, with Isabel Best, Nicolas Humphrey, and Marion Pauck (Minneapolis: Fortress Press, 2012), 98.

95. Root, 101.

96. **Ibid.**

97. Root, *Bonhoeffer as Youth Worker*, 102.

98. Ibid., 6.

99. Ibid., 4.

100. Strong's *Concordance of the Bible*, 7.

101. Browning, "Altruism and Christian Love," 422.

102. Ibid.

103. Dietrich Bonhoeffer, *Ethics* (New York: Touchstone, 1995), 66.

104. Bonhoeffer, *Works*, 8, *Letters and Papers from Prison*, 45.

105. Erickson, *Christian Theology*, 518–19.

106. Ibid., 523. The other views, which are beyond the scope of this conversation, are the relational view and the functional view.

107. Ibid., 532.

108. Ibid., 535.

109. Hirsch and Hirsch, *Untamed (Shapevine)*, 198.

110. Ibid., 194.

111. Philip Mercer, *Sympathy and Ethics: A Study of the Relationship Between Sympathy and Morality with Special Reference to Hume's Treatise* (Oxford: Clarendon Press, 1972), 127.

112. Søren Kierkegaard, *Kierkegaard's Writings*, XVI, *Works of Love*, ed. Howard V. Hong and Edna H. Hong (Princeton: Princeton University Press, 1995).

113. Kierkegaard, *Writings*, XVI, *Works of Love*, 66.

114. Ibid., 89.

115. Ibid.

116. Ibid., 63.

117. Ibid., 74.

118. Ibid.

119. Ibid.

120. Browning, "Altruism and Christian Love," 422.

121. C. S. Lewis, *Mere Christianity* (New York: Harper and Row, 1952), 129.

122. Lewis, Mere Christianity, 129.

123. Bonhoeffer, *Works*, 8, *Letters and Papers from Prison*, 26.

124. Ibid., 27.

125. Ibid., 1, Bonhoeffer, Works, 1, *Sanctorum Communio*, 136fn.

126. Christopher R.J. Holmes, "The Holy Spirit," in The Oxford Handbook of Dietrich Bonhoeffer, 168–78, ed. Michael Mawson and Philip G. Ziegler (New York: Oxford University Press, 2019), 172; Bonhoeffer, *Works*, 4, *Discipleship*, 209–10.

127. Holmes, "The Holy Spirit," 173.

128. Bonhoeffer, *Works*, 4, *Discipleship*, 260.

129. Holmes, "The Holy Spirit," 178.

130. Dietrich Bonhoeffer, *Works*, 8, *Letters and Papers from Prison*, 362.

131. In classical Reformed Calvinism, this grace is extended to the elect and empowers them to respond (thus it is also called "irresistible grace" or "efficacious grace"). In the Wesleyan-Arminian understanding, by contrast, prevenient grace is resistible and therefore offered with the proviso that not all will respond. My own view is a conflicted one. I believe in the existence of prevenient grace generally. I come from a Calvinist tradition but am not a strict Calvinist because I struggle with the concept of limited atonement. Neither do I fall into the Arminian camp because I reject the position held by some Arminians that salvation can be forfeited. This leaves me in a position of soteriological liminality, which might explain my quest for a theology that goes beyond "religious" doctrinal sectarianism.

132. Calvin wrote that this grace "is a powerful impulse of the Holy Spirit, which makes men willing who formerly were unwilling and reluctant." John Calvin, *Commentary on John*, cf. John 6:41–45, https://www.ccel. org/ccel/calvin/calcom34.xii.vii.html, accessed January 28, 2021; Roger Olson, a prominent Arminian theologian, wrote about the Holy Spirit's role: "[Prevenient grace is] the illuminating, convicting, calling, enabling power of the Holy Spirit working on the sinner's soul and making them free to choose saving grace (or reject it)." Roger Olson, *Against Calvinism* (Grand Rapids: Zondervan Academic, 2011), 67.

133. David Kinnaman and Mark Matlock, *Faith for Exiles: 5 Ways for a New Generation to Follow Jesus in Digital Babylon* (Grand Rapids: Baker, 2019), 33.

134. Kinnaman and Matlock, *Faith for Exiles*, 33.

135. J. H. Wright, *The Mission of God* (Downers Grove, Ill.: InterVarsity Press, 2006), 62.

136. Hirsch, *The Forgotten Ways*, 84.

137. Lesslie Newbigin, *The Open Secret: An Introduction to the Theology of Mission*, rev. ed. (Grand Rapids: Eerdmans, 1995), 61.

138. Newbigin, *The Open Secret*, 20.

139. Bonhoeffer, *Works*, 1, *Sanctorum Communio*, 143.

140. Holmes, "The Holy Spirit," 171–74.

141. Zscheile, "A Missional Theology of Spiritual Formation," 21. Zscheile contrasts this definition with that of many congregations who describe discernment as an "episodic or extraordinary" activity, such as calling a new pastor or launching a capital campaign—activities that have a specific goal or outcome. Zscheile's missional understanding is a more open-ended willingness to be carried along by the Spirit, suspending one's own plans in order to discern where God is moving in the lives of others in the world (23). This was the type of discernment observed in my fieldwork.

142. The disciples were sent out by Jesus in the power of the Spirit, with the promise that he would be their counsellor and guide (Acts 1:8; John 14). Paul wrote in 1 Corinthians 12:10 that discernment is a gift from the Spirit.

143. Newbigin cites this passage as an emblematic example of the Holy Spirit's work in missional advance. Newbigin, *The Open Secret*, 48.

144. Wayne Grudem presents a four-view taxonomy of the gifts of the Holy Spirit in *Are Miraculous Gifts for Today?* (Grand Rapids: Zondervan, 1996): (1) Cessationist—no miraculous gifts exist today; (2) Open-But-Cautious—unconvinced by cessationist arguments, open to possibility of miraculous gifts, but concerned about possibility of abuses; (3) Third Wave—so called because it is the third renewal movement, Pentecostal being the first and charismatic being the second, which believes that the proclamation of the gospel should be accompanied by signs and wonders and that baptism of the Holy Spirit happens at conversion; (4) Pentecostal/Charismatic—all gifts of the Holy Spirit are for today, one should seek the baptism of the Holy Spirit, and *glossalia* is the sign of baptism of the Holy Spirit. Grudem's research found that the Open-But-Cautious group "was gigantic in the evangelical world" and reflects probably "the position held by the majority of evangelicals today, at least in the U.S." Grudem, *Are Miraculous Gifts for Today?* 11, 13. My own pneumatology, which falls somewhere between Open-But-Cautious and Third Wave in Grudem's taxonomy, makes allowances for these subjective experiences. I believe that all the gifts are operational today, but I am wary of abuses and believe that evangelism, Bible study, and faithful obedience should be emphasized as means to spiritual maturity and church growth. I therefore accept the possibility that the experiences of research participants were authentic interactions with the Holy Spirit.

145. Gary Tyra, *The Holy Spirit in Mission* (Downers Grove, Ill.: InterVarsity Press, 2011), loc. 162, Kindle.

146. In Karina Kremenski, "The Discipline of Discerning the Holy Spirit," Missio Alliance, August 20, 2013, https://www.missioalliance.org/the-discipline-of-discerning-the-holy-spirit/.

147. Ibid.

148. Kremenski, "The Discipline of Discerning the Holy Spirit."

149. Bonhoeffer, *Ethics*, 41.

150. Bonhoeffer, *Works*, 11, *Ecumenical, Academic, and Pastoral Works*, 299–300.

151. Lisa E. Dahill, "Probing the Will of God: Bonhoeffer and Discernment," *Dialog: A Journal of Theology* 41, no. 1 (Spring 2002): 42–49, 42, https://onlinelibrary.wiley.com/doi/epdf/10.1111/1540-6385.00098.

152. Bonhoeffer, *Ethics*, 193.

153. Dahill, "Probing the Will of God," 43. It should not be misconstrued that Bonhoeffer's pneumatology was in line with missional theology here. Bonhoeffer believed that the Holy Spirit's activity was confined to the church, which explains his fervency for the need to bear witness to Christ in the world. This stands in contrast to missional theology, which believes that the Holy Spirit is working in the world beyond the church, and it is the church's duty to discover it and join him.

154. Bonhoeffer, *Life Together*, 32.

155. Ibid.

156. Ibid., 37.

157. I base this observation on the definition of "sectarian" found in the *Oxford Dictionary of Difficult Words* (Oxford: Oxford University Press, 2014), 394: "(of an action) carried out on the grounds of membership of a sect, denomination, or other group." For example, D. A. Carson laments in *Showing the Spirit* that charismatics and non charismatics "cherish neat stereotypes of the other," which is a "painful, indeed embarrassing" situation. (Grand Rapids: Baker, 1987), 12. Wayne Grudem writes in *Are Miraculous Gifts for Today?* that there is "little consensus" on the question "How is the Holy Spirit working in churches today?" (9).

158. It is unlikely that Zach ever witnessed snake-handling, as it is extremely uncommon. There are no known churches in the state of Texas that engage in this practice. He was likely using the most stereotypical example of Pentecostalism that came to mind.

159. Bonhoeffer, *Cost of Discipleship*, 40.

160. This is the fruit of the Spirit described in Galatians 5:22–23 (NET): "But the fruit of the Spirit is love, joy, peace, patience, kindness, gentleness, goodness, faithfulness, and self-control. Against such things there is no law."

161. A. W. Tozer, *The Pursuit of God: The Human Thirst for the Divine* (Camp Hill, Pa.: Christian Publications, 1993), 33.

162. Erickson, *Christian Theology*, 875. The Bible speaks of him as God (Acts 5; 1 Cor 3:16–17; 6:19–20), He possess the same attributes John 16:8–13; Luke 1:35; Rom 15:19 ; 1 Cor 2:10–11) and performs the same functions as God (Gen 1:2; Job 26:13; Ps 104:30).

163. Erickson names these as the "three fundamental elements of personhood." Erickson, *Christian Theology*, 878.

164. Ibid., 885–886.

165. Ibid., 874, 889.

166. Ibid., 890.

167. Ibid., 891–892.

168. Both the Westminster and Baptist Confessions of Faith say that "our full persuasion and assurance of the infallible truth, and divine authority thereof, is from the inward work of the Holy Spirit bearing witness by and with the Word in our hearts," accessed March 3, 2021, https:// www.kx.church/second-london-confession-1689-chapter-1/.

169. Dietrich Bonhoeffer, "Sermon for Whitsunday, 1940", quoted in Geffrey B. Kelly and F. Burton Nelson, *The Cost of Moral Leadership: The Spirituality of Dietrich Bonhoeffer* (Grand Rapids: Eerdmans, 2003), 51.

170. Bonhoeffer, *Life Together*, 32; Bonhoeffer, "Sermon for Whitsunday," 51.

171. In several works, including *Act and Being*, Bonhoeffer tackled ontological and transcendental challenges posed by Idealist and Kantian transcendental philosophy, which understood the human being to be fundamentally autonomous, free, and self-creating through one's own reason (Dahl, 76). Bonhoeffer's theological reflection dismissed these philosophies as an "illusion of the autonomous human individual who is alone and self-constituting" (Dahl, 86). He wrote, "Man's whole spirituality becomes evident only along with others" (*Sanctorum Communio*, 48). "Freedom" is found not in autonomy, but in relationship: "Being free," wrote Bonhoeffer, "is being free for the other." (Dietrich Bonhoeffer, *Creation and Fall/Temptation: Two Biblical Studies*, trans. by Kathleen Downham (London: SCM, 1959), 37). Bonhoeffer believed that when believers are located within a community of faith, they are made free for one another and, through Christ, free from themselves and their sinful man.

172. Jürgen Moltmann, *The Spirit of Life: A Universal Affirmation* (Minneapolis: Fortress, 1992), 2.

173. Moltmann, *The Spirit of Life*, 2.

174. Bonhoeffer, *Works*, 1, *Sanctorum Communio*, 143, 226–50.

175. Holmes, "The Holy Spirit," 178.

176. Moltmann, *The Spirit of Life*, 2.

177. Ibid. 2-3.

178. Ibid.

179. Hywel R. Jones, "The Doctrine of the Holy Spirit in 20th Century Ecumenism," *The Banner of Truth*, November 17, 2003, https://banner

oftruth.org/us/resources/articles/2003/the-doctrine-of-the-holy-spirit-in-20th-century-ecumenism/.

180. For example, see works by Jürgen Moltmann, Alister McGrath, Clark Pinnock, J. I. Packer, and Sinclair Ferguson. Ferguson credits the charismatic/Pentecostal movement for the rise, while Jones cites the Eastern Orthodox tradition as an additional impetus. Sinclair Ferguson, *The Holy Spirit: Contours of Christian Theology* (Downers Grove, Ill.: InterVarsity Press, 1996), 11; Jones, "The Doctrine of the Holy Spirit in 20th Century Ecumenism."

181. Abraham Kuyper, in his landmark book *The Work of the Holy Spirit*, claimed the opposite (New York: Funk and Wagnalls Company, 1900), ix.

182. Ferguson, *The Holy Spirit*, 12.

183. Kinnaman and Matlock, *Faith for Exiles*, 181.

184. Seel, *The New Copernicans*, 181.

185. Setran and Kiesling, *Spiritual Formation in Emerging Adulthood*, 44–52.

186. Michael D. Langford, "Spirit-Driven Discipleship: A Pneumatology of Youth Ministry," *Theology Today* 71, no. 3 (September 16, 2014): 323, https://doi.org/10.1177%2F0040573614542309.

187. Langford, "Spirit-Driven Discipleship of Youth," 328.

188. Ibid., 323.

189. Ibid., 333.

190. Ibid.

191. Ibid.

192. Ferguson, *The Holy Spirit*, 91; Langford, "Spirit-Driven Discipleship," 323.

193. Bonhoeffer, The Cost of Discipleship, 47.

CHAPTER 6

1. Craig Dykstra and Dorothy C. Bass, "A Theological Understanding of Christian Practices," *Lifelong Faith* 2, no. 2 (Summer 2008): 3, 5, https://www.lifelongfaith.com/uploads/5/1/6/4/5164069/lifelong_faith_journal_2.2.pdf.

2. Dykstra and Bass, "A Theological Understanding of Christian Practices," 7.

3. Ibid.

4. Ibid., 6.

5.   Gordon S. Mikoski, "Educating and Forming Disciples for the Reign of God: Reflections on Youth Pilgrimages to the Holy Land," in *For Life Abundant: Practical Theology, Theological Education, and Christian Ministry*, ed. Dorothy C. Bass and Craig Dykstra (Grand Rapids: Eerdmans, 2008), 339.

6.   Mikoski, "Educating and Forming Disciples for the Reign of God," 340.

7.   Hoyt, "Testimony," 90.

8.   **Dykstra and Bass, "A Theological Understanding of Christian Practices," 18.**

9.   Thomas Hoyt, Jr., "Testimony," in *Practicing Our Faith: A Way of Life for a Searching People*, 2nd ed, Dorothy C. Bass, ed. (San Francisco: Jossey-Bass, 2010), 90.

10.   Hoyt, "Testimony," 90.

11.   "'uwd," Bible Study Tools, accessed August 19, 2020, https://www.bible studytools.com/lexicons/hebrew/nas/uwd-2.html; "martureo," Bible Study Tools, accessed August 19, 2020, https://www.biblestudytools.com/lexicons/greek/nas/martureo.html.

12.   "Witness," The Bible Project, accessed November 29, 2019, https://thebibleproject.com/explore/witness/.

13.   Eugene Peterson, "Living into God's Story," accessed April 17, 2020, https://static1.squarespace.com/static/55a6400fe4b0062f1359e218/t/581ef178d2b85747b9dd2e7c/1478422904361/Living+into+God%27s+Story.pdf.

14.   Dykstra and Bass, "A Theological Understanding of Christian Practices," 17; Ana Maria Pineda, "Hospitality," in *Practicing Our Faith: A Way of Life for a Searching People*, 2nd ed., Dorothy C. Bass, ed. (Jossey-Bass, 2010), 31.

15.   Pineda, "Hospitality," 33.

16.   Christine D. Pohl, *Making Room: Recovering Hospitality as a Christian Tradition* (Grand Rapids: Eerdmans, 1999), 42.

17.   Pohl, *Making Room*, 61.

18.   Dykstra and Bass, "A Theological Understanding of Christian Practices," 10.

19.   Ibid.

20.   Henri Nouwen, *Reaching Out: The Three Movements of the Spiritual Life* (New York: Doubleday, 1975), 8.

21.   "From Hostility to Hospitality" is one of three movements described by Nouwen. The other two are "From Loneliness to Solitude," which deals

with "reaching out to our inmost self," and "From Illusion to Prayer," which deals with "reaching out to God." Nouwen, *Reaching Out*, 7.

22. Ibid, 46.
23. Ibid., 51.
24. Ibid., 69.
25. Ibid., 70.
26. Pohl, *Making Room*, 58.
27. Indeed, Fresh Expressions has introduced the concept of "Dinner Church," a creative and decidedly missional approach to hospitality in the home.
28. John Swinton, "Time, Hospitality, and Belonging: Towards a Practical Theology of Mental Health," *Word & World* 35, no. 2 (Spring 2015), 178, https://wordandworld.luthersem.edu/issues.aspx?article_id=3849.
29. Switon, "Time, Hospitality, and Belonging," 177.
30. Ibid., 177–178.
31. Ibid., 180.
32. Ibid., 178.
33. Willie James Jennings, *The Christian Imagination: Theology and the Origins of Race* (Yale University Press: 2011), 8.
34. Jennings, *The Christian Imagination*, 4, 36.
35. Ibid., 5.
36. Ibid., 33–34. This section does not begin to do justice to the complexity and sophistication of Jennings's work, in particular on the origin of race, implications of replacement theology, and critique of Christian social imagination. I have had to limit the discussion to his points that most directly deal with hospitality.
37. Nancy E. Bedford, "Little Moves against Destructiveness: Theology and the Practice of Discernment," *Practicing Theology: Beliefs and Practices in Christian Life*, ed. by Miroslav Volf and Dorothy C. Bass (Grand Rapids: Eerdmans, 2001), 158.
38. Henri Nouwen, *Discernment: Reading the Signs of Daily Life* (New York: Harper One, 2013), 84.
39. Ibid.
40. Strong's *Concordance of the Bible*, Greek 5611, Fair, beautiful, blooming. From hora, belonging to the right hour or season, i.e., flourishing (figuratively), Bible Hub, accessed November 26, 2019, https://biblehub.com/greek/strongs_5611.htm.

41. From my fieldwork journal, February 17, 2018.

42. David F. White, *Practicing Discernment with Youth: A Transformative Youth Ministry Approach* (Eugene, Ore.: Wipf & Stock, 2005), 6.

43. Frank Rogers Jr. "Discernment," in *Practicing Our Faith: A Way of Life for a Searching People*, ed. Dorothy C. Bass (San Francisco: Jossey-Bass, 2010), 105.

44. Rogers, "Discernment," 106.

45. Ibid., 110.

46. Ibid., 109.

47. Ibid., 110.

48. Curtis R. Love and Cornelius J. P. Niemandt, "Led by the Spirit: Missional Communities and the Quakers on Communal Vocation Discernment," *Herv. teol. Stud.* 70, no.1 (January 2014): 8, http://www.scielo.org.za/scielo.php?script=sci_arttext&pid=S0259-94222014000100051&lng=en&nrm=iso.

49. Love and Niemandt, "Led by the Spirit," 8.

50. Conan Rainwater, "Christian Base Communities in Peru: Lessons for North America," *Quest: A Journal of Undergraduate Research 5* (2015): 85, https://dspace2.creighton.edu/xmlui/bitstream/handle/10504/111837/Article_6.pdf?sequence=1&isAllowed=y.

51. Rainwater, "Christian Base Communities in Peru," 88.

52. Erickson, *Christian Theology*, 283.

53. Ibid., 282.

54. Bonhoeffer, *Works*, 11, *Ecumenical, Academic, and Pastoral Works*, 378.

55. Ibid.

56. White, *Practicing Discernment with Youth*, xii, 46–47.

57. Rainwater, "Christian Base Communities in Peru," 87.

CHAPTER 7

1. Hirsch, *The Forgotten Ways*, 145.

2. This metaphor was shared at Urban Life Church, but I recall hearing it in other sermons and teachings.

3. Kinnaman, *You Lost Me*, 19; Dunn and Sundene, *Shaping the Journey of Emerging Adults*, 19.

4. Osmer, Practical Theology.

5. Kimball, *They Like Jesus but Not the Church*, 60.

6. Setran and Kiesling, *Spiritual Formation in Emerging Adulthood*, 25.

www.ingramcontent.com/pod-product-compliance
Lightning Source LLC
Chambersburg PA
CBHW062055080426
42734CB00012B/2662